Blank Comic Book

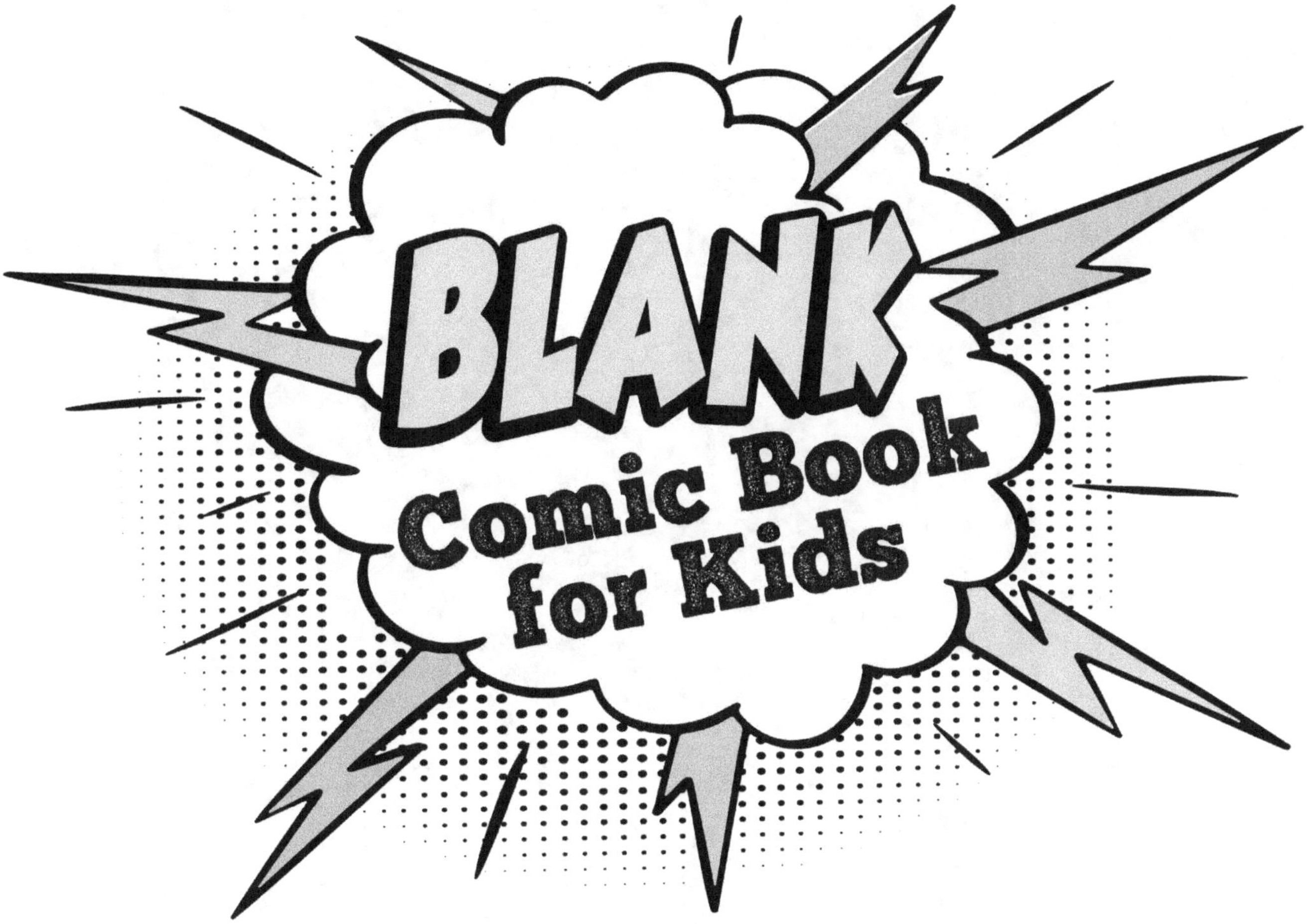

Blank Comic Book

Blank Comic Book

This book belongs to:

_____

Start date: _____

The Blank Comic Book for Kids Copyright 2020
All rights reserved. No part of this book may be reproduced, or stored in a retrieval system, or transmitted in any form or by any means, electronic, mechanical, photocopying, recording, or otherwise, without express written permission of the publisher.

Developing Story Components

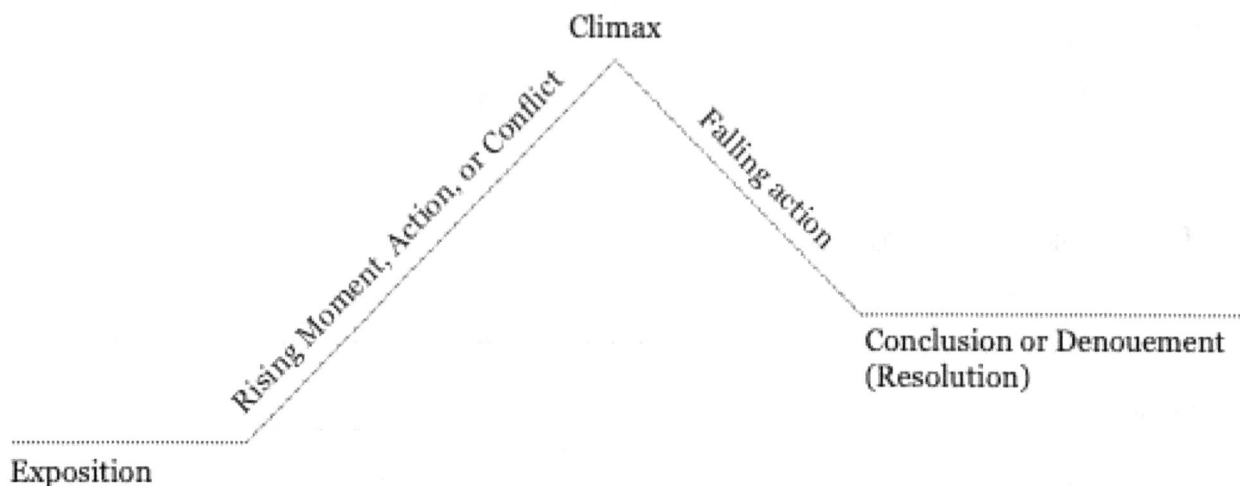

The dramatic structure of a story, play, TV show, movie, or novel can take many different forms to create a story arc. Some movie and TV show makers look outside the traditional structure of drama, comedy, or love story.

One of the most commonly taught ways of structuring a story of Freytag's Pyramid was in place since 1863 as a way of understanding dramatic structure. Since being published, Freytag's Pyramid has become one of the most popular forms of exploring the different stories from screenplays to novels, short stories, and narrative poems.

What is Freytag's Pyramid?

The basis of Freytag's Pyramid is that there are five basic principles to the use of this dramatic structure:

- Exposition
- Rising moment, action, or conflict
- Climax
- Falling action
- Conclusion or Denouement (Resolution)

German poet and dramatist first used these five fundamental aspects of a story, Gustav Freytag, to develop his pyramid. Initially, the expert in dramatic poetry positioned his five points within the structure of the popular form or story of the time, tragedy.

Expanding on the Work of Aristotle

When Gustav Freytag wrote his "Freytag's Technique of The Drama" in 1863, he expanded on the ideas of the Ancient Greek philosopher, Aristotle. Where Freytag used a pyramid to explore the options within his dramatic structure, Aristotle had described a similar set of events in the form of a triangle.

Exposition

Some may think the exposition or introduction, to any story as an optional aspect, for well based narrative, you should begin any tale by introducing the characters and location to your viewers or readers. The use of an introduction or exposition as the first point that allows the viewer to feel for the mood and characters in the story, which will enable them to feel they are drawing closer to them as the stories move forward.

Rising Moment, Action, or Conflict

In "Freytag's Technique of the Drama," the rising moment or movement is a continuation of every critical character introduced by the end of this second sector. The rising action is an integral part of the story because, by this part of the story, the mood of the overall drama and the life of the characters should be clear to all readers or viewers.

Climax

What differs in the work of Gustav Freytag to other dramatists is his belief that the climax to the story comes in the central portion of the arc of the main character. At this point, the main character or characters have a dramatic event occur that makes their life better or worse and sets in motion the events that define the remainder of the story.

The climax can take many different forms depending on the genre of the story being told. In the form of a tragedy, the climax is when an event occurs that sees the life of the main character or characters take a dramatic turn that sees them descend into more severe problems. In a comedy, the usual turn taken is that a character has a tough life but sees their fortunes take a turn for the second half of the story.

Blank Comic Book

Blank Comic Book

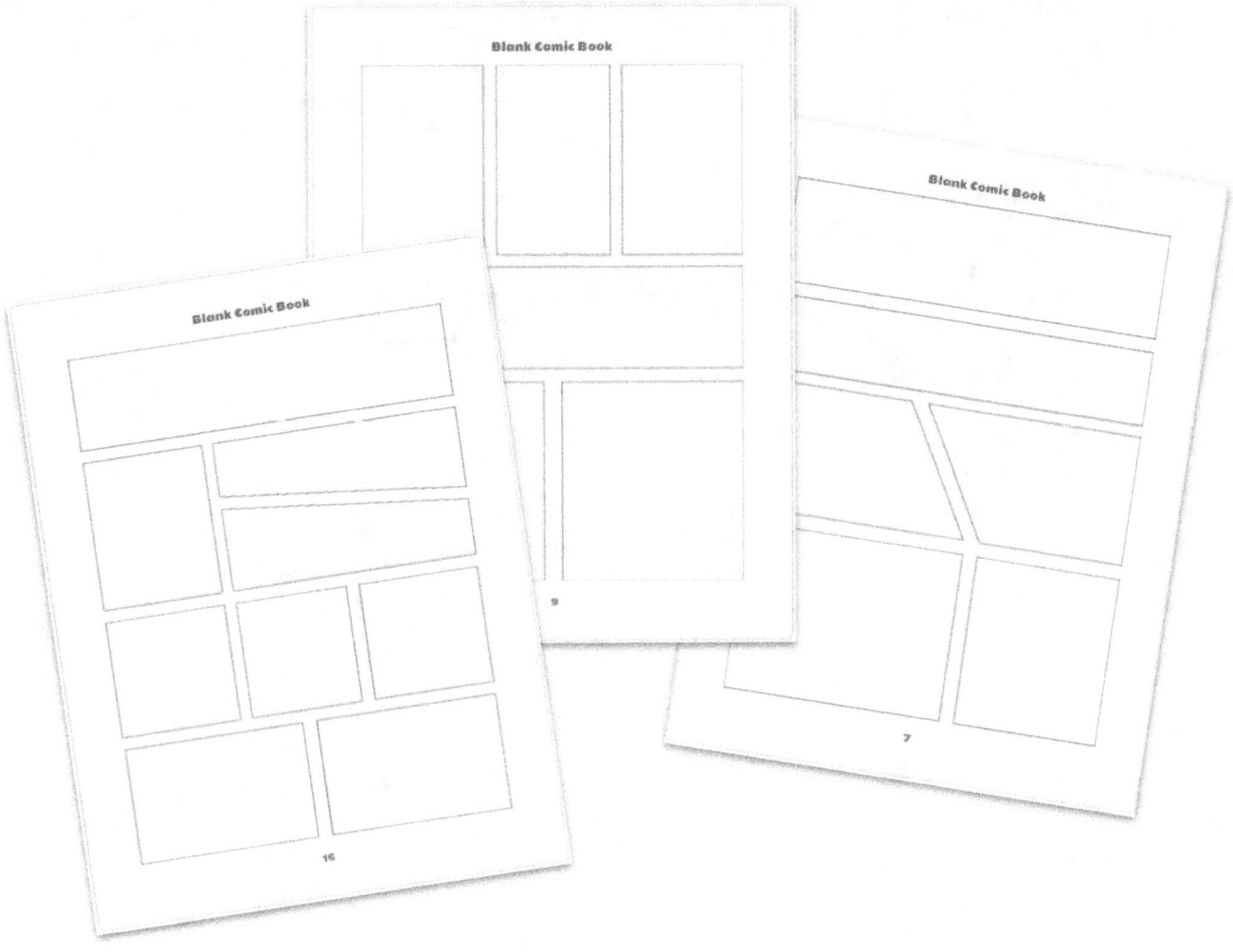

Every comic starts with a story. This book is the 1st step in bringing your comic book story to life. Incorporate the five-story elements described in the previous pages.

Each block represents an idea or scene to move the story forward if you need to rest or change direction, jump to a page into the book.

Blank Comic Book

Blank Comic Book

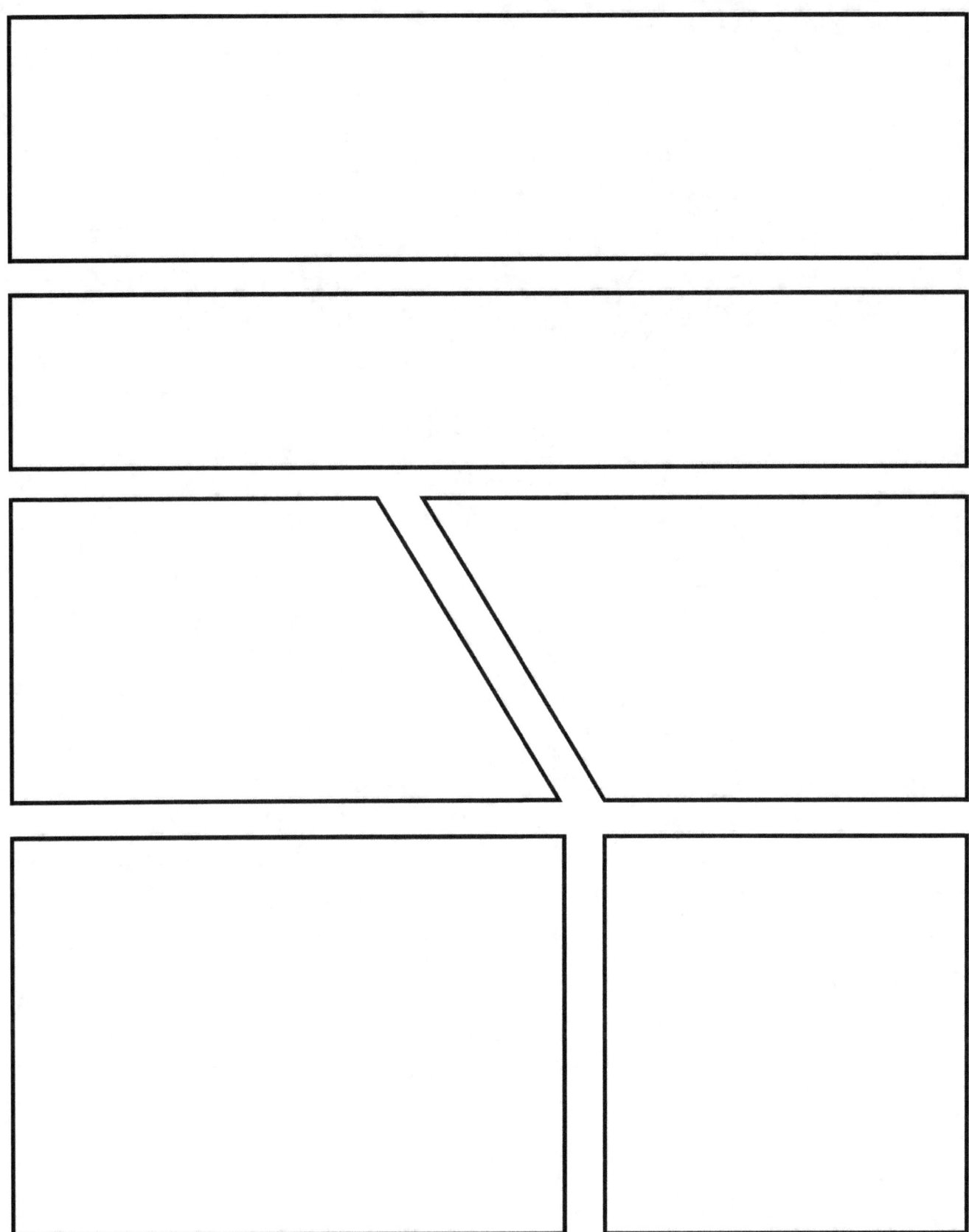

9

Blank Comic Book

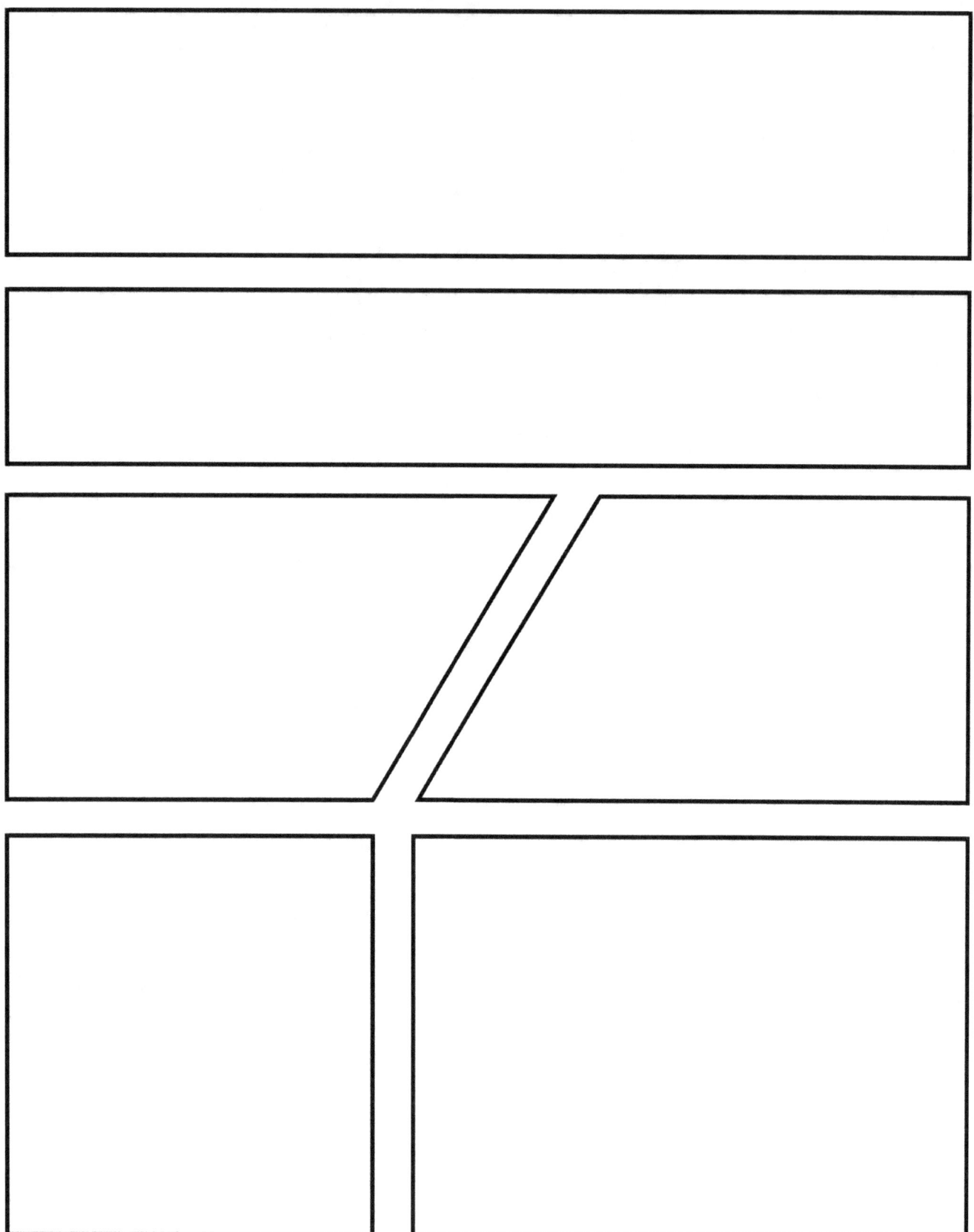

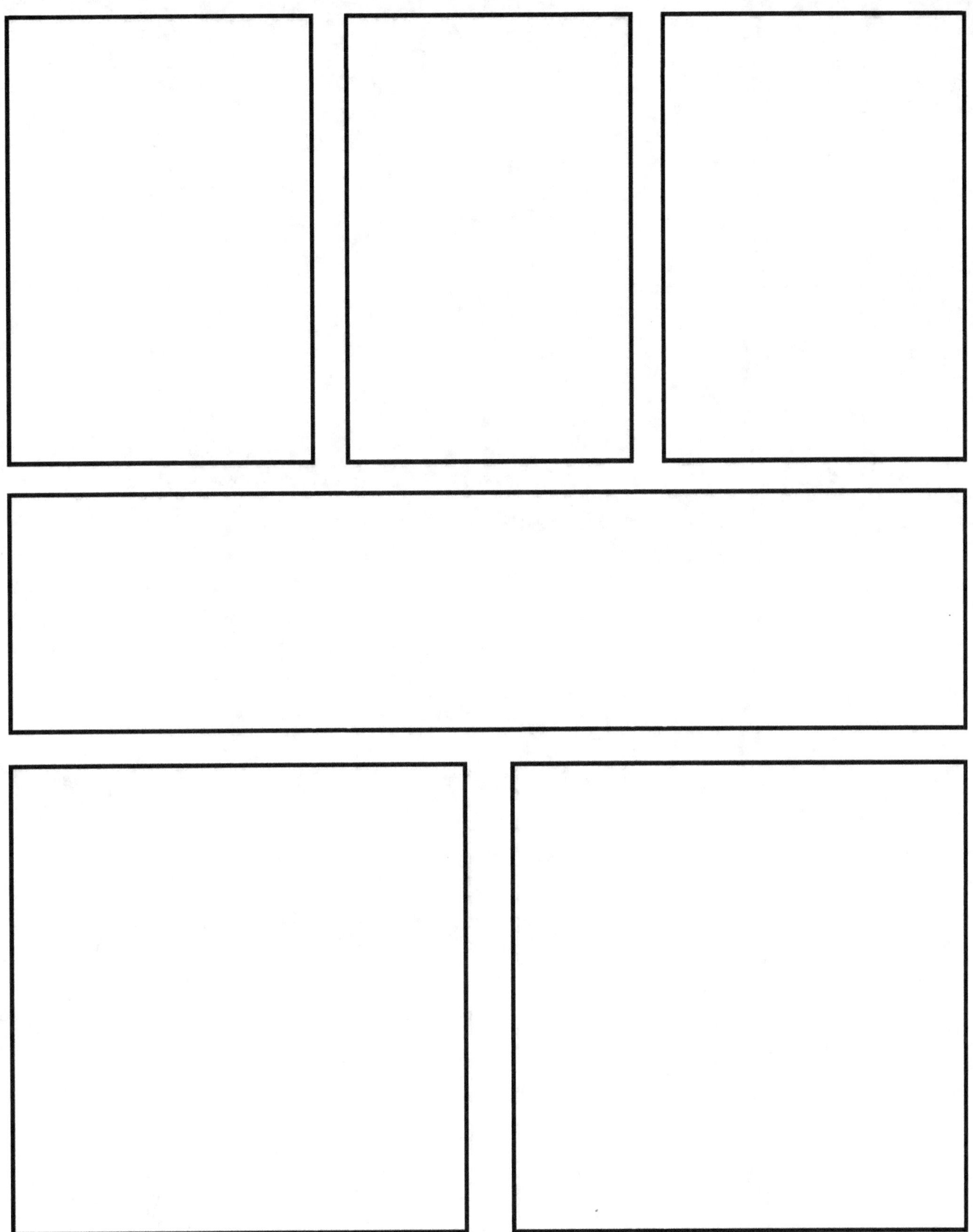

Blank Comic Book

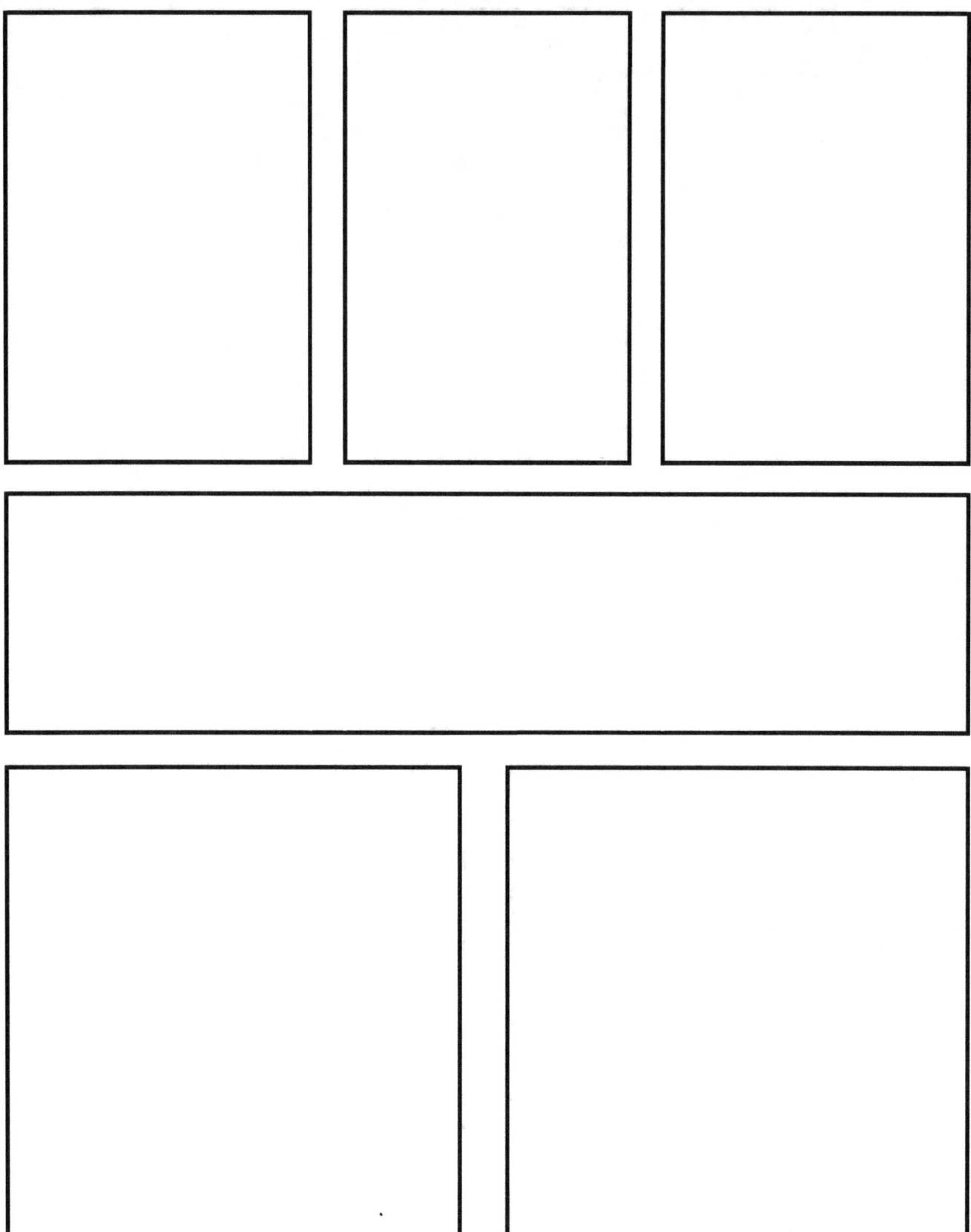

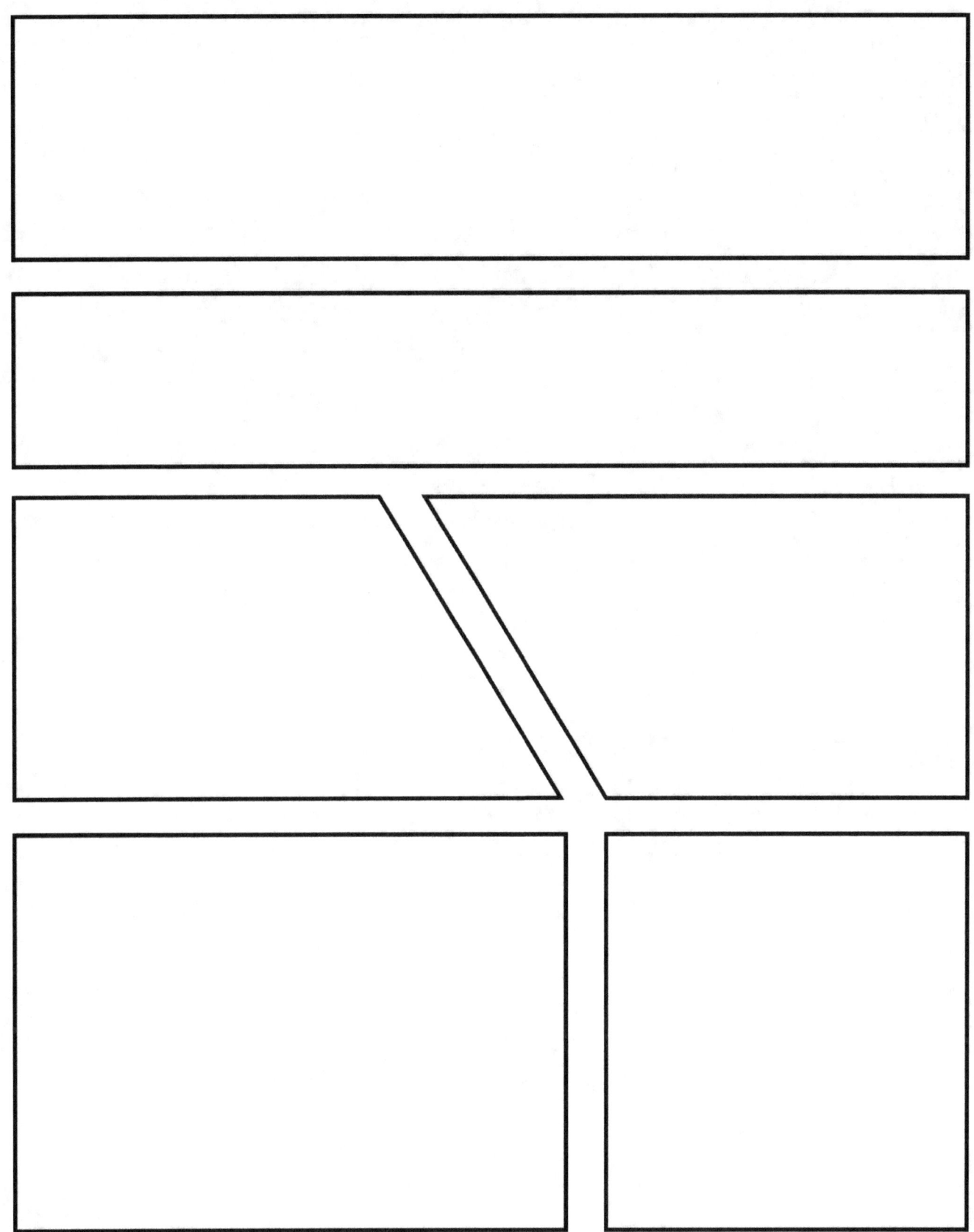

Blank Comic Book

Blank Comic Book

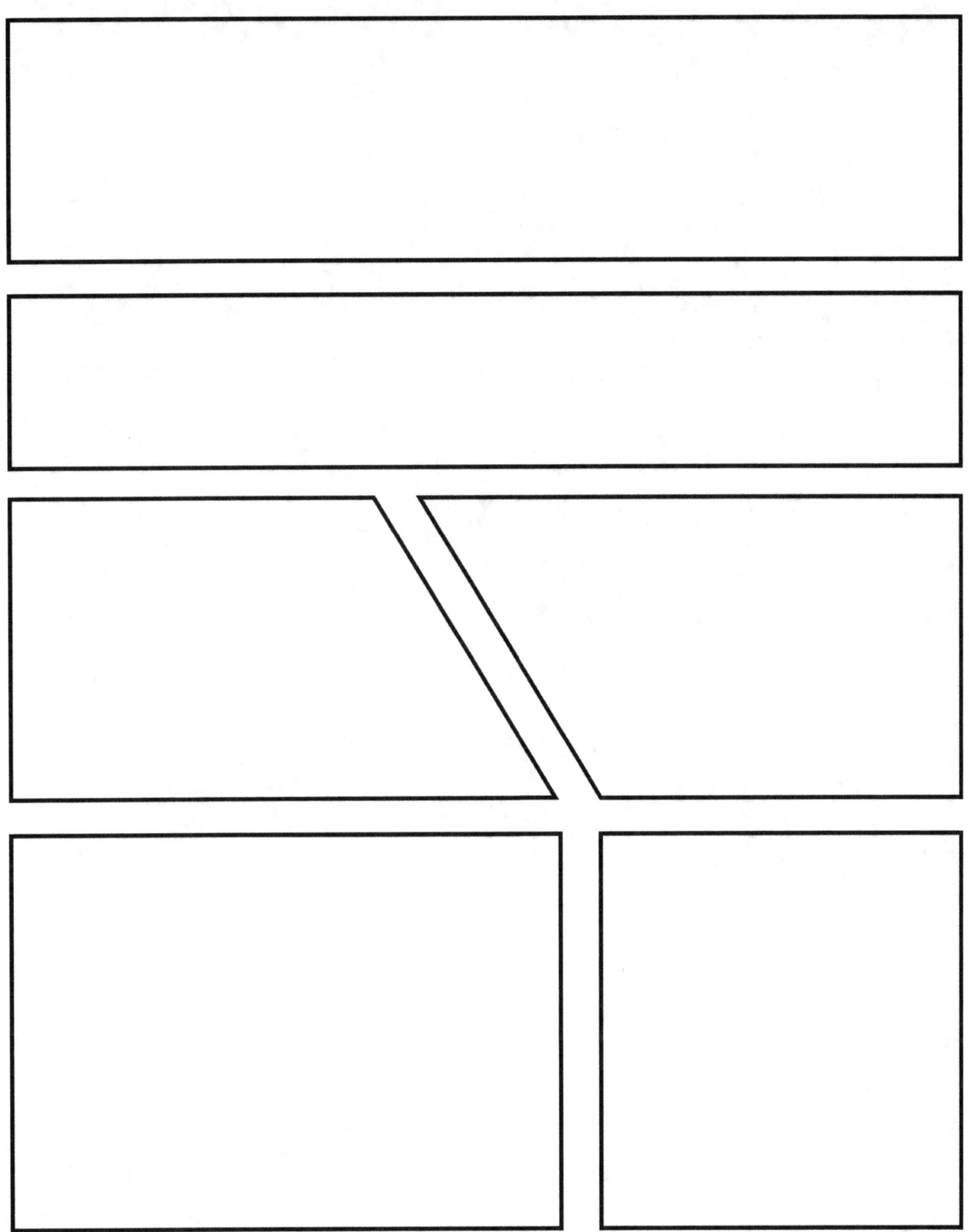

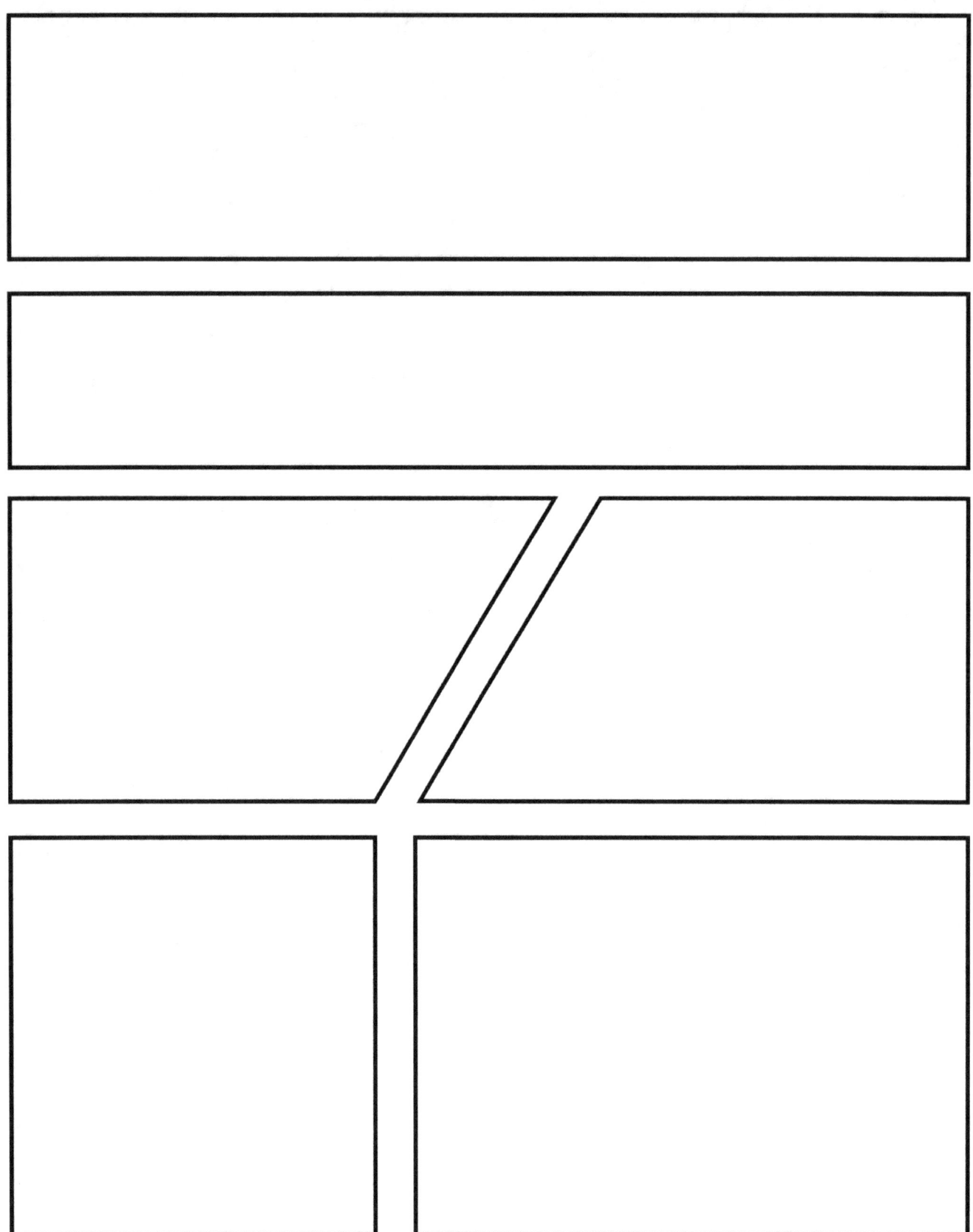

Blank Comic Book

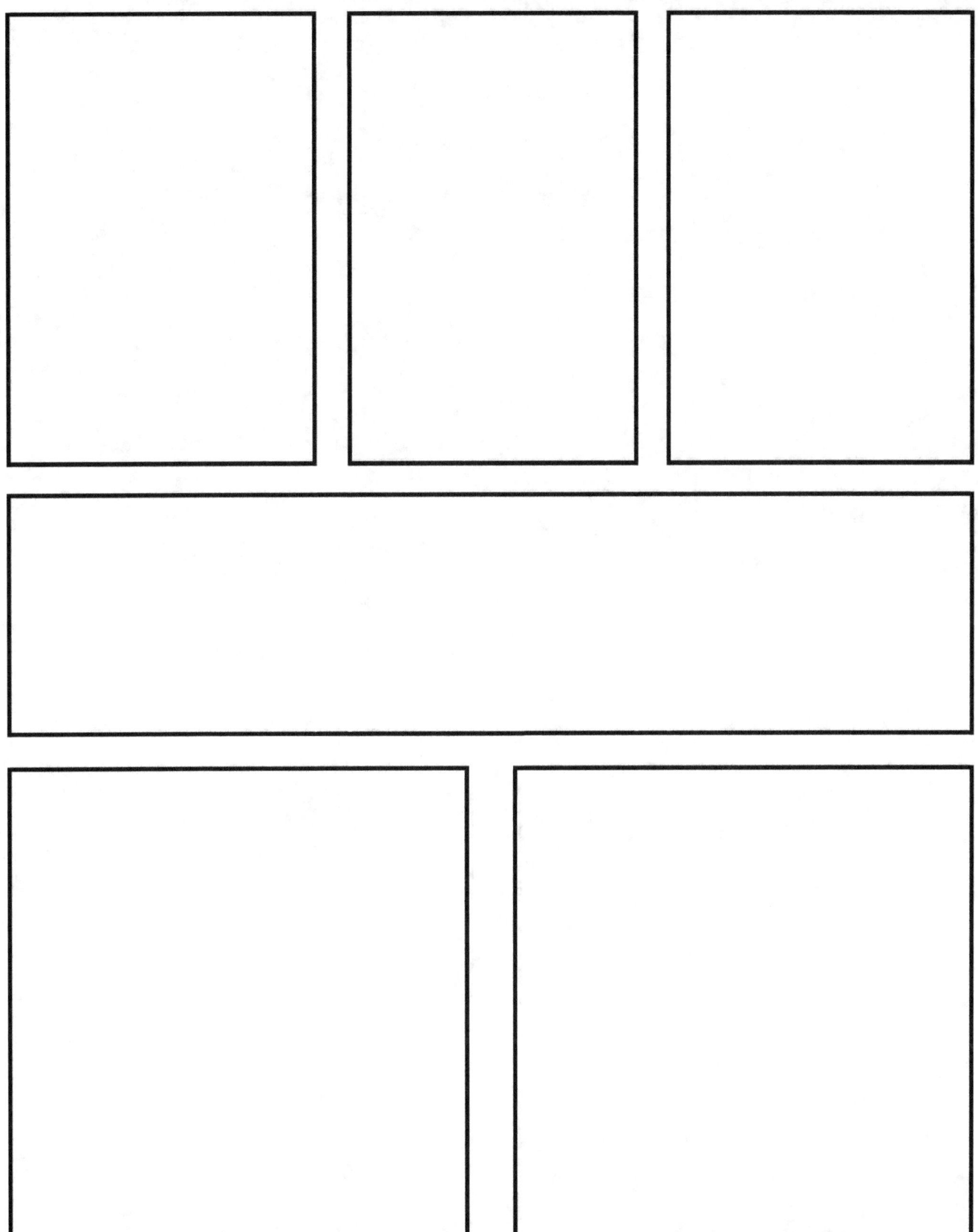

Blank Comic Book

Blank Comic Book

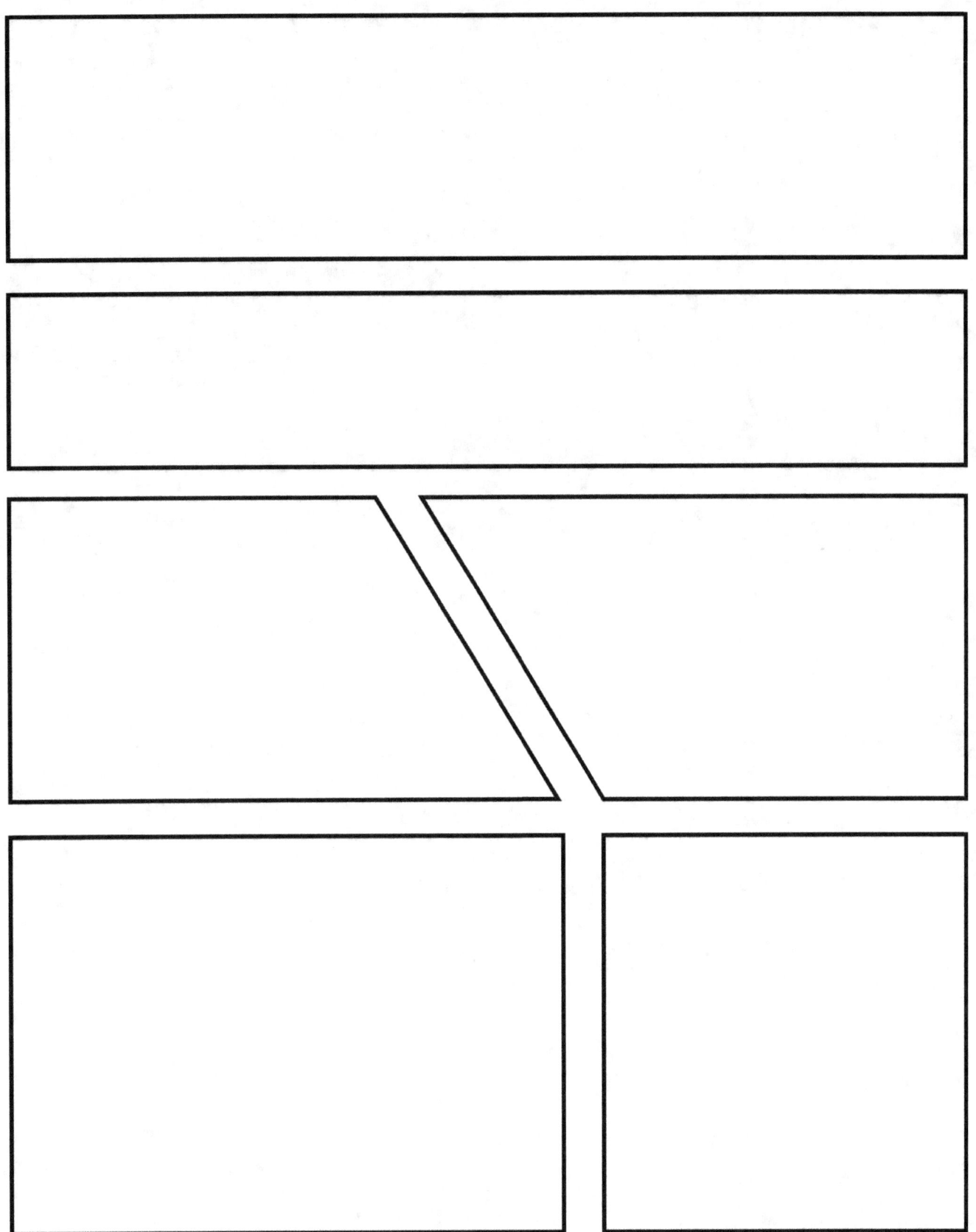

Blank Comic Book

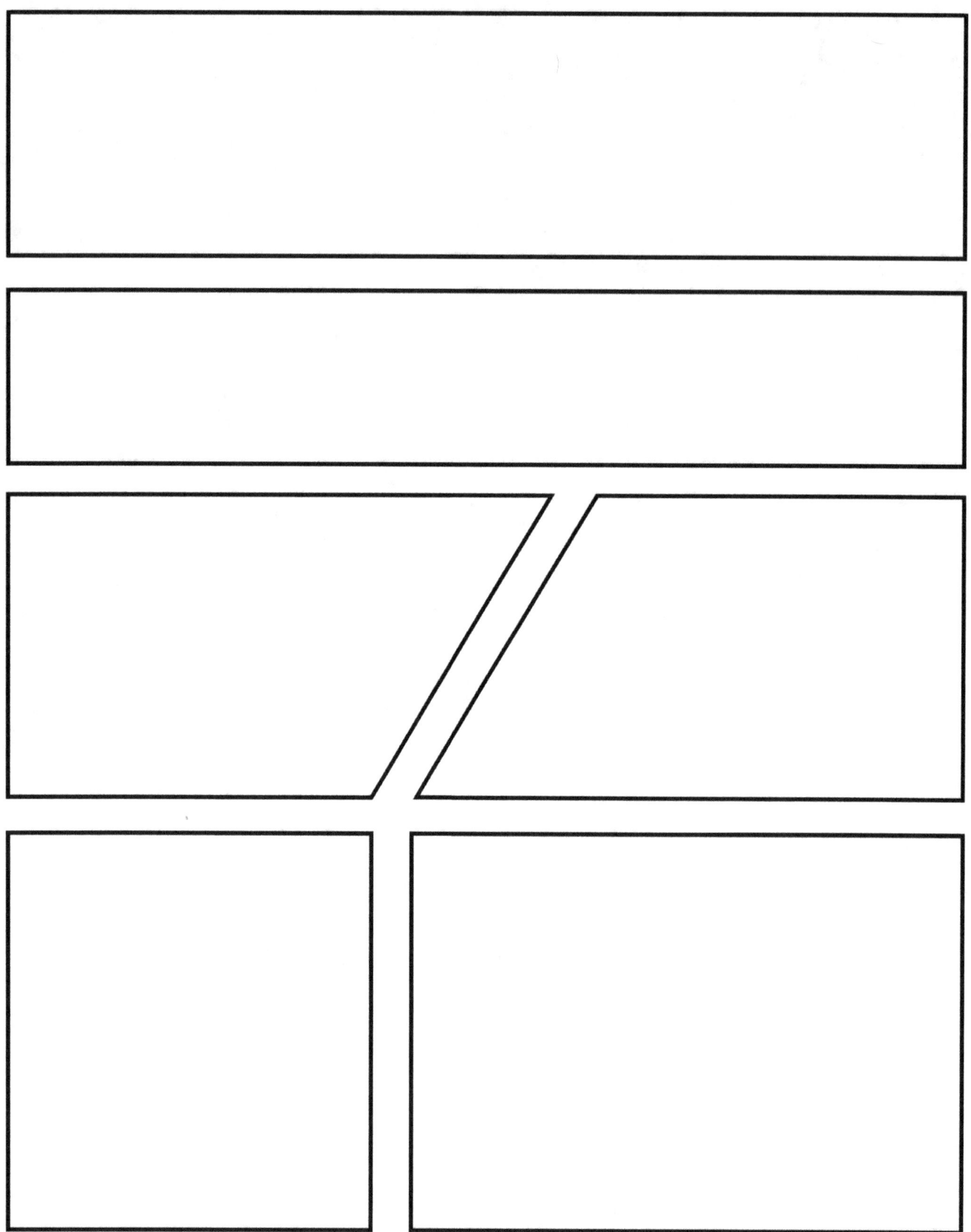

20

Blank Comic Book

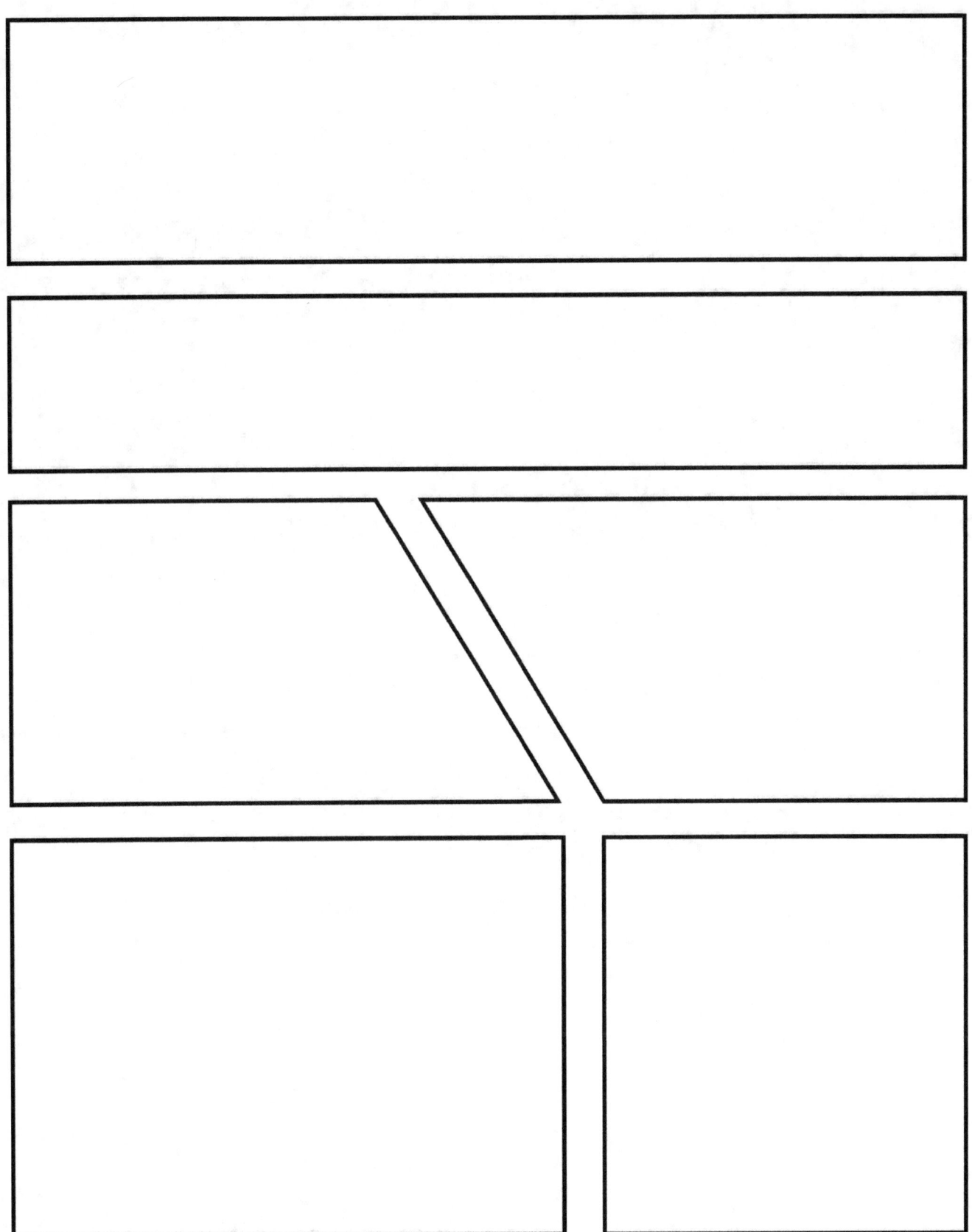

21

Blank Comic Book

Blank Comic Book

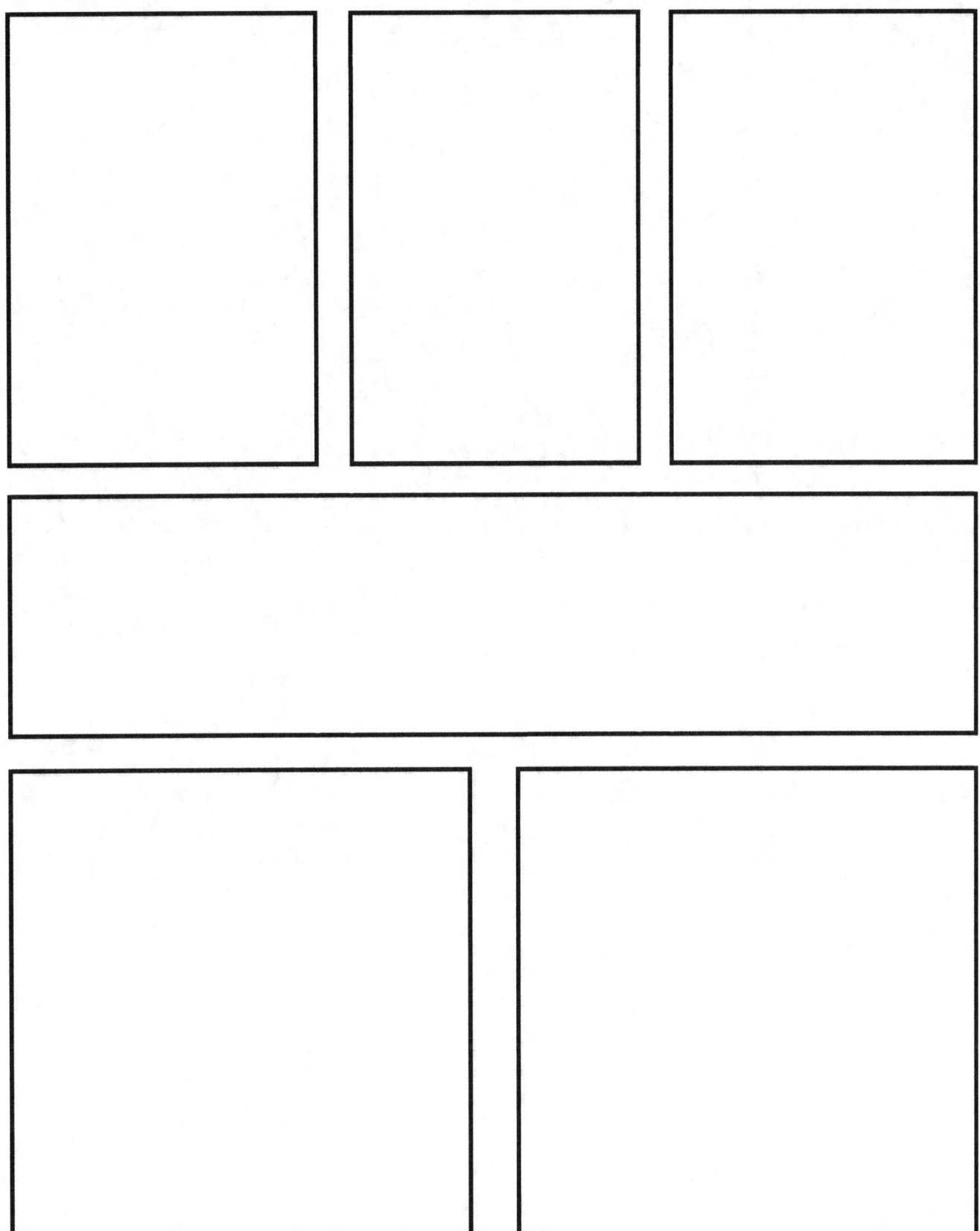

23

Blank Comic Book

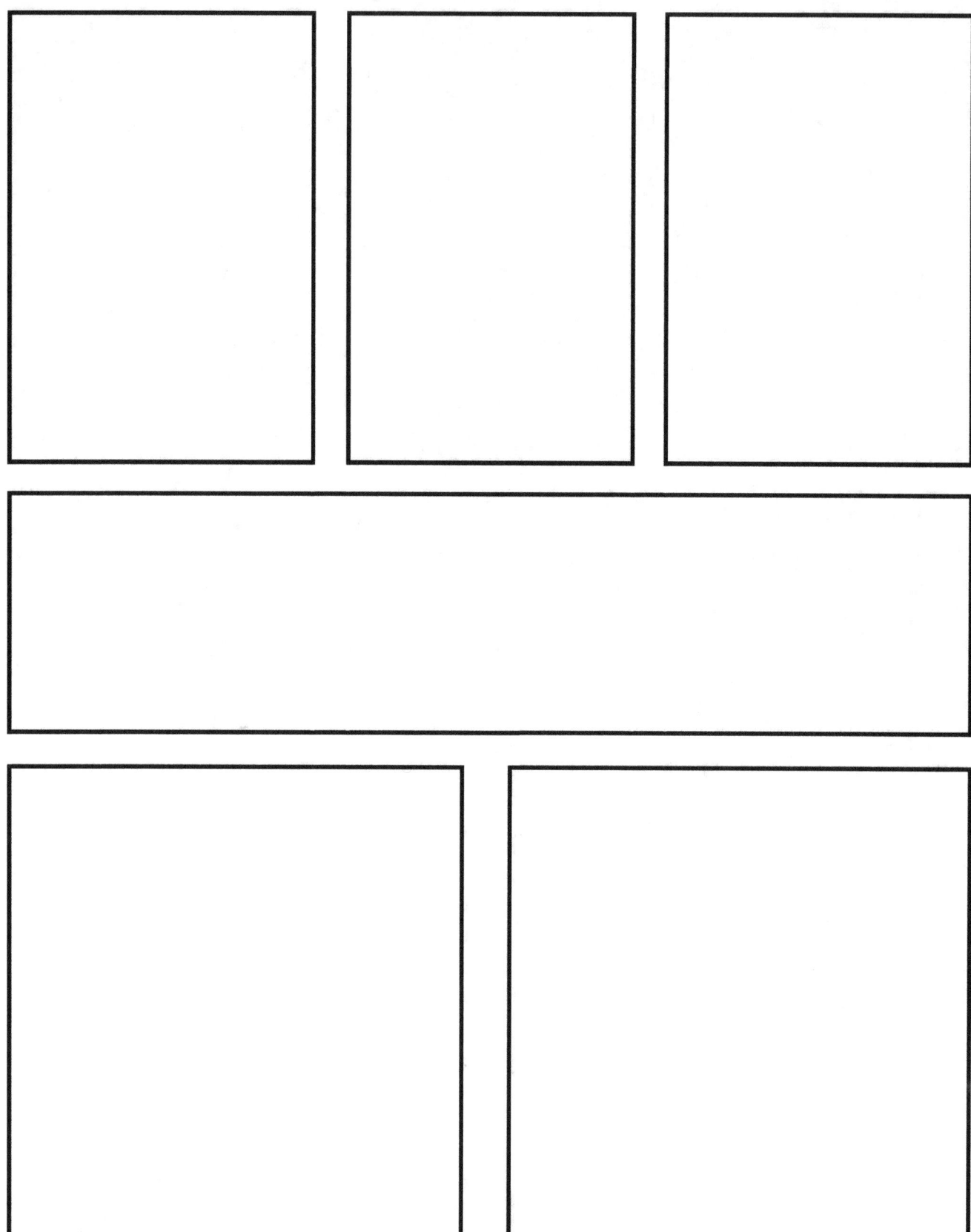

24

Blank Comic Book

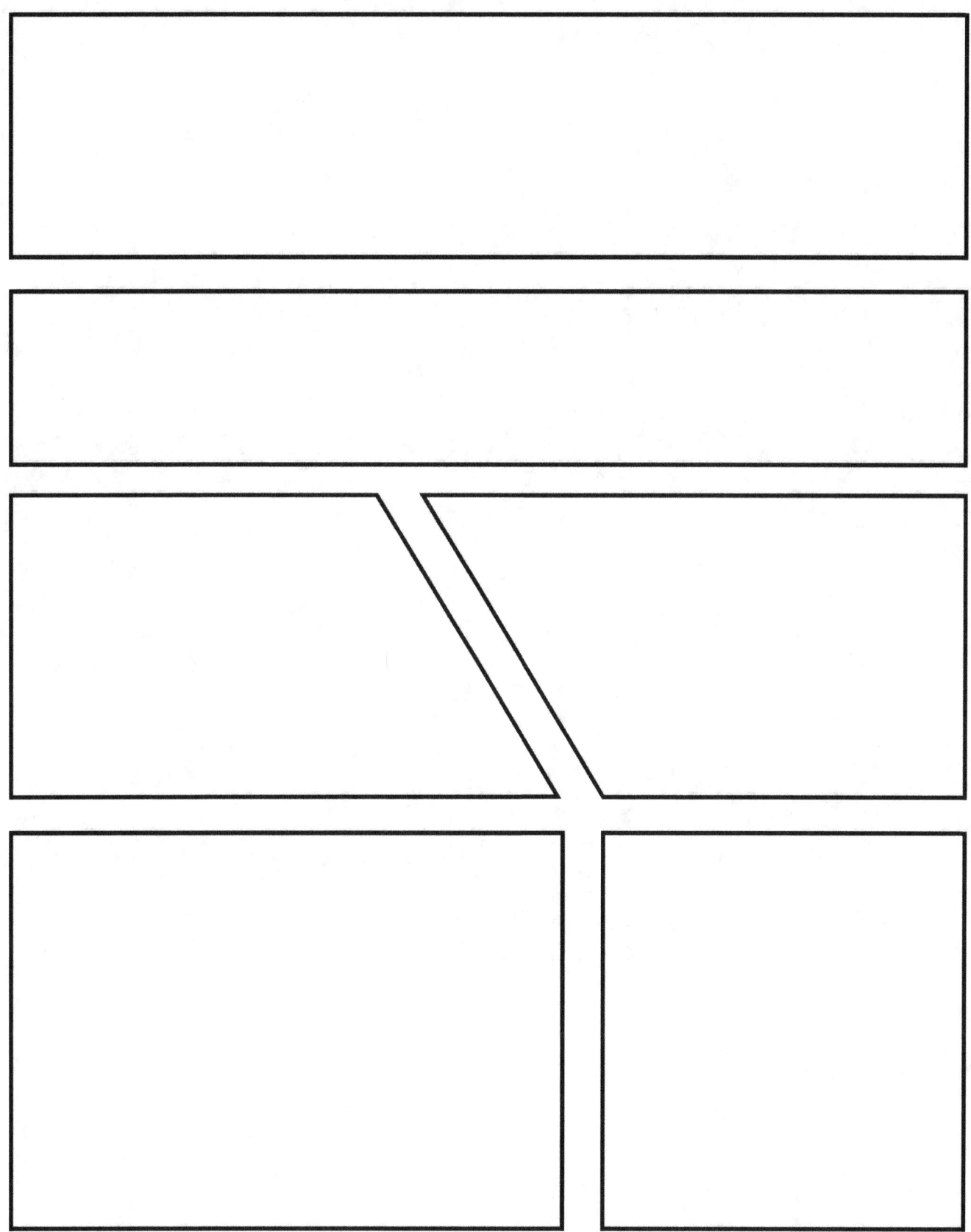

25

Blank Comic Book

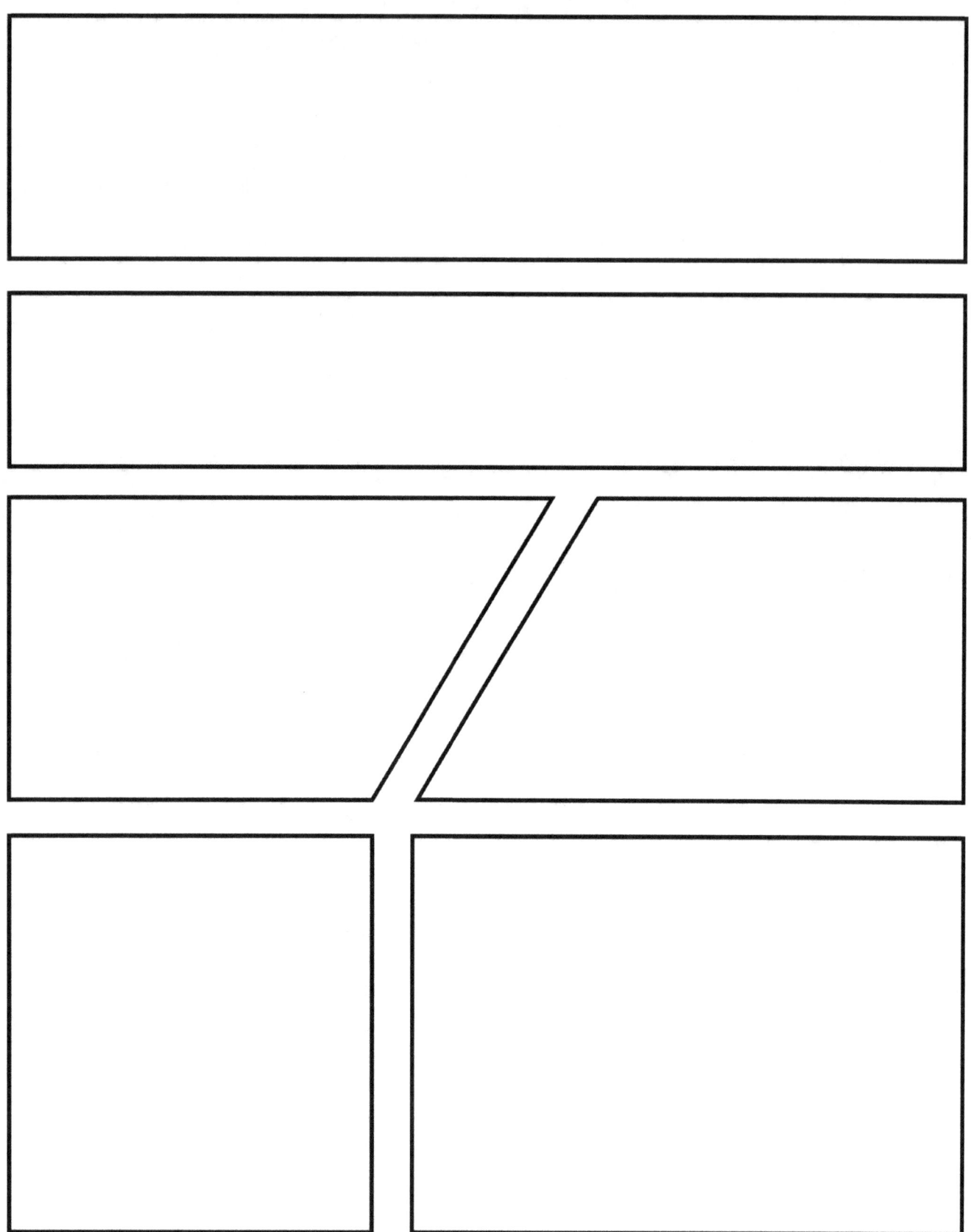

Blank Comic Book

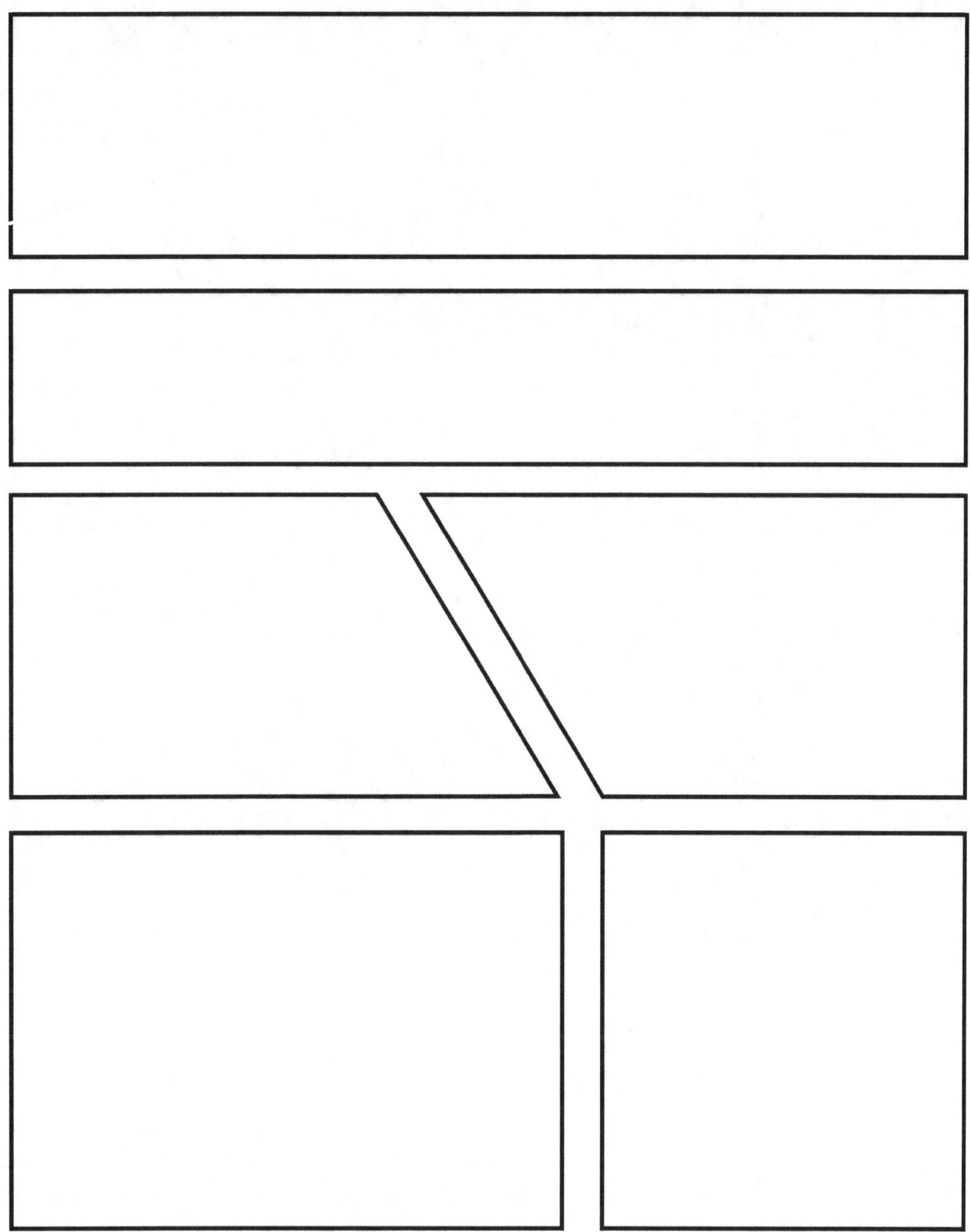

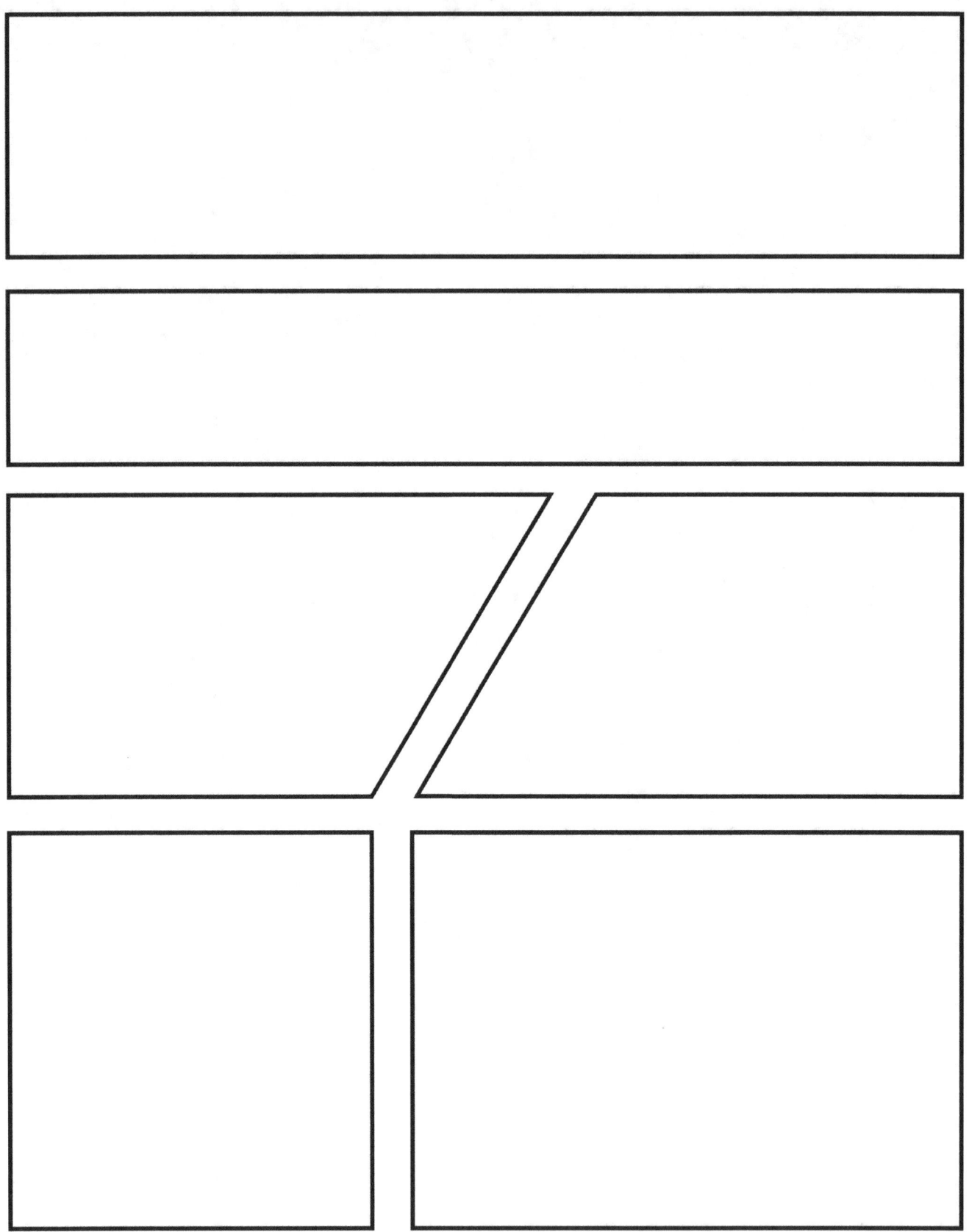

Blank Comic Book

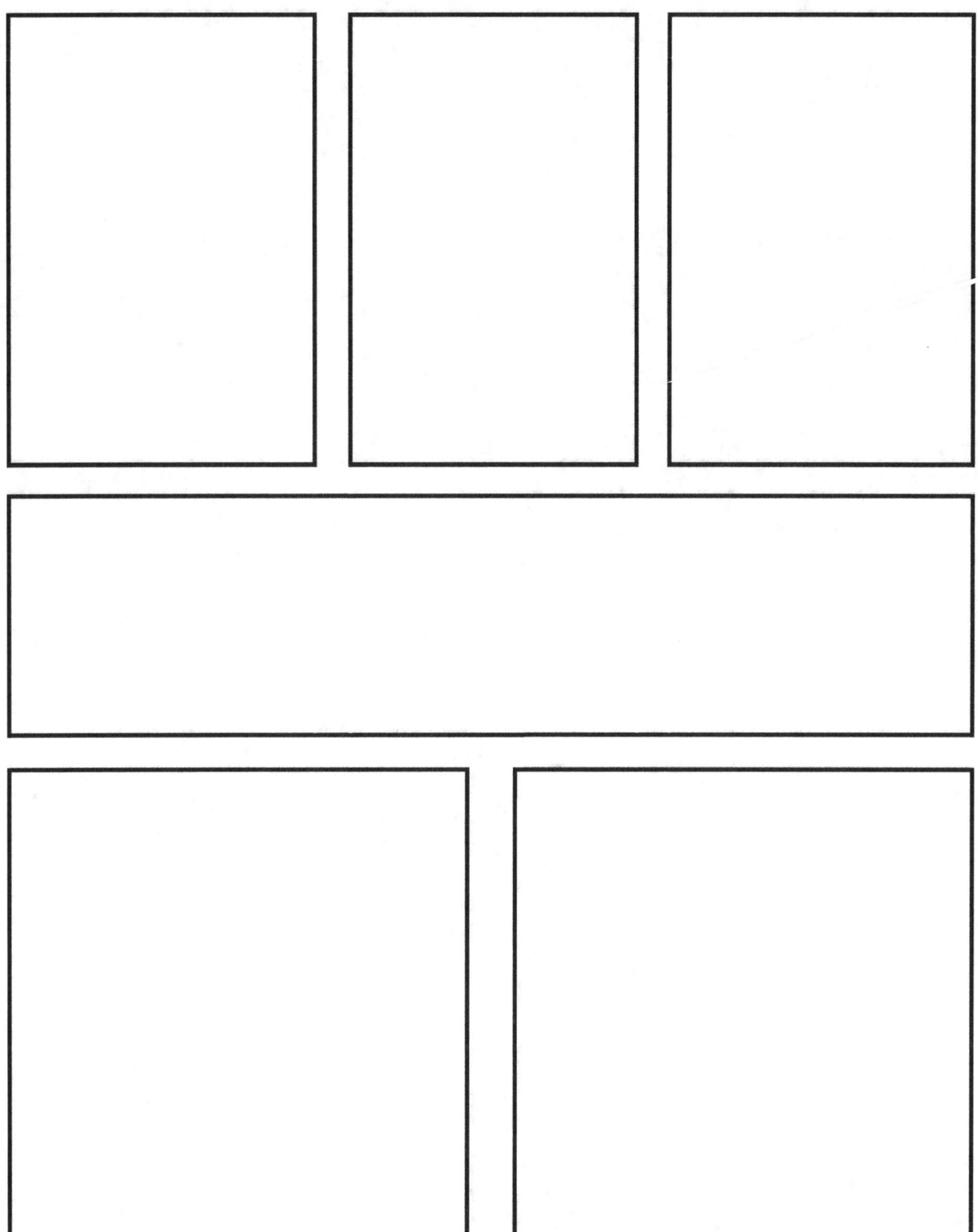

Blank Comic Book

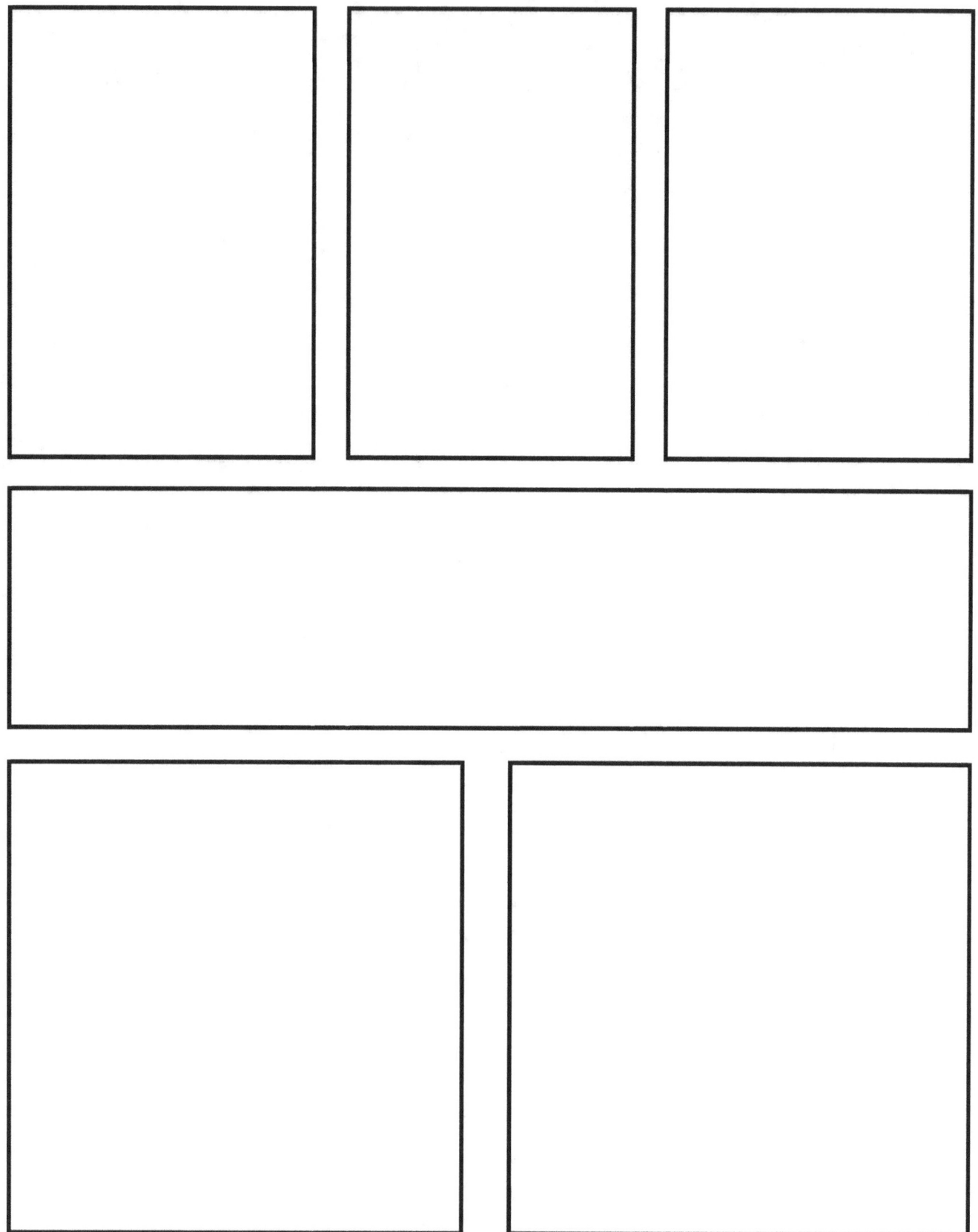

30

Blank Comic Book

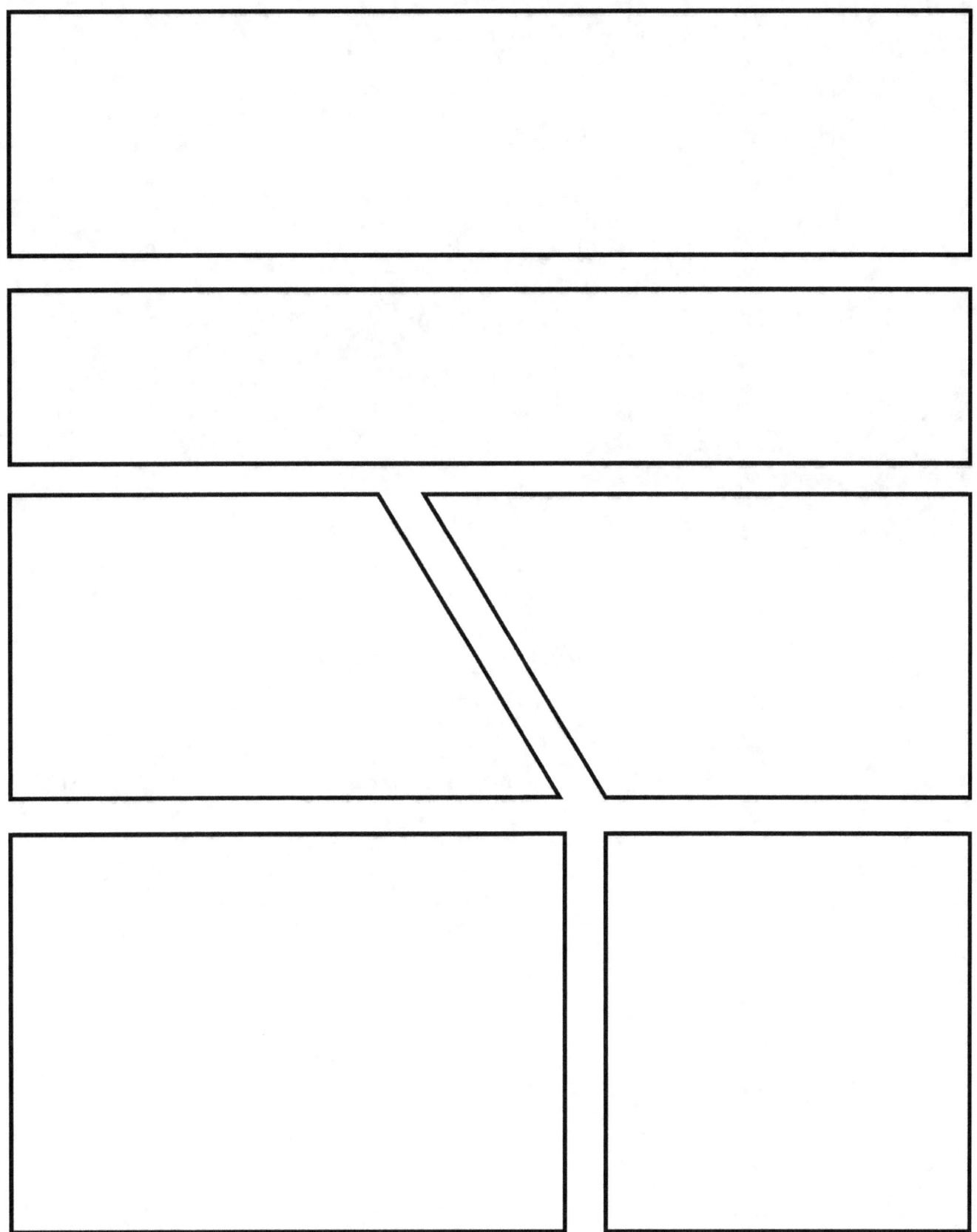

31

Blank Comic Book

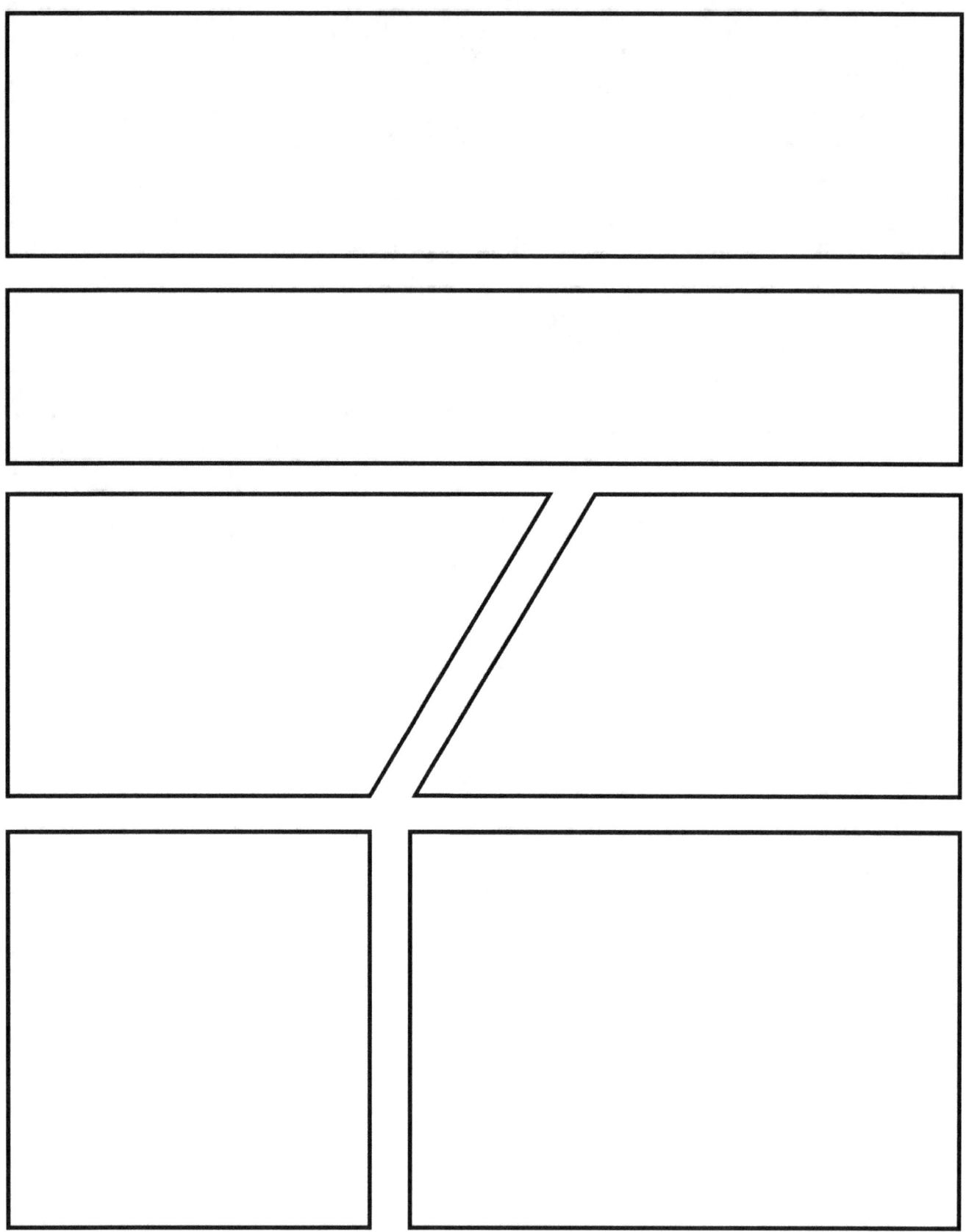

Blank Comic Book

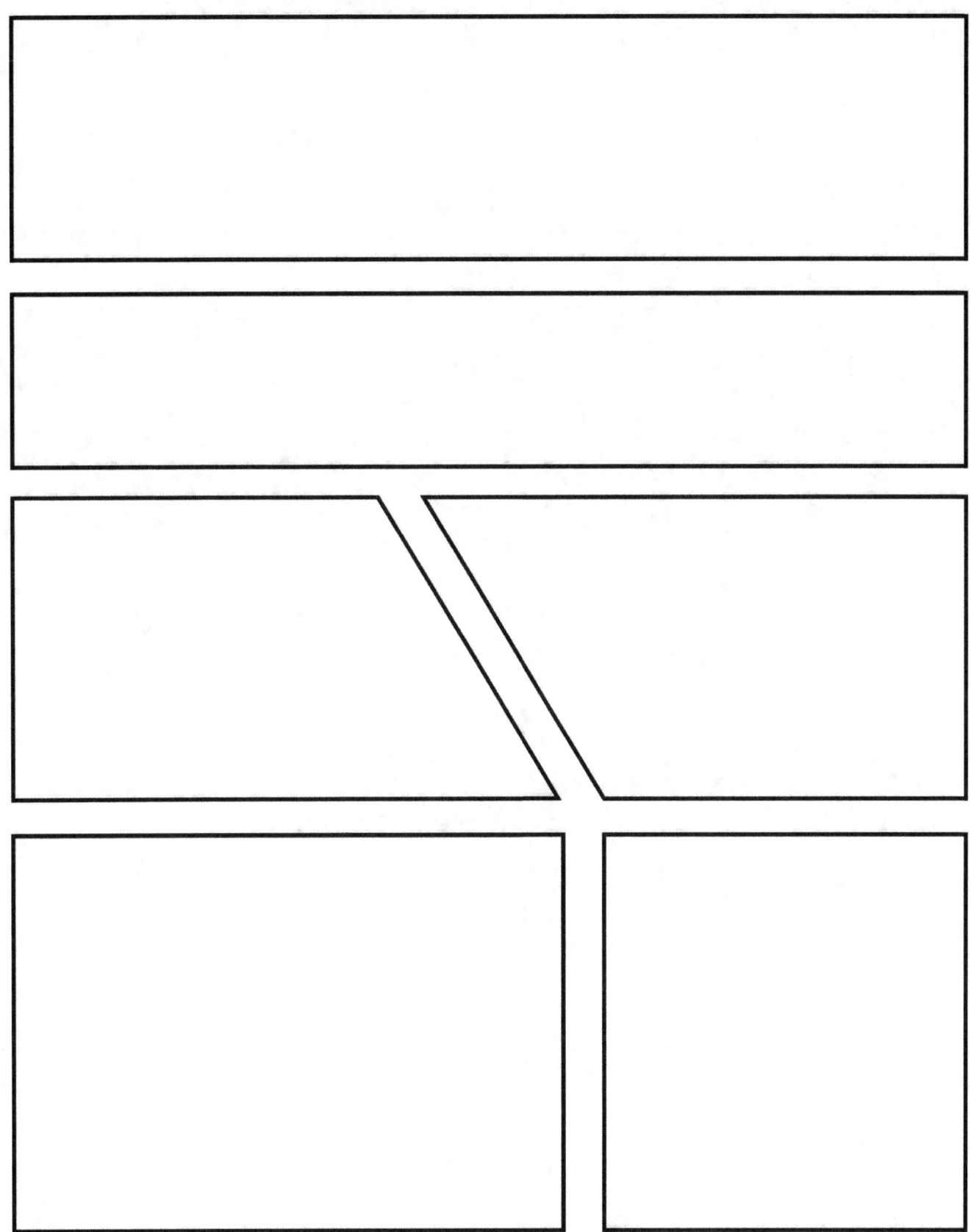

Blank Comic Book

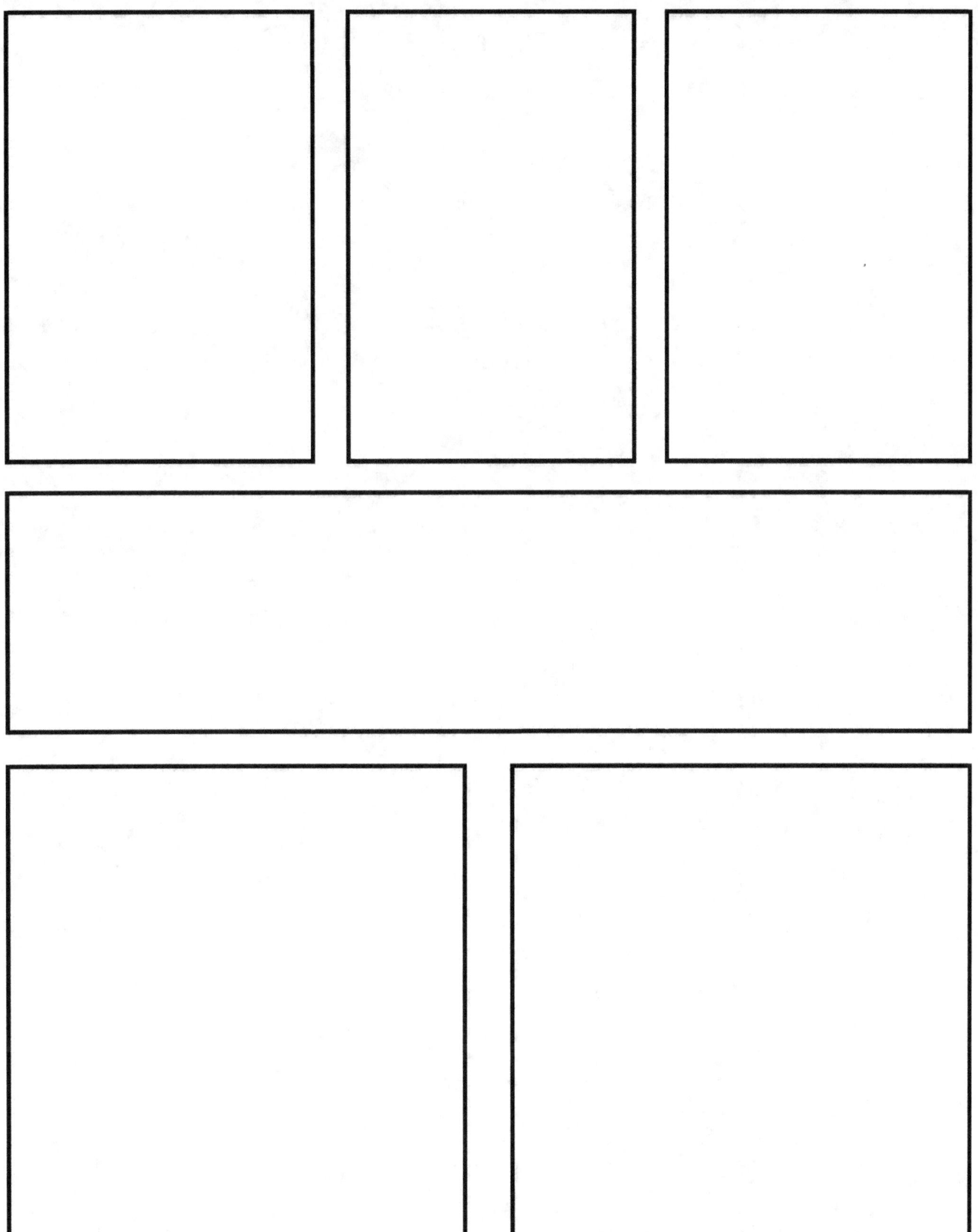

Blank Comic Book

Blank Comic Book

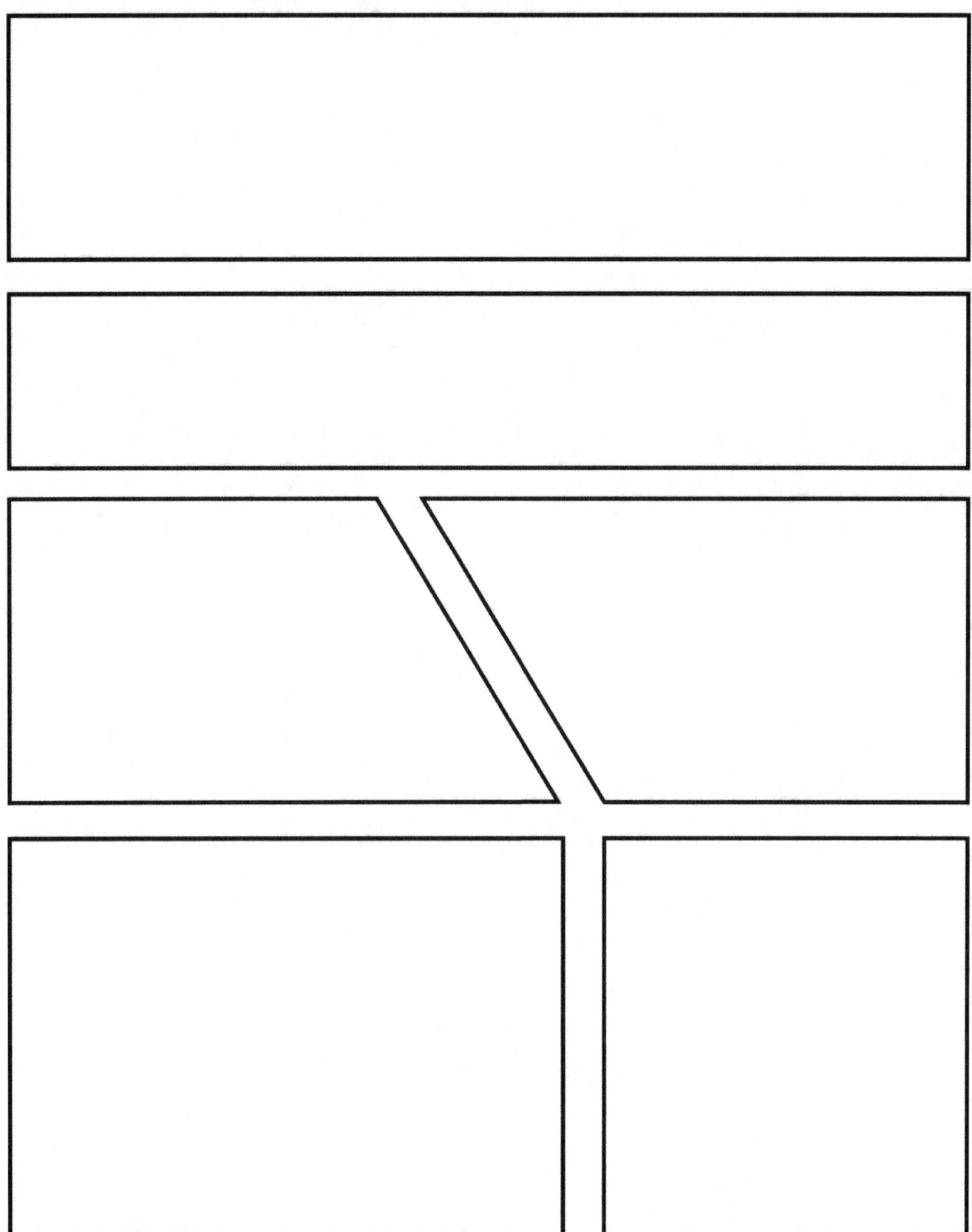

Blank Comic Book

38

Blank Comic Book

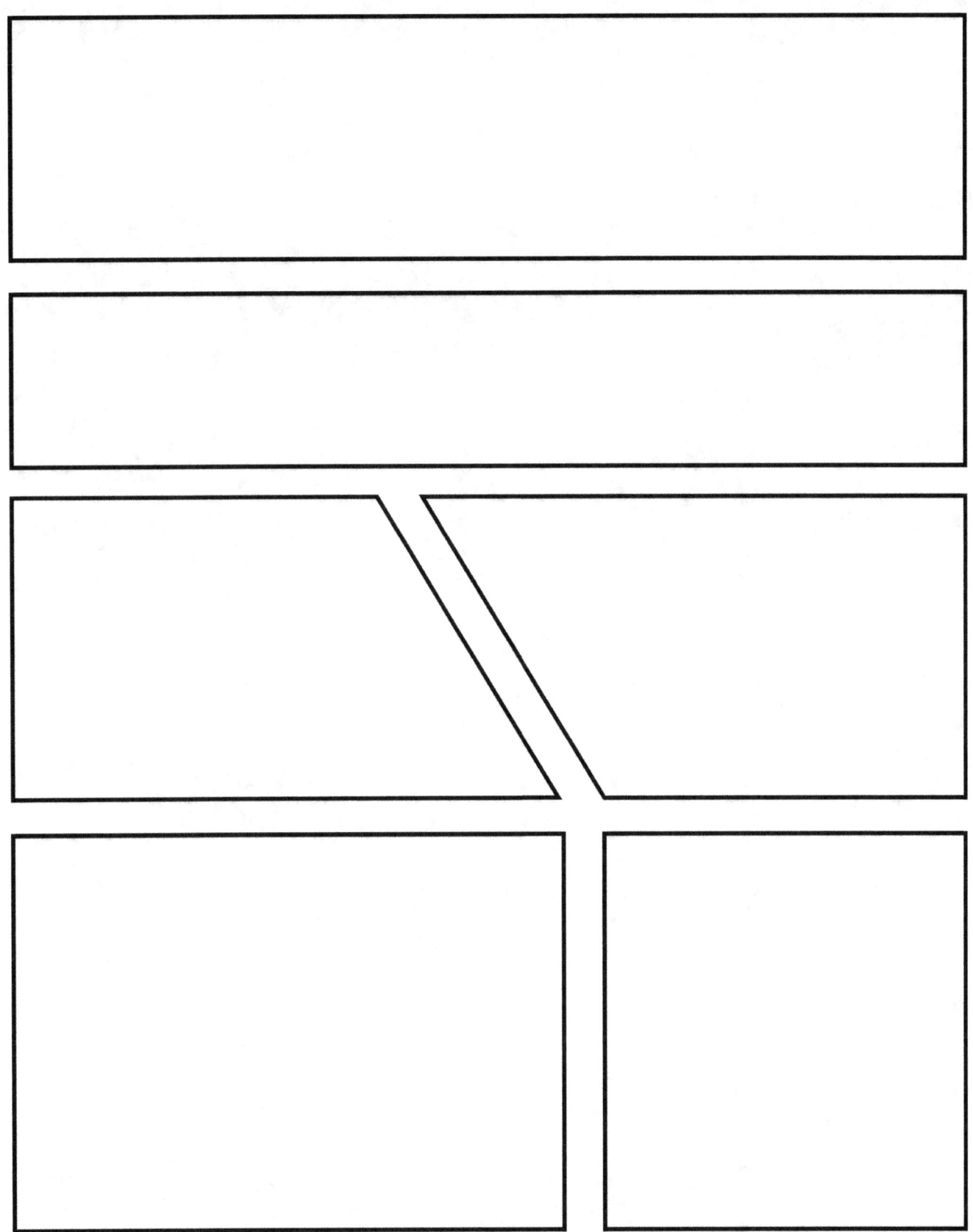

Blank Comic Book

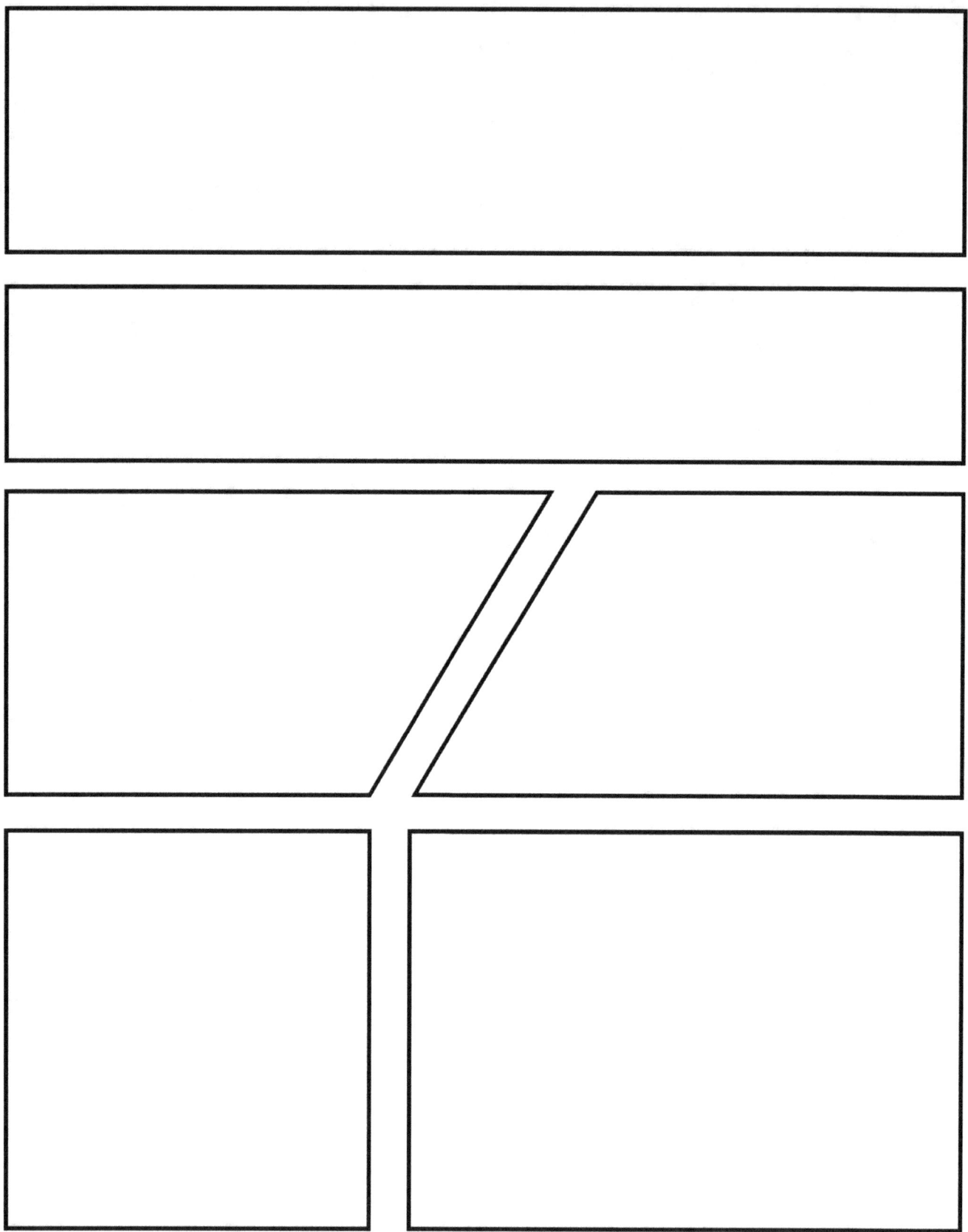

40

Blank Comic Book

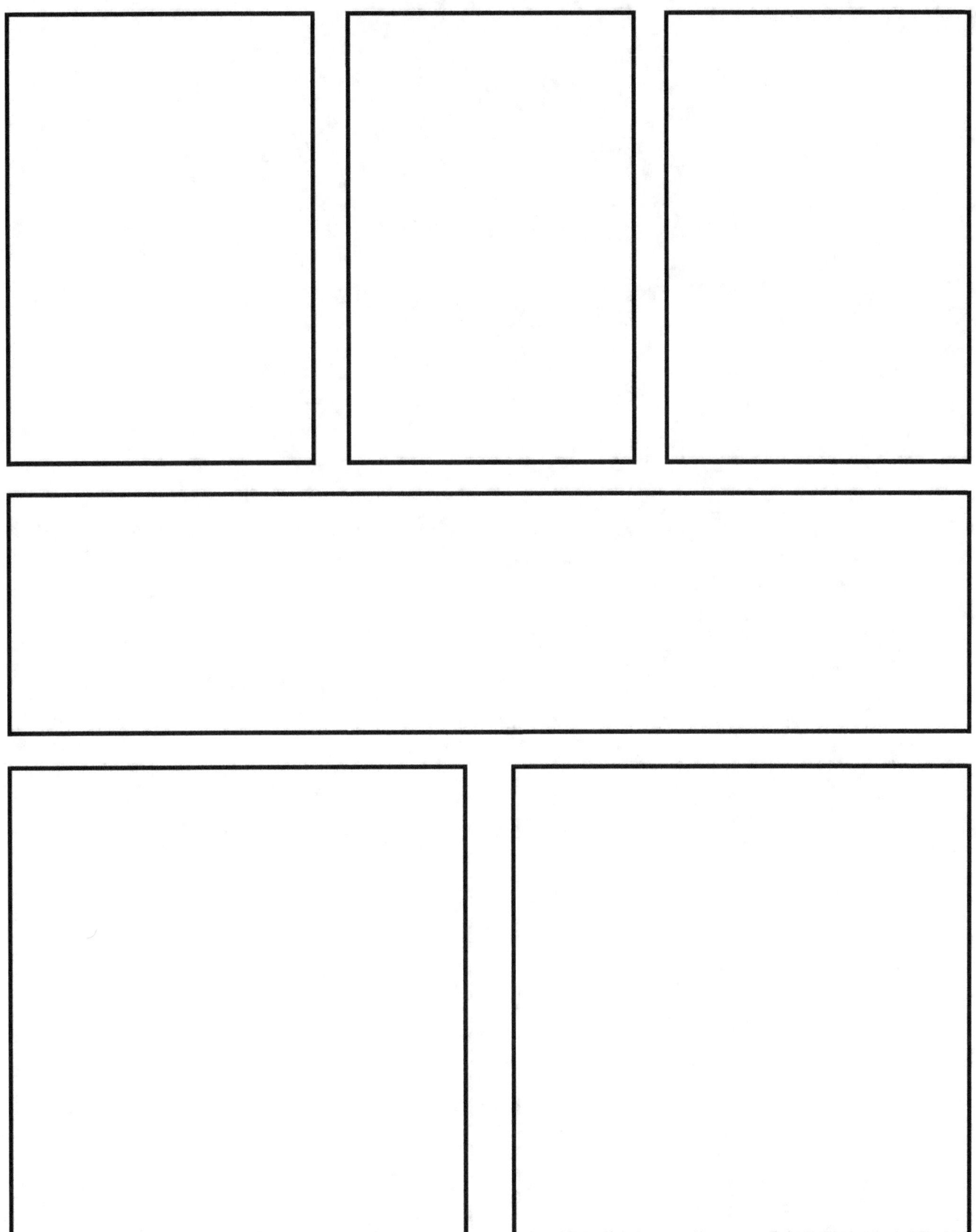

Blank Comic Book

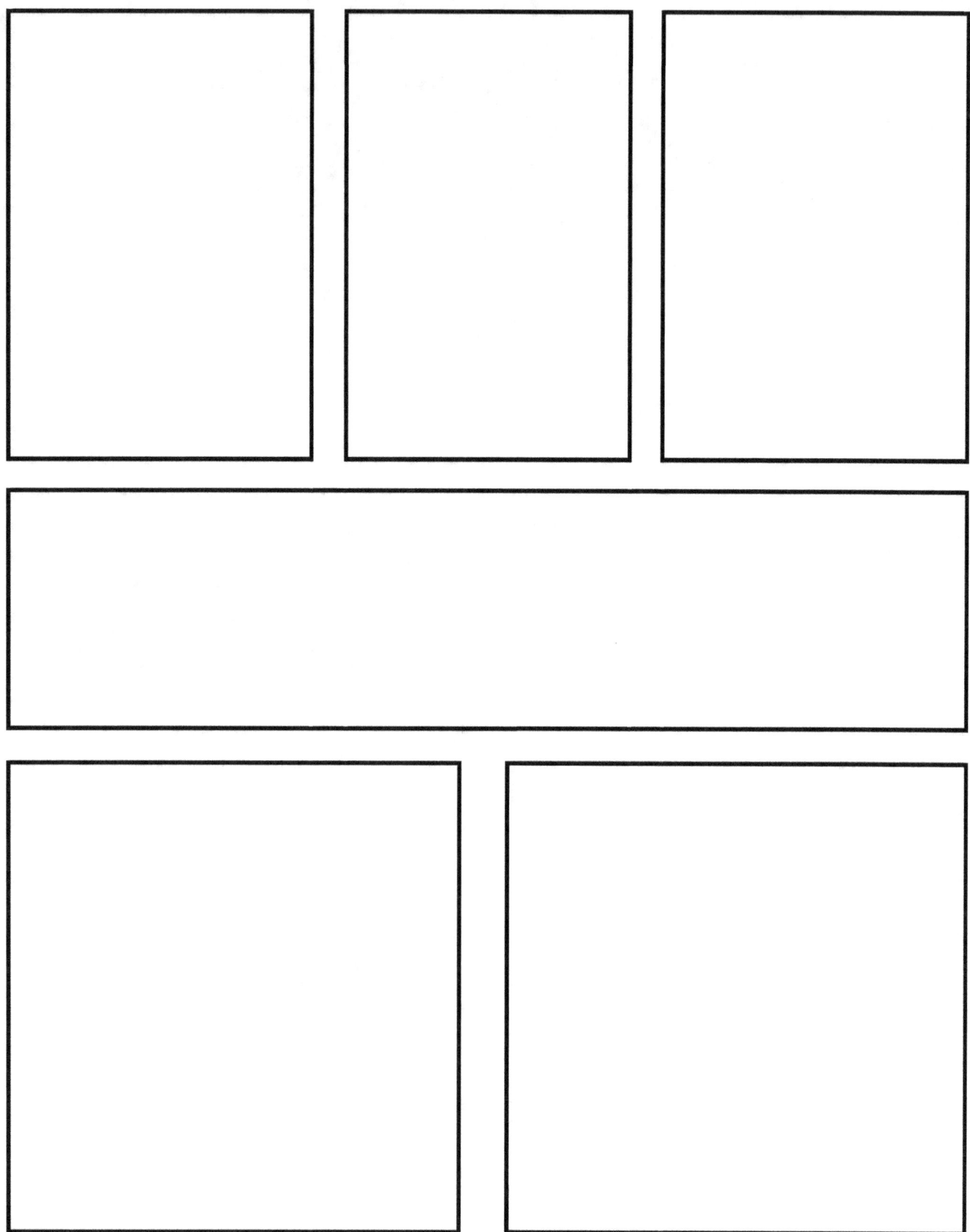

42

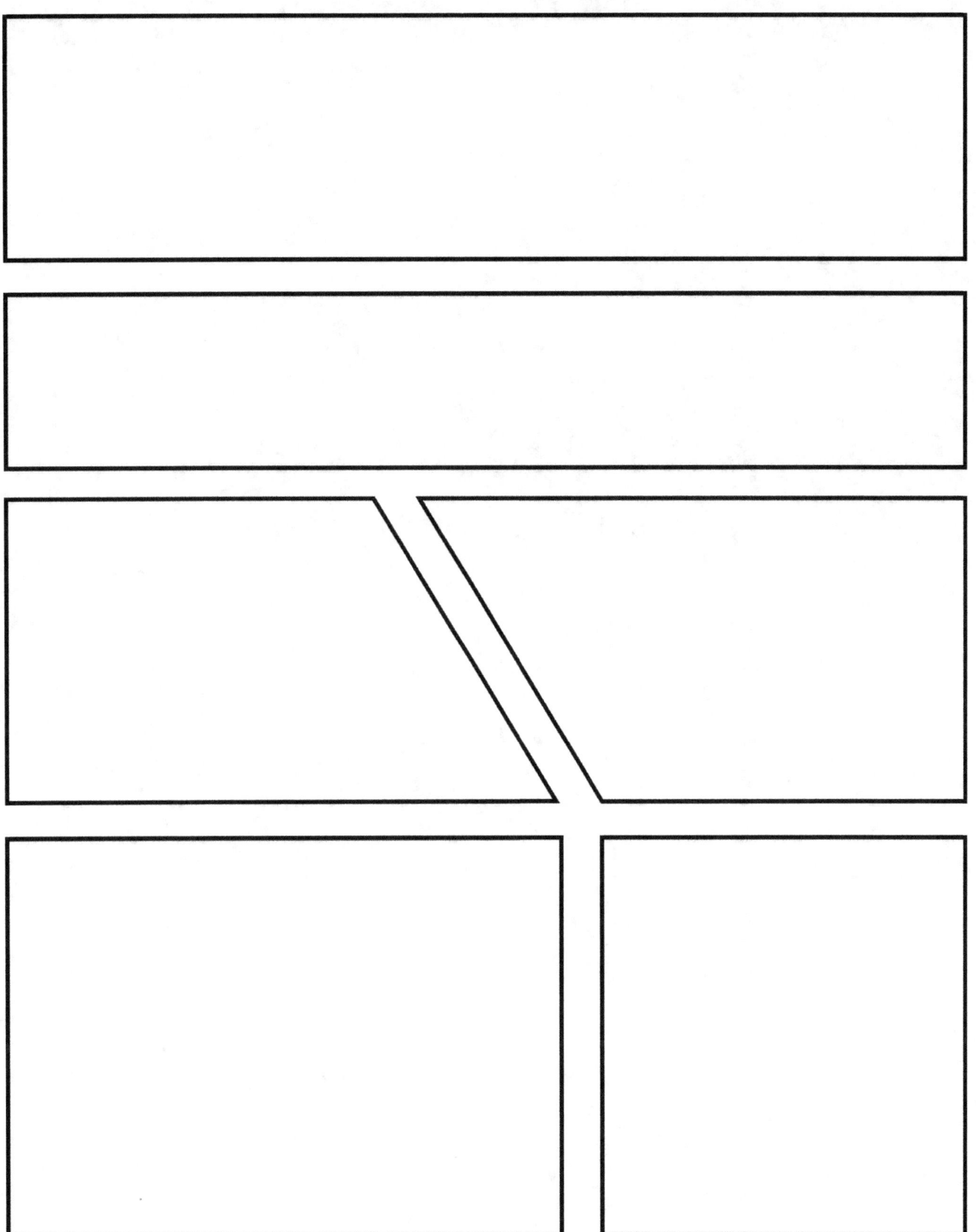

Blank Comic Book

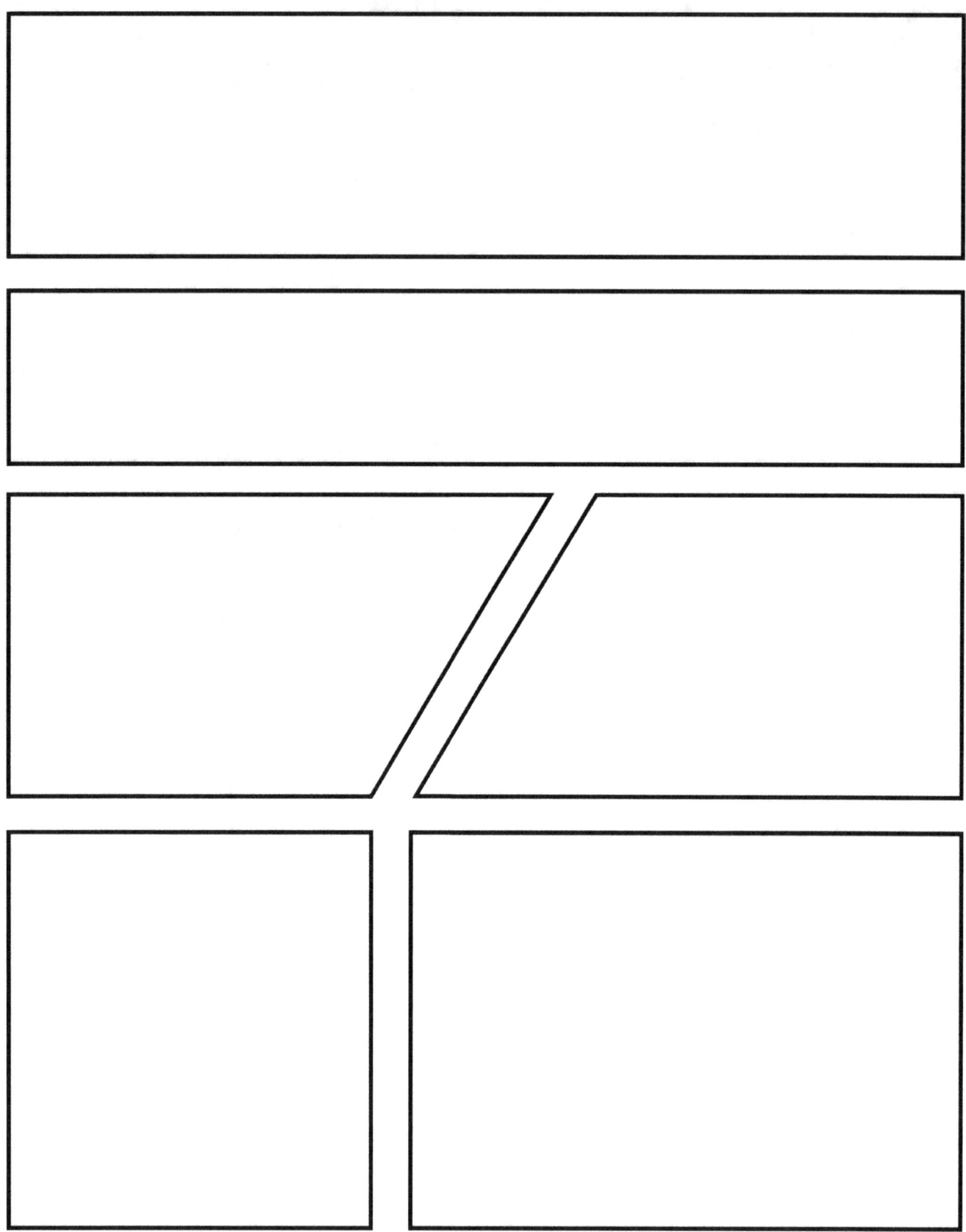

Blank Comic Book

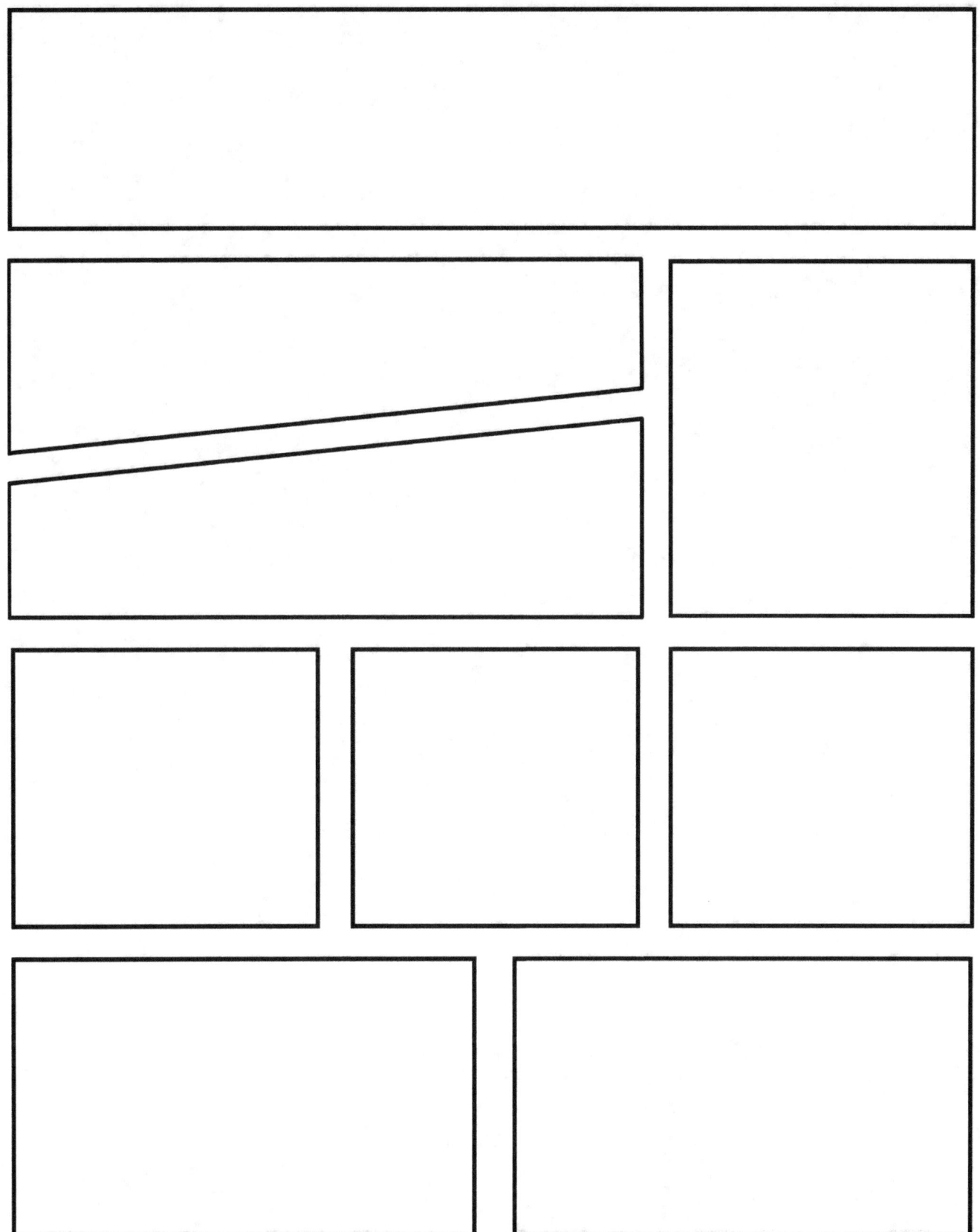

45

Blank Comic Book

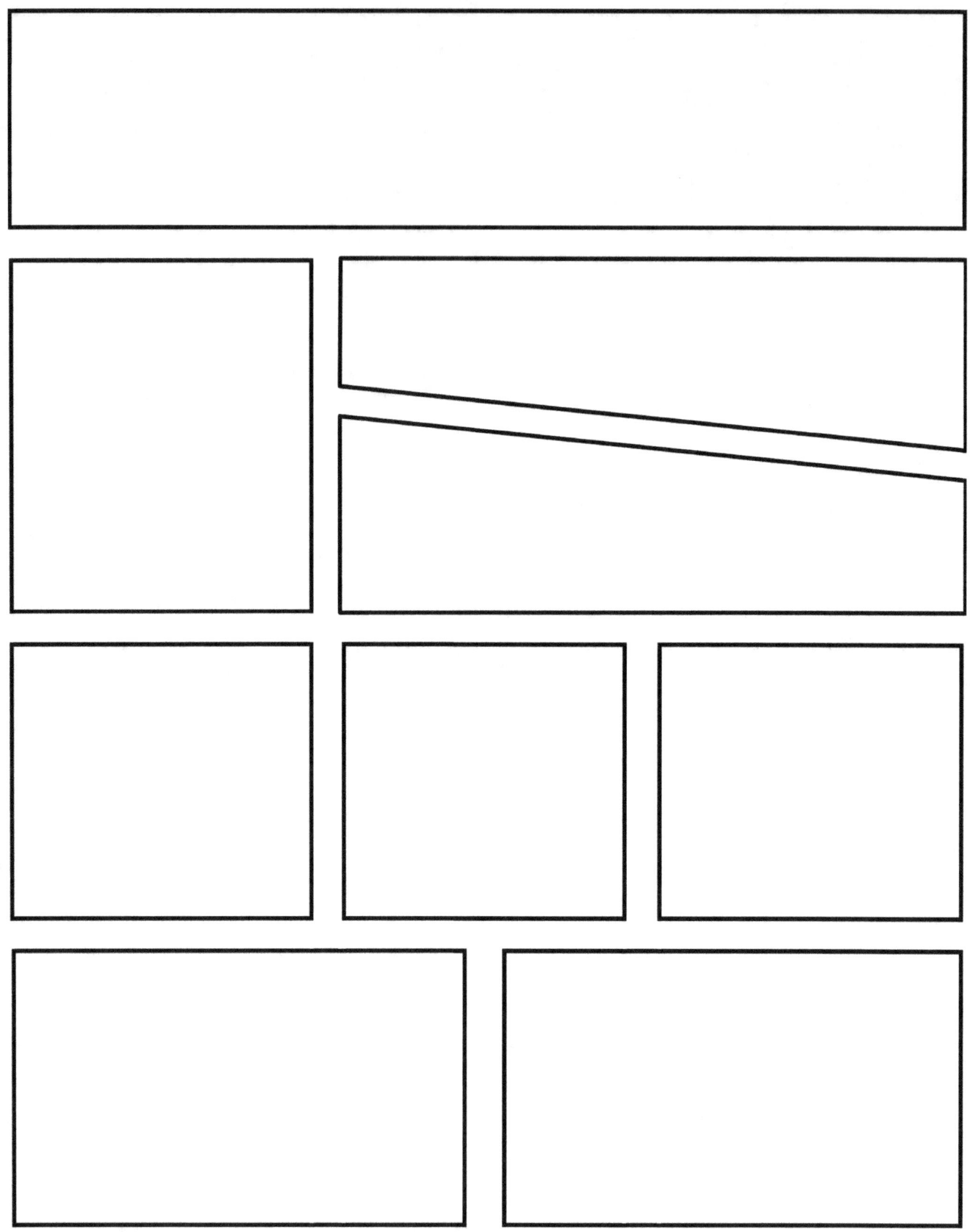

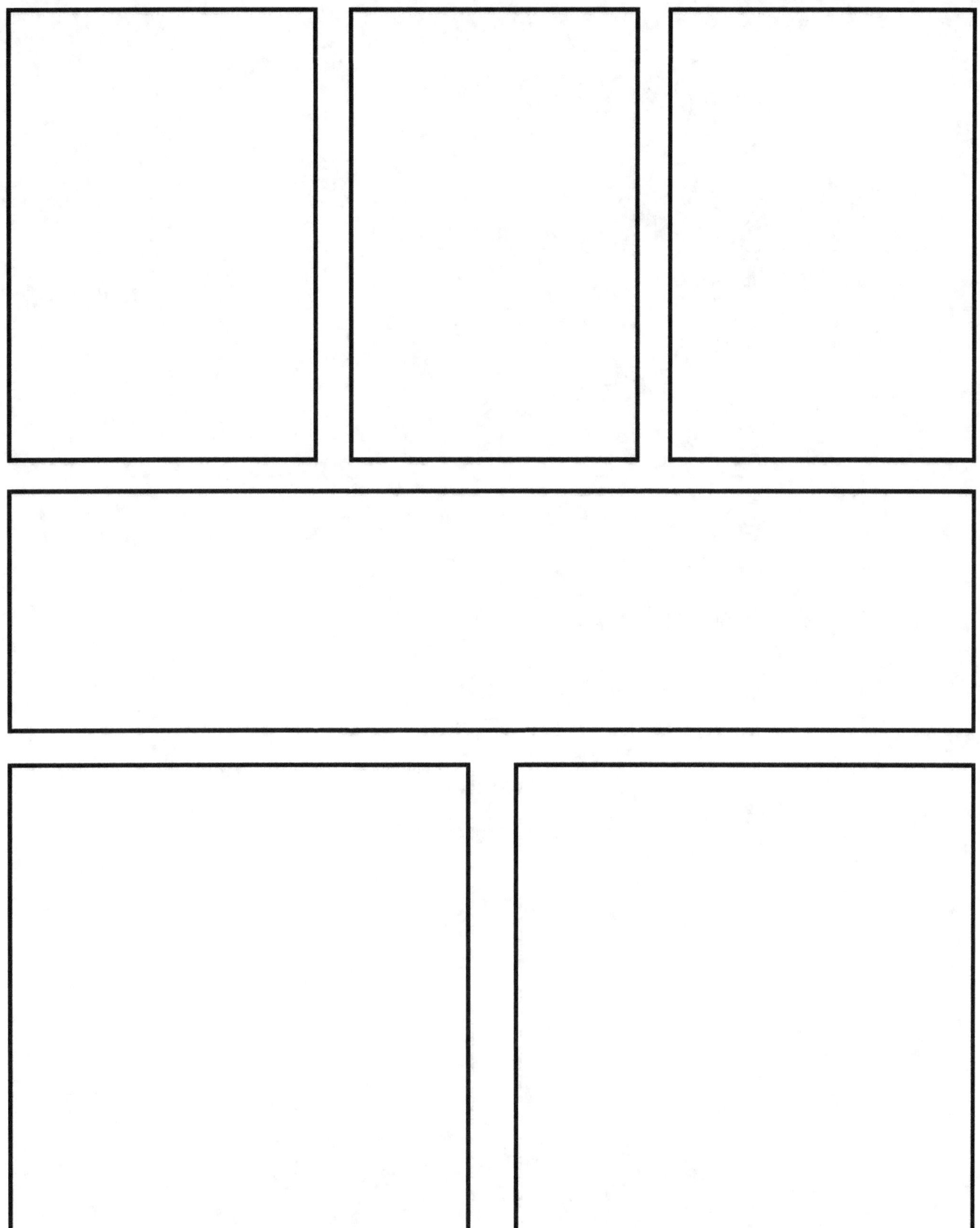

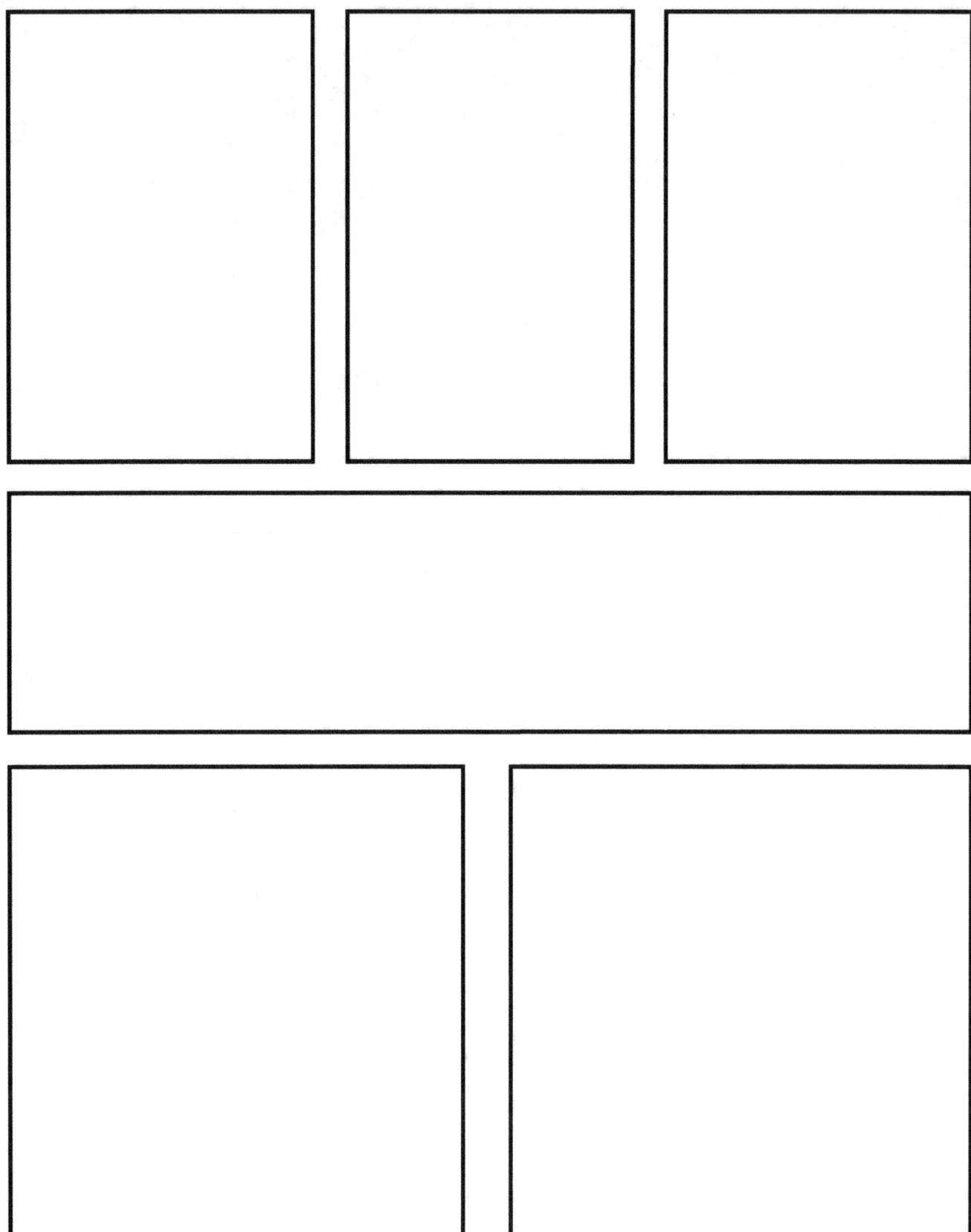

Blank Comic Book

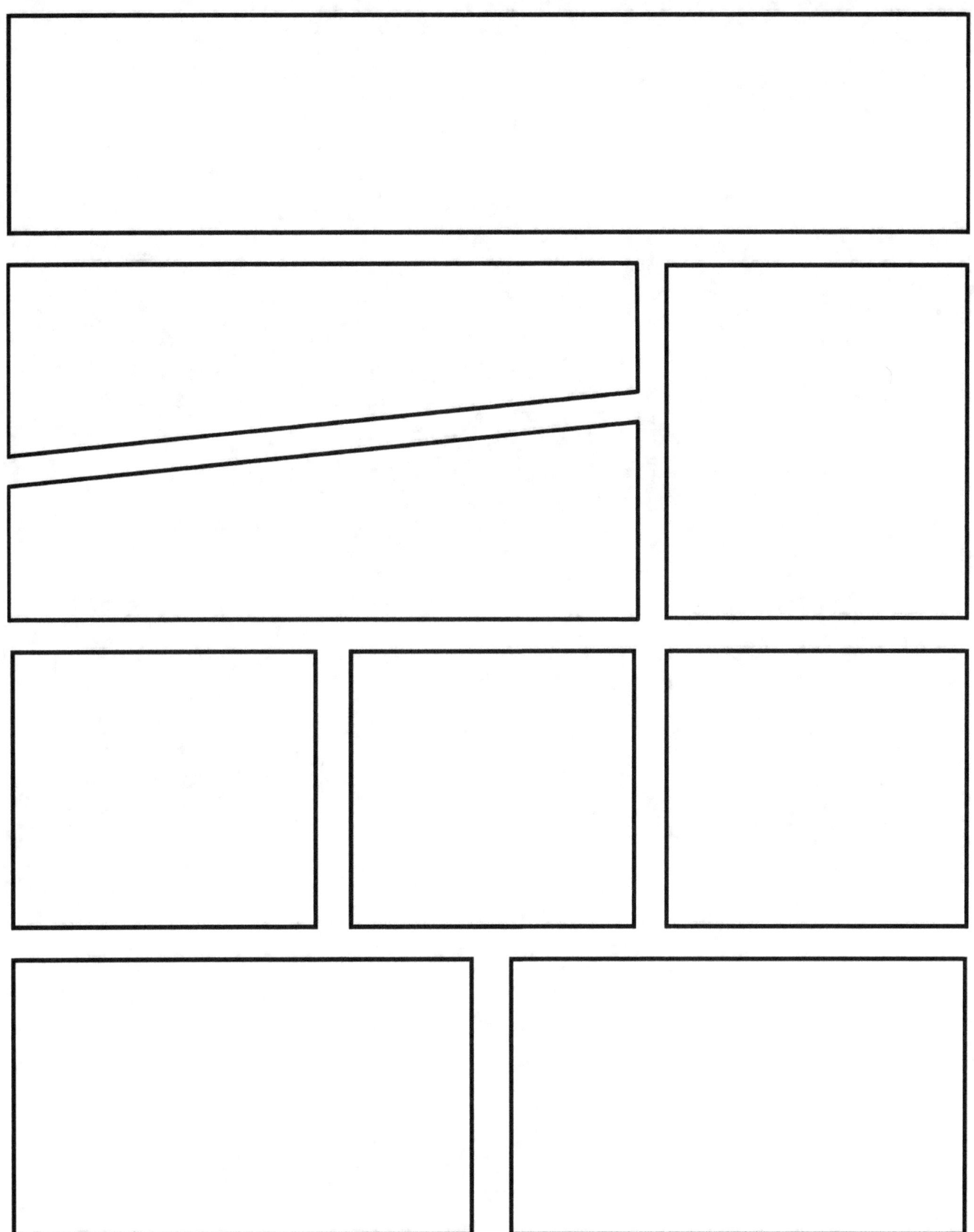

49

Blank Comic Book

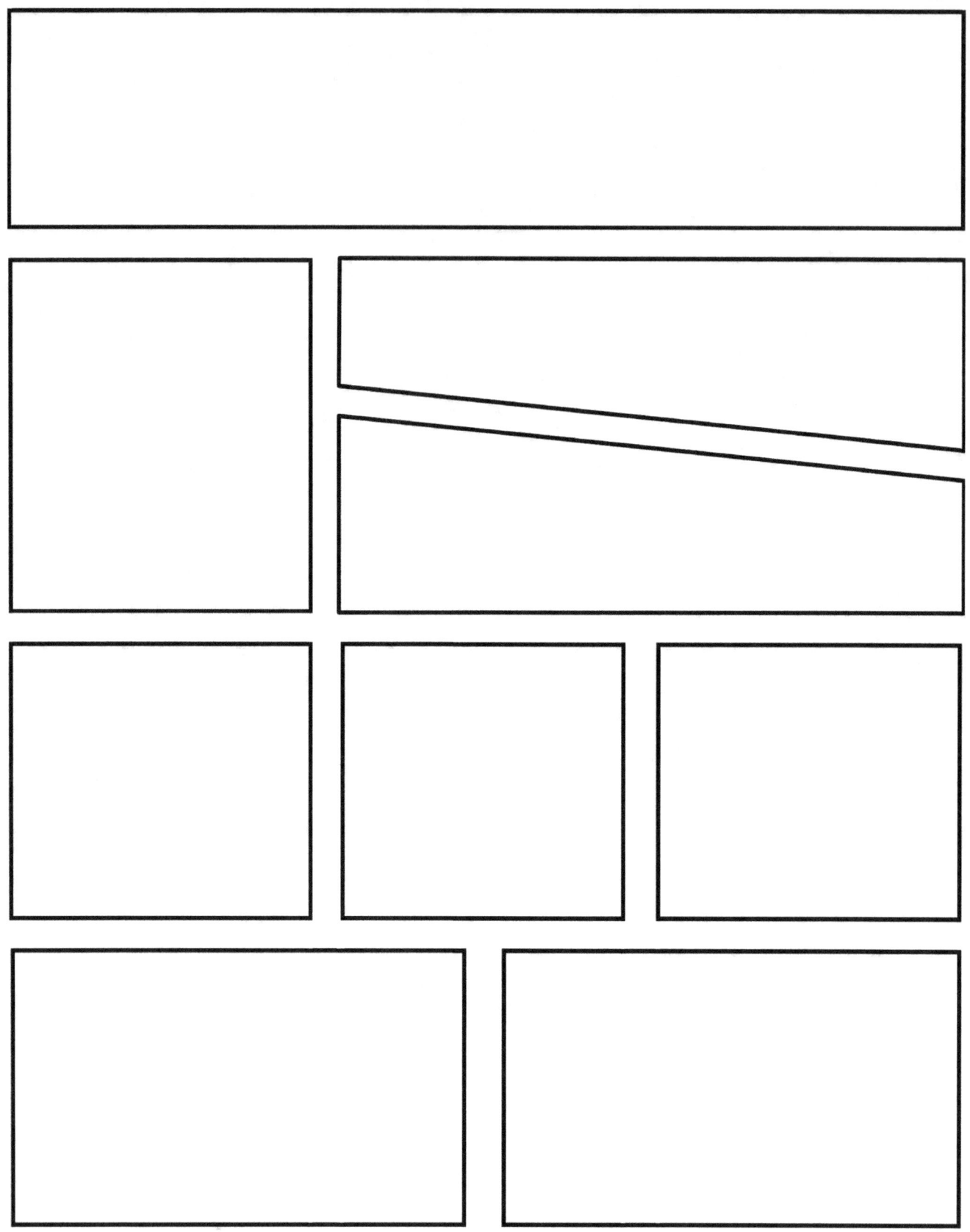

50

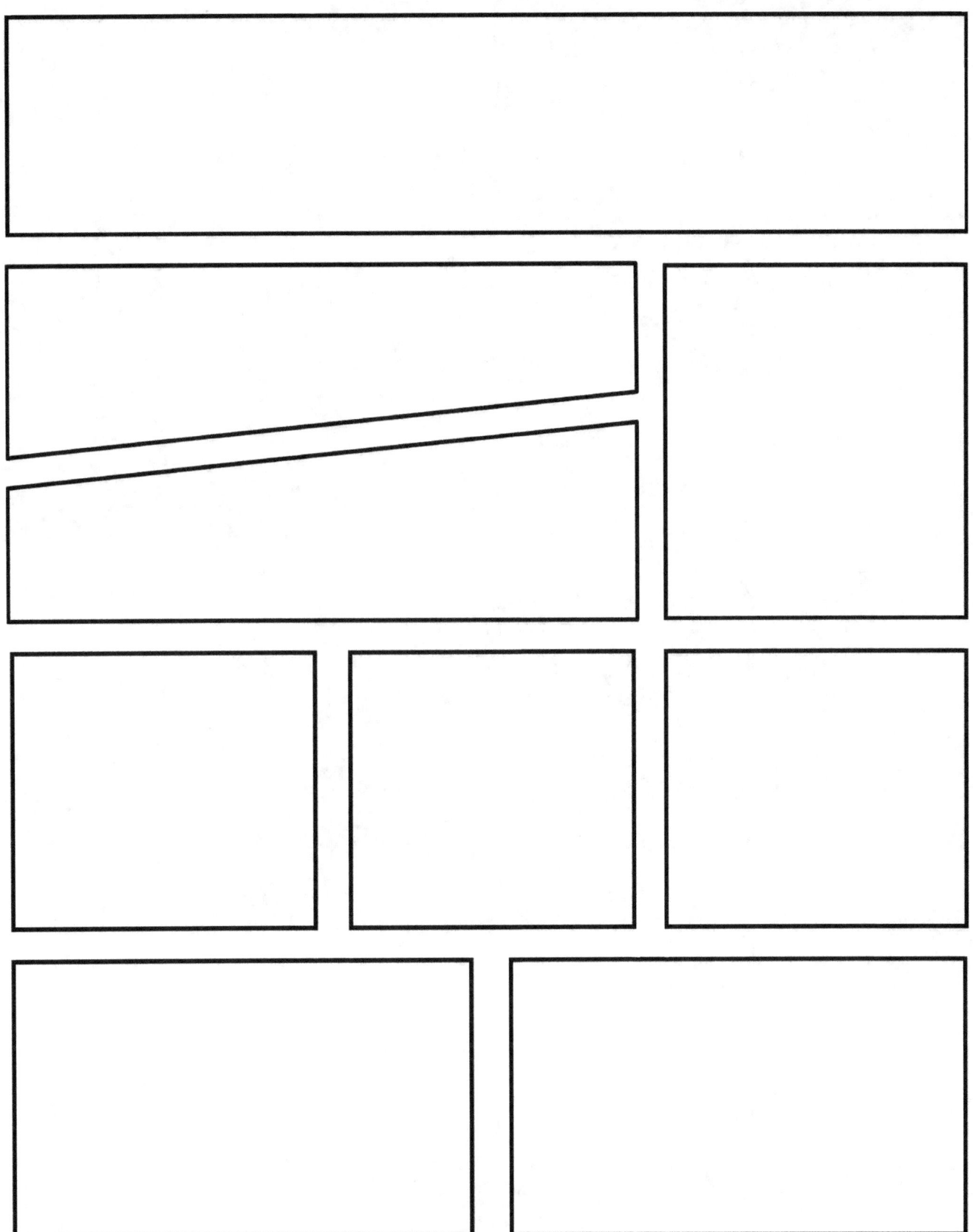

Blank Comic Book

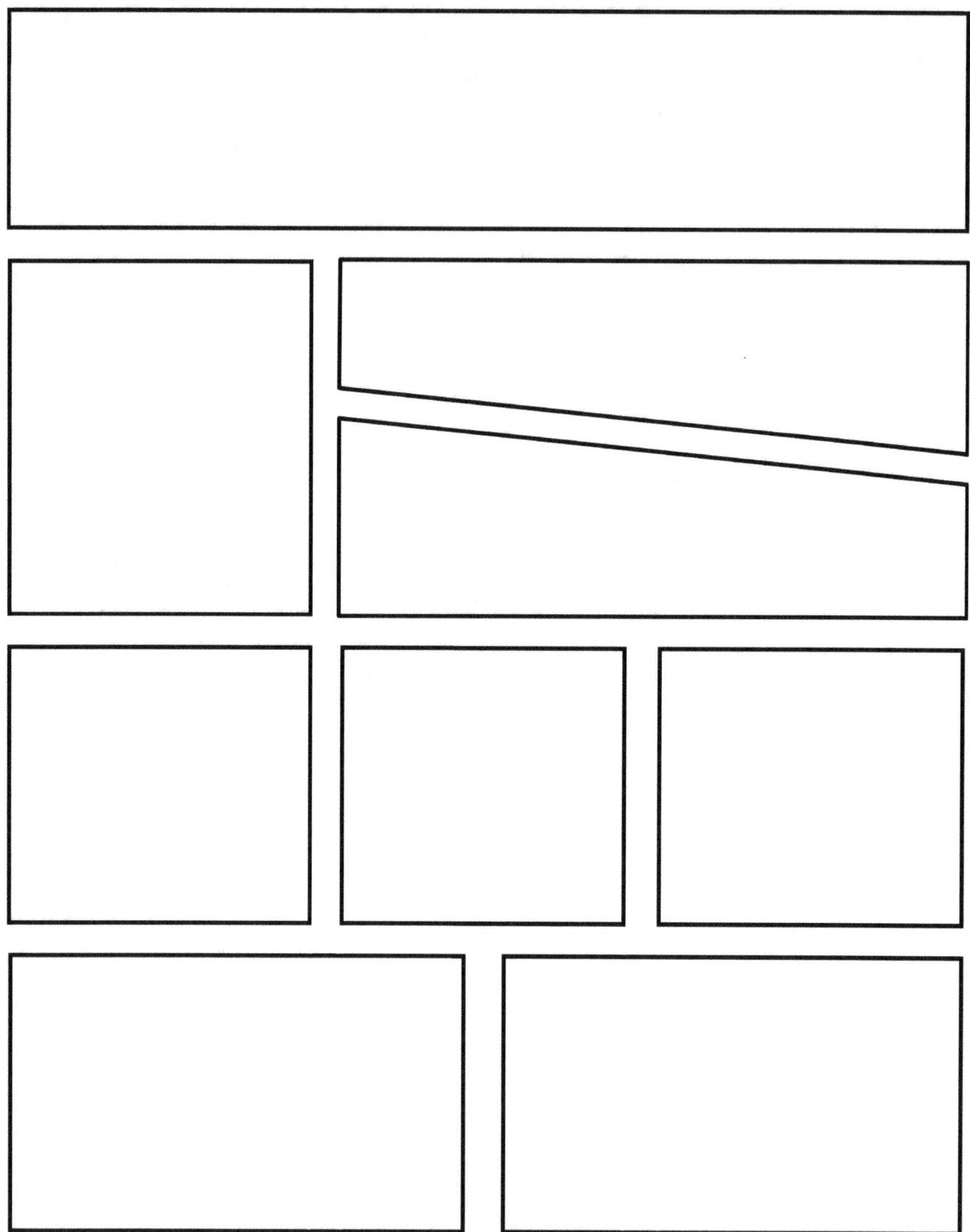

52

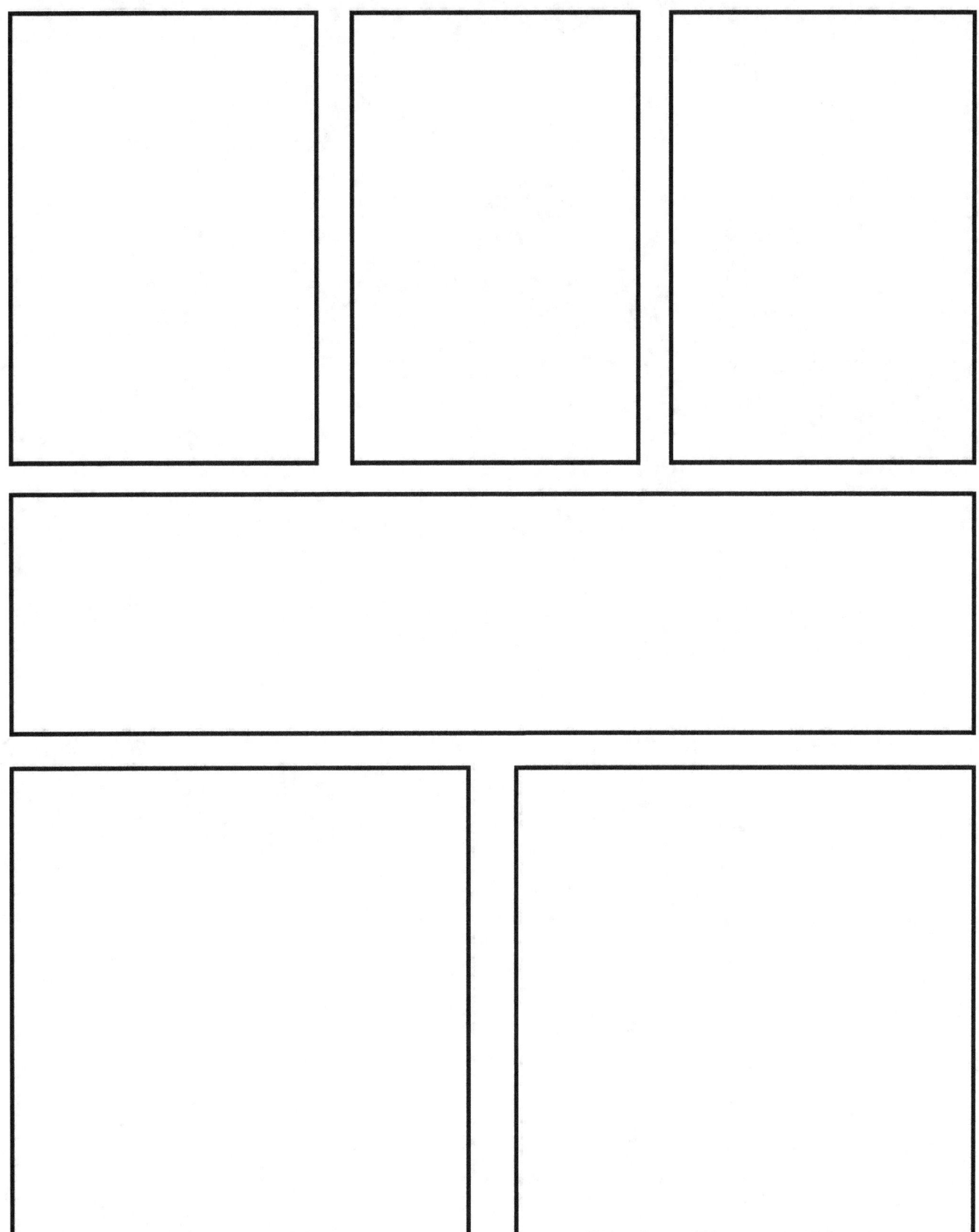

Blank Comic Book

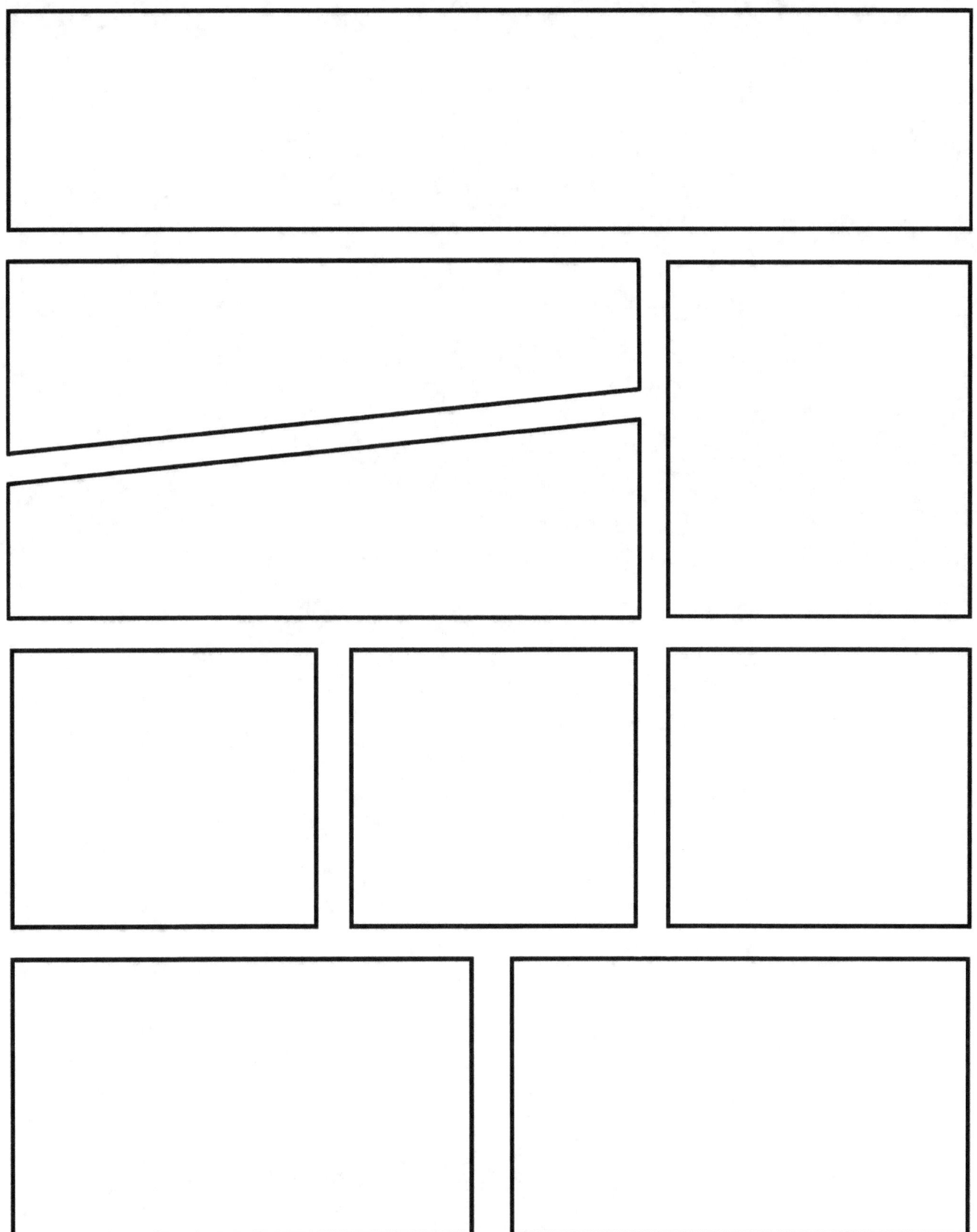

Blank Comic Book

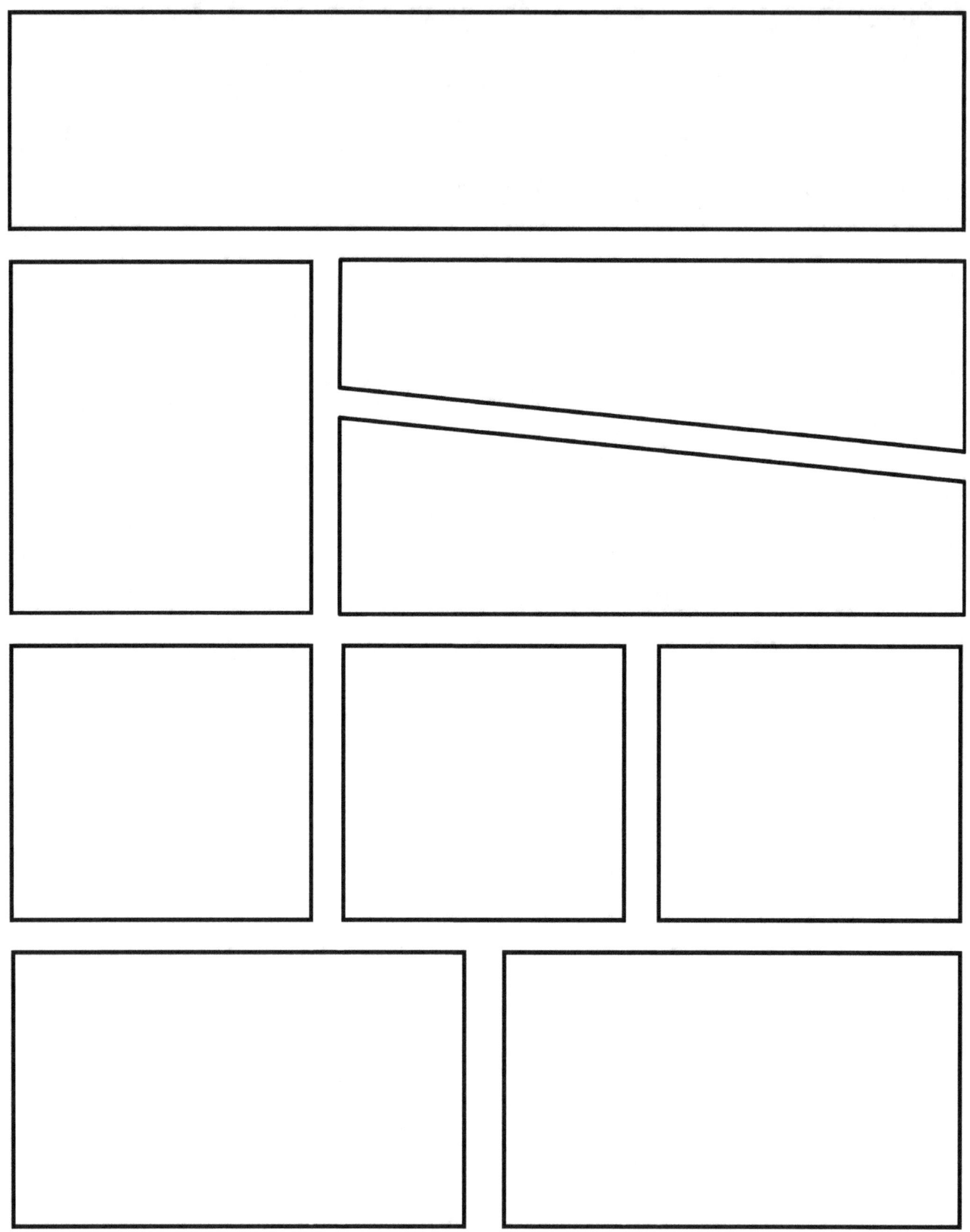

Blank Comic Book

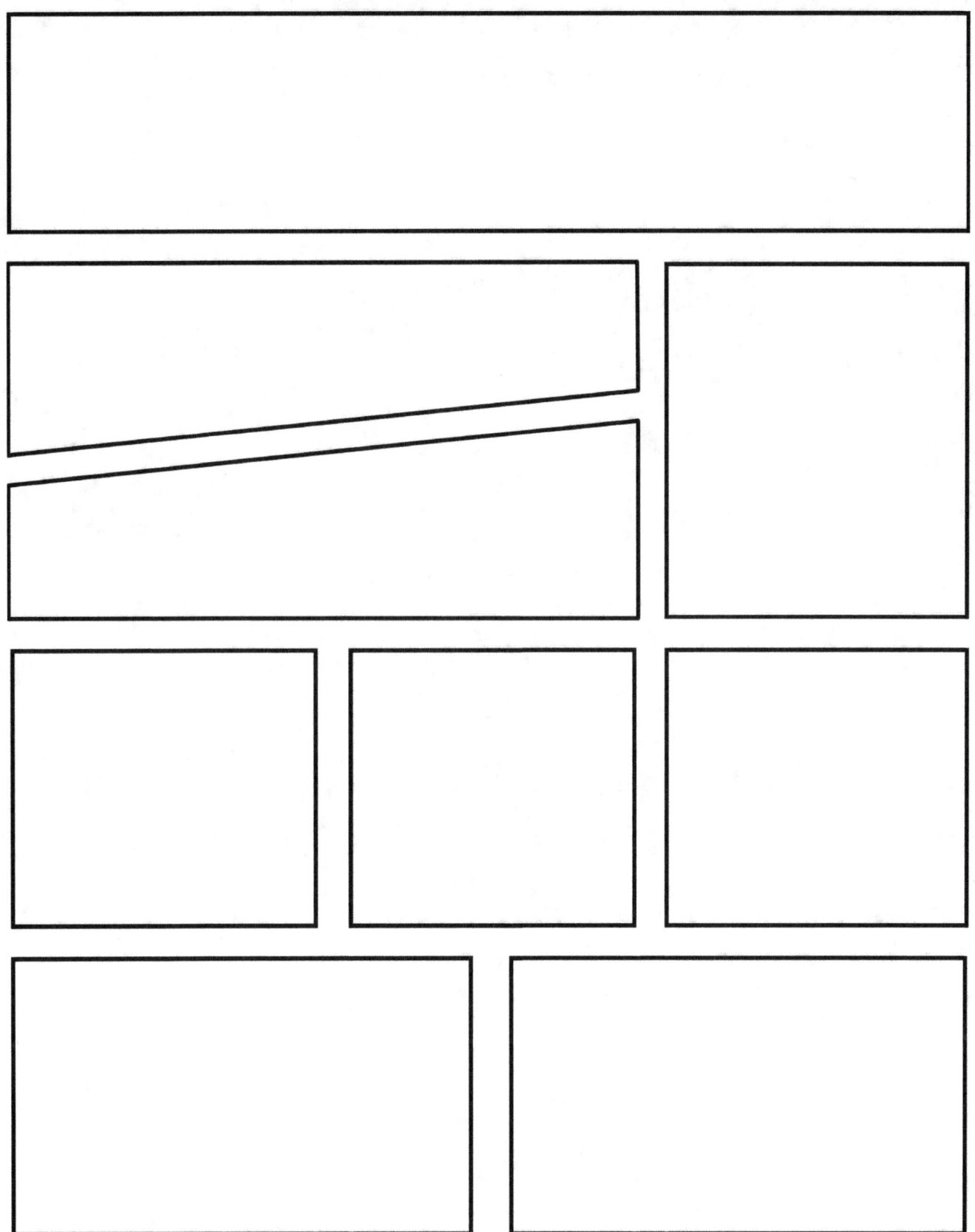

Blank Comic Book

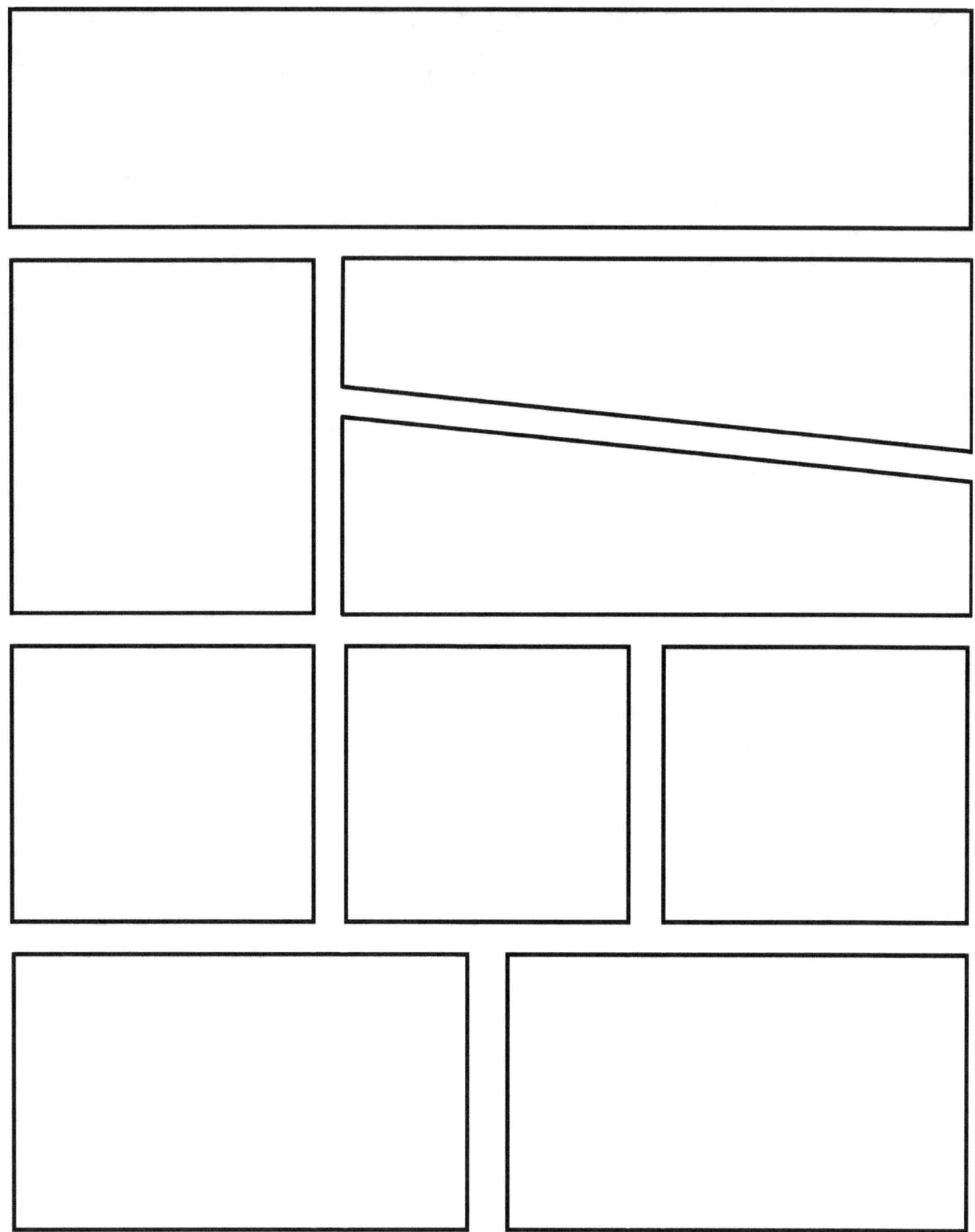

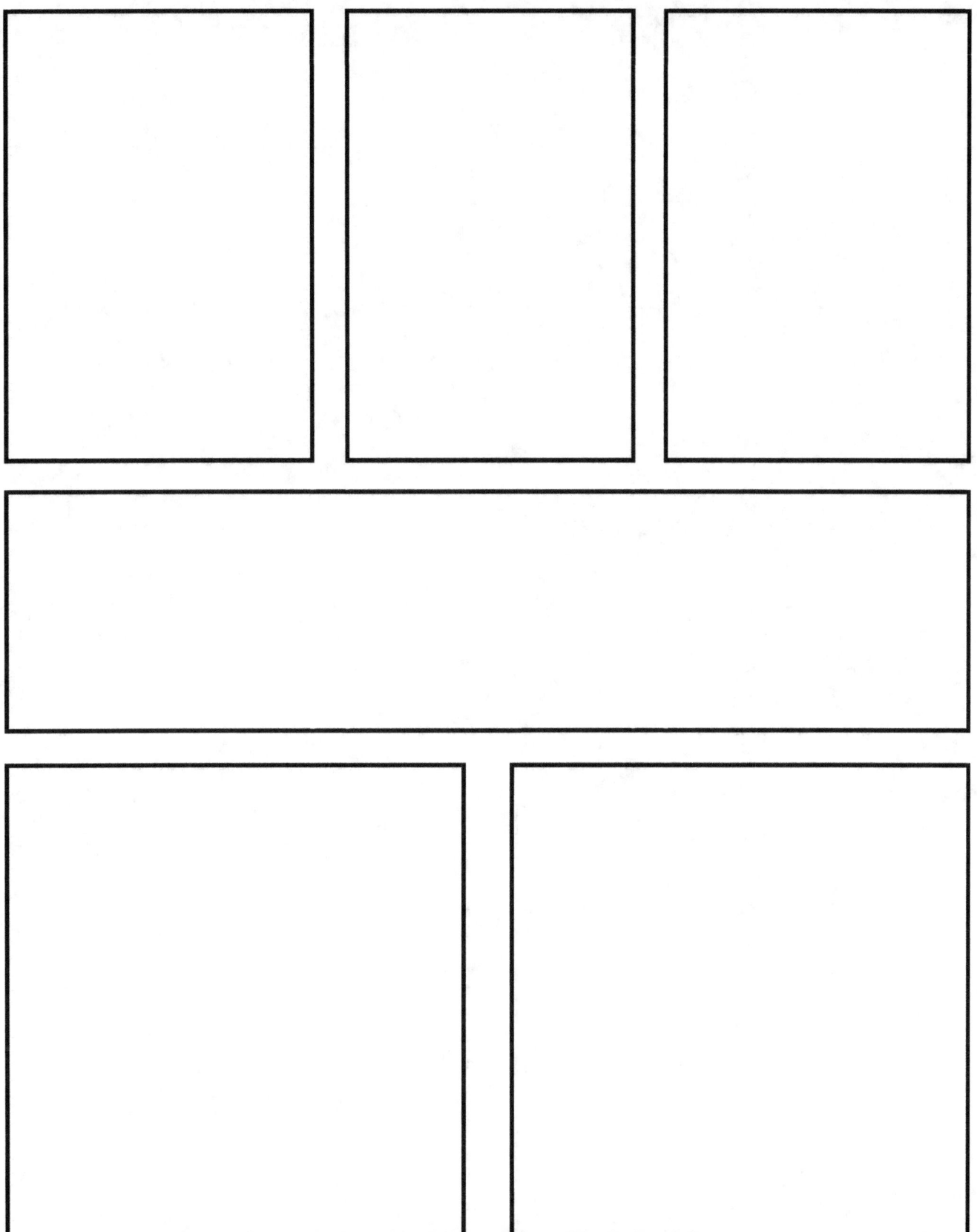

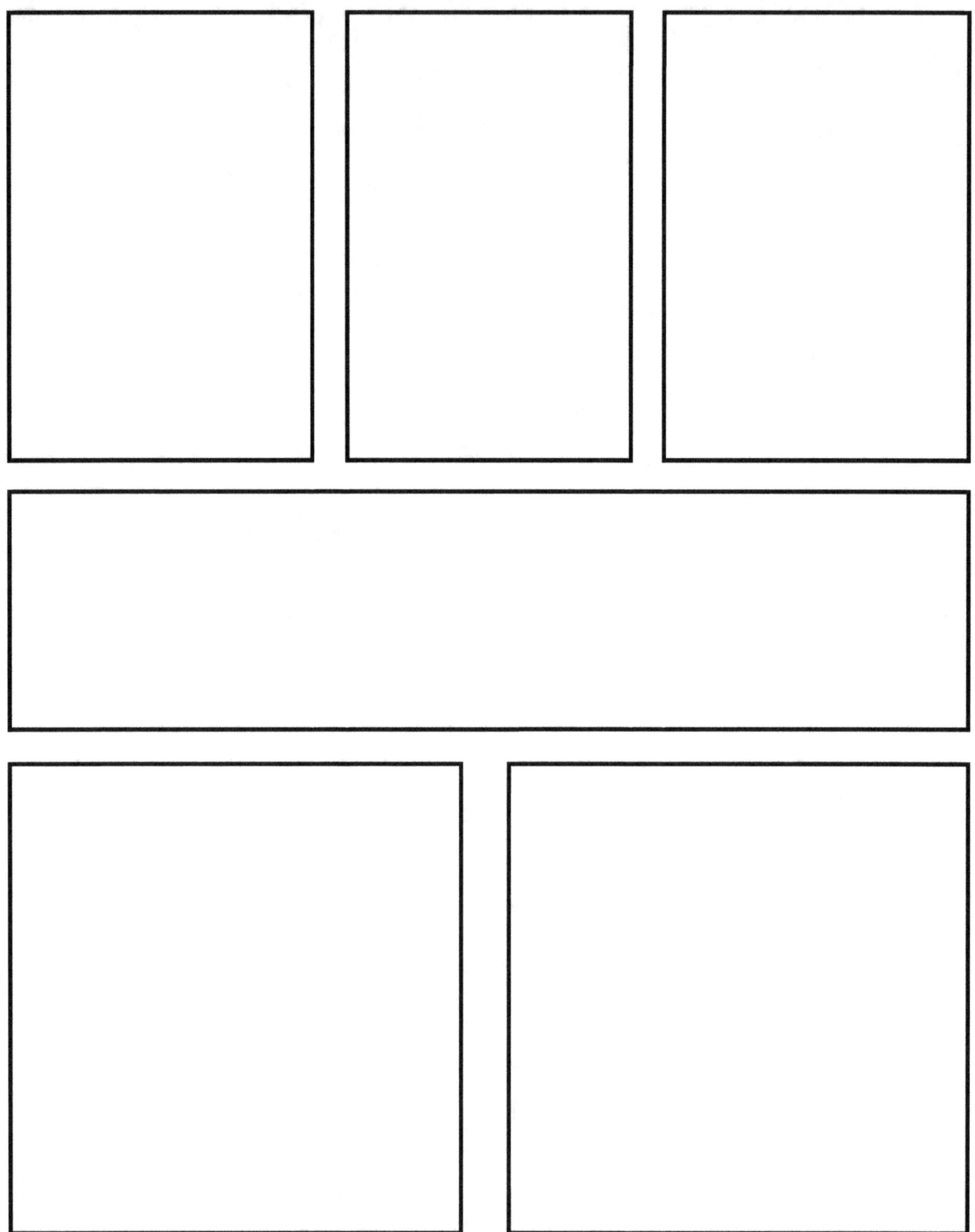

Blank Comic Book

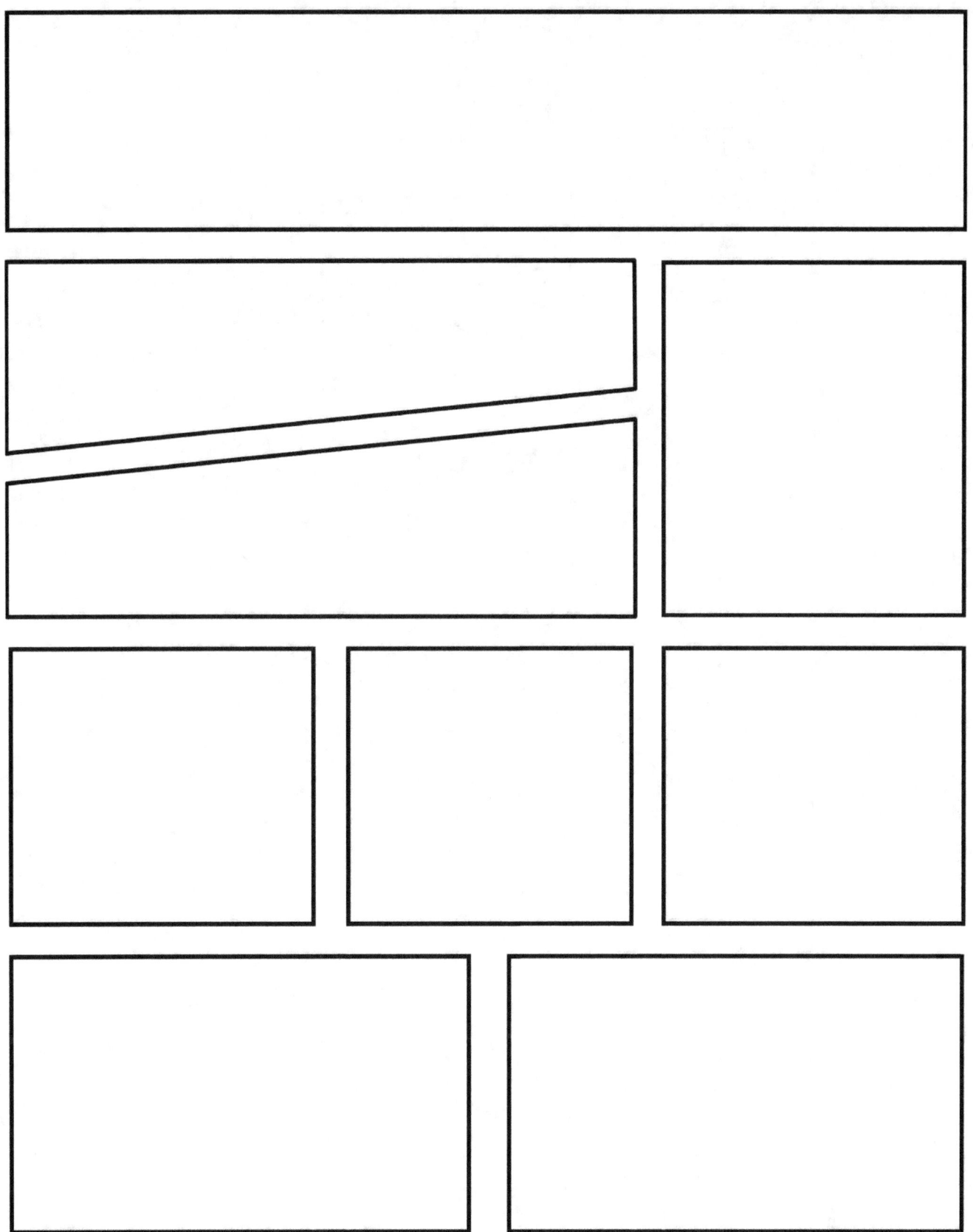

Blank Comic Book

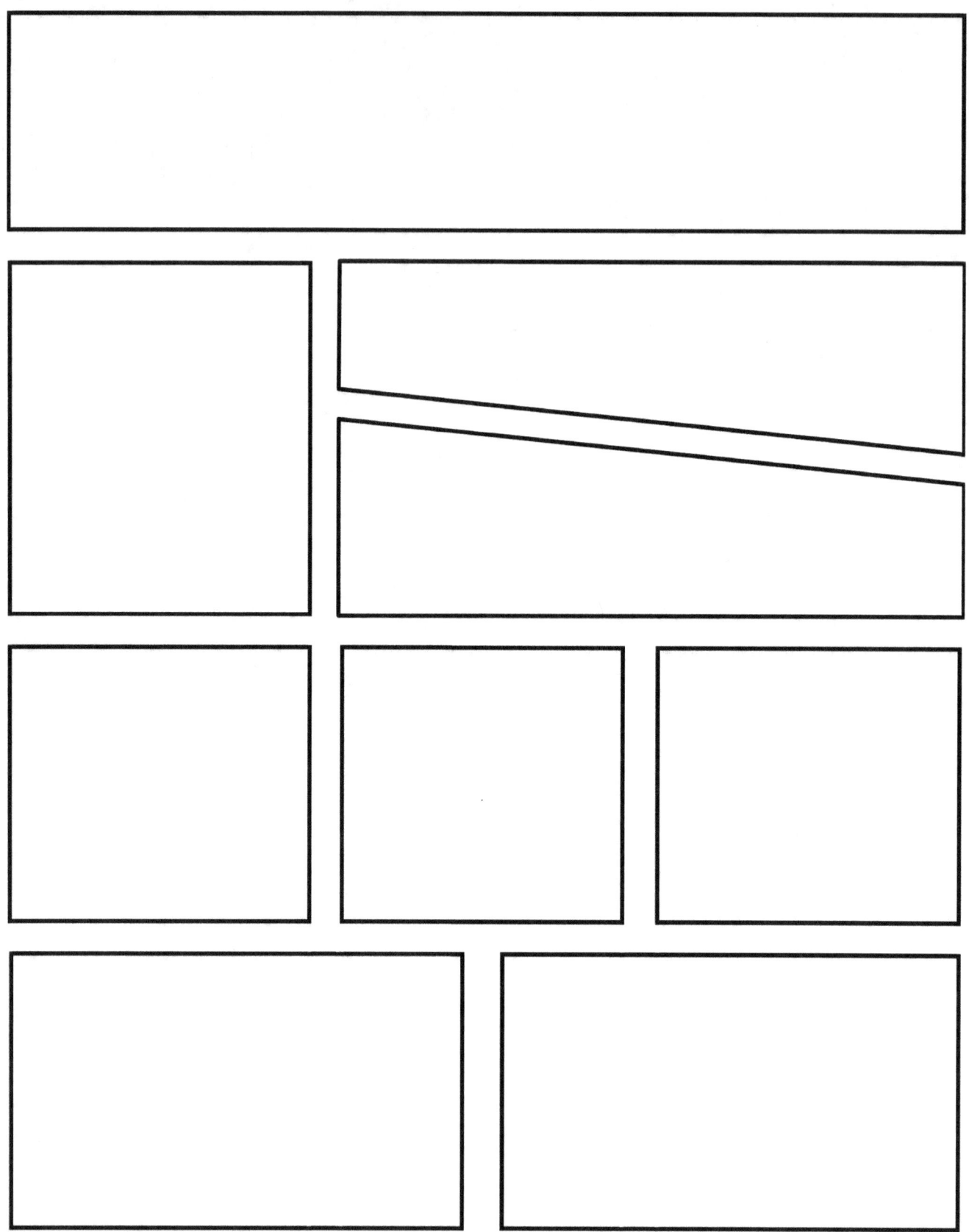

62

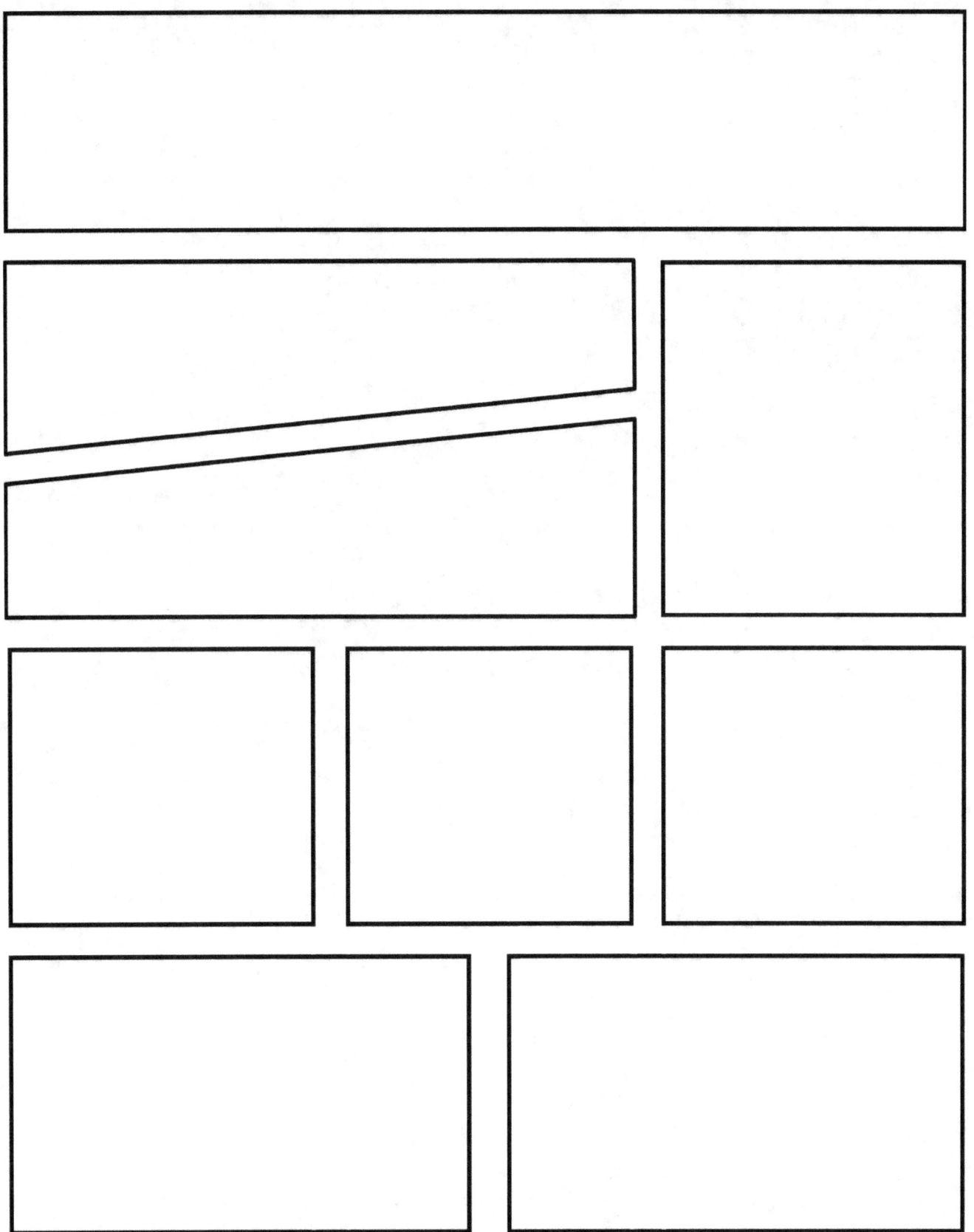

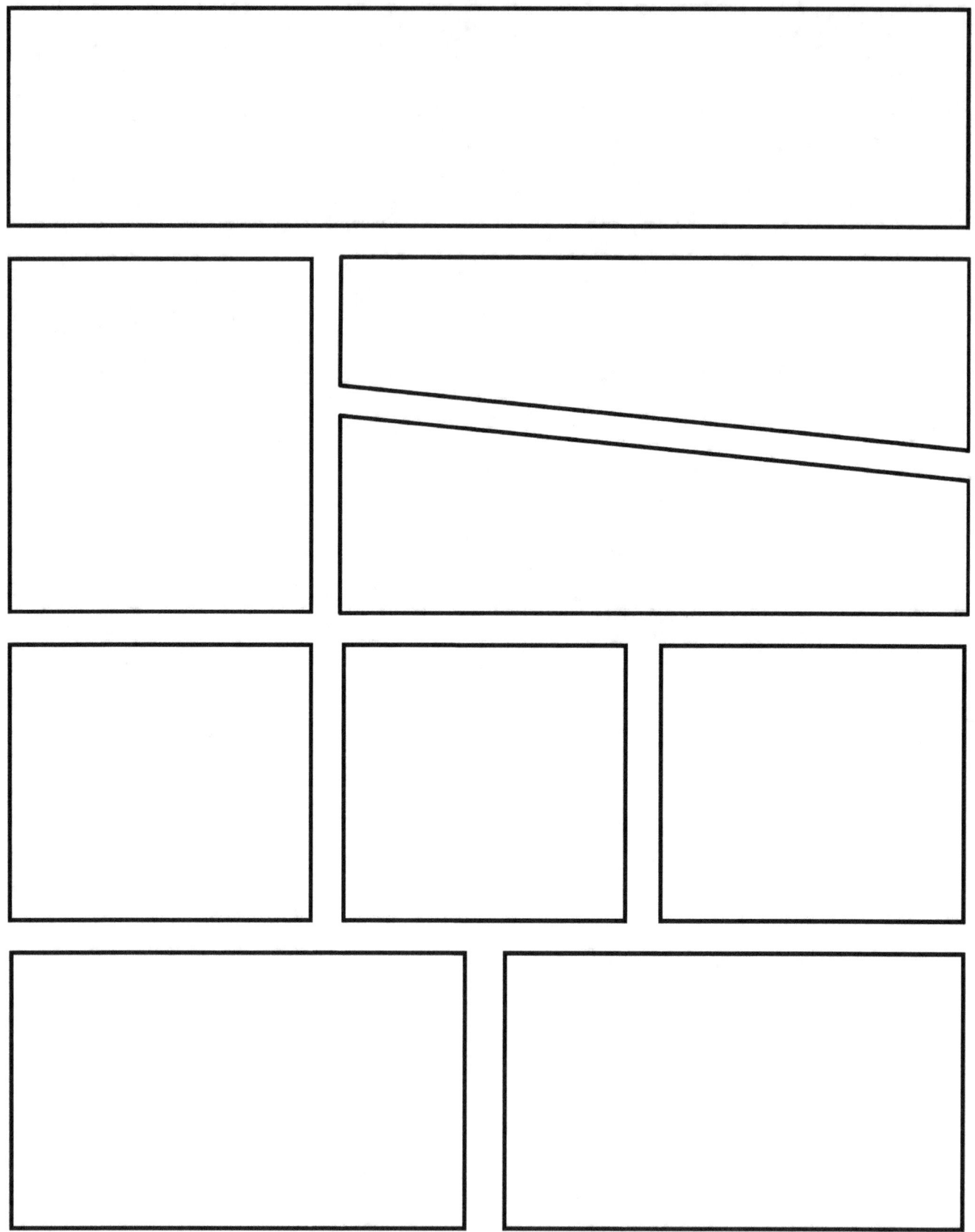

Blank Comic Book

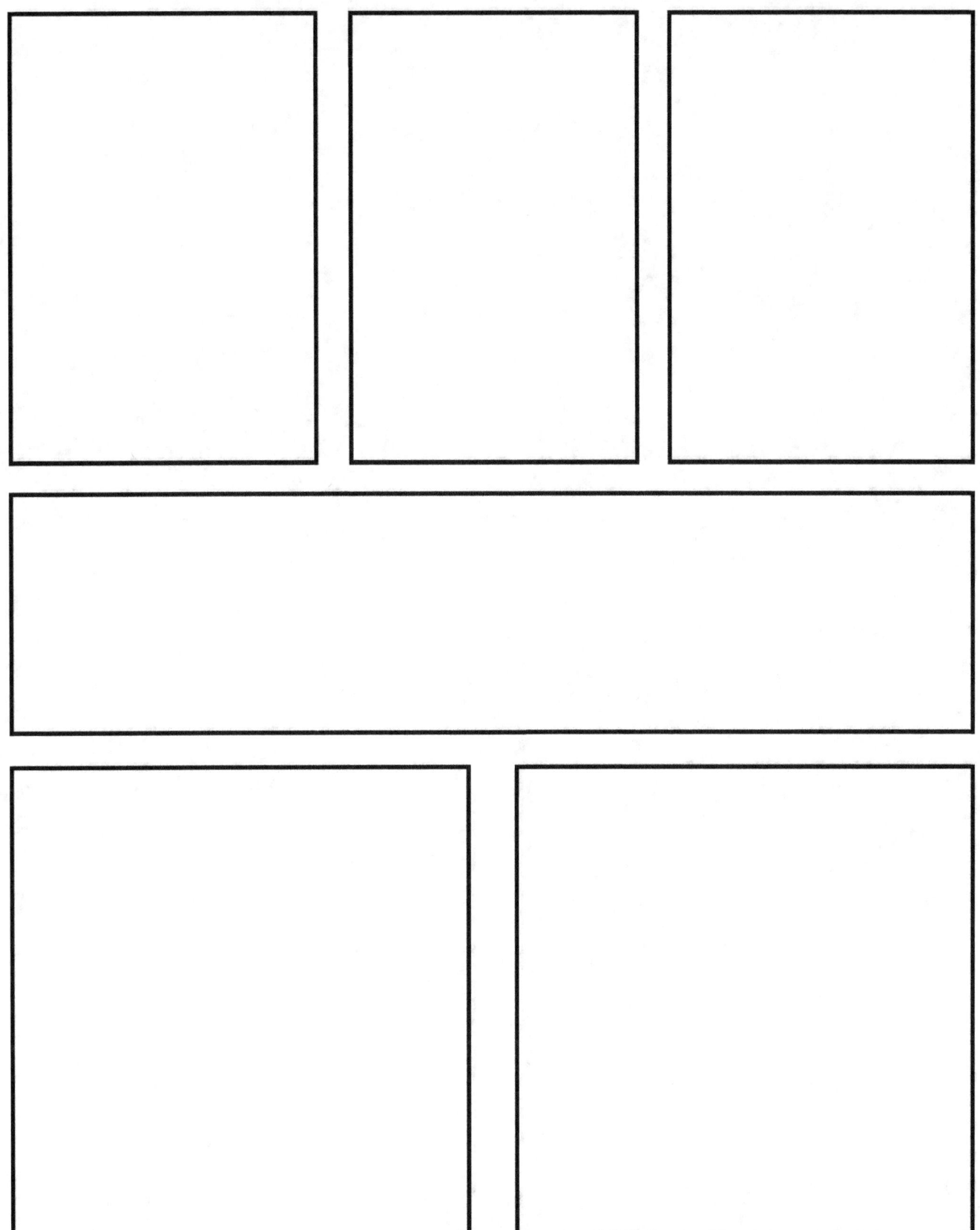

Blank Comic Book

Blank Comic Book

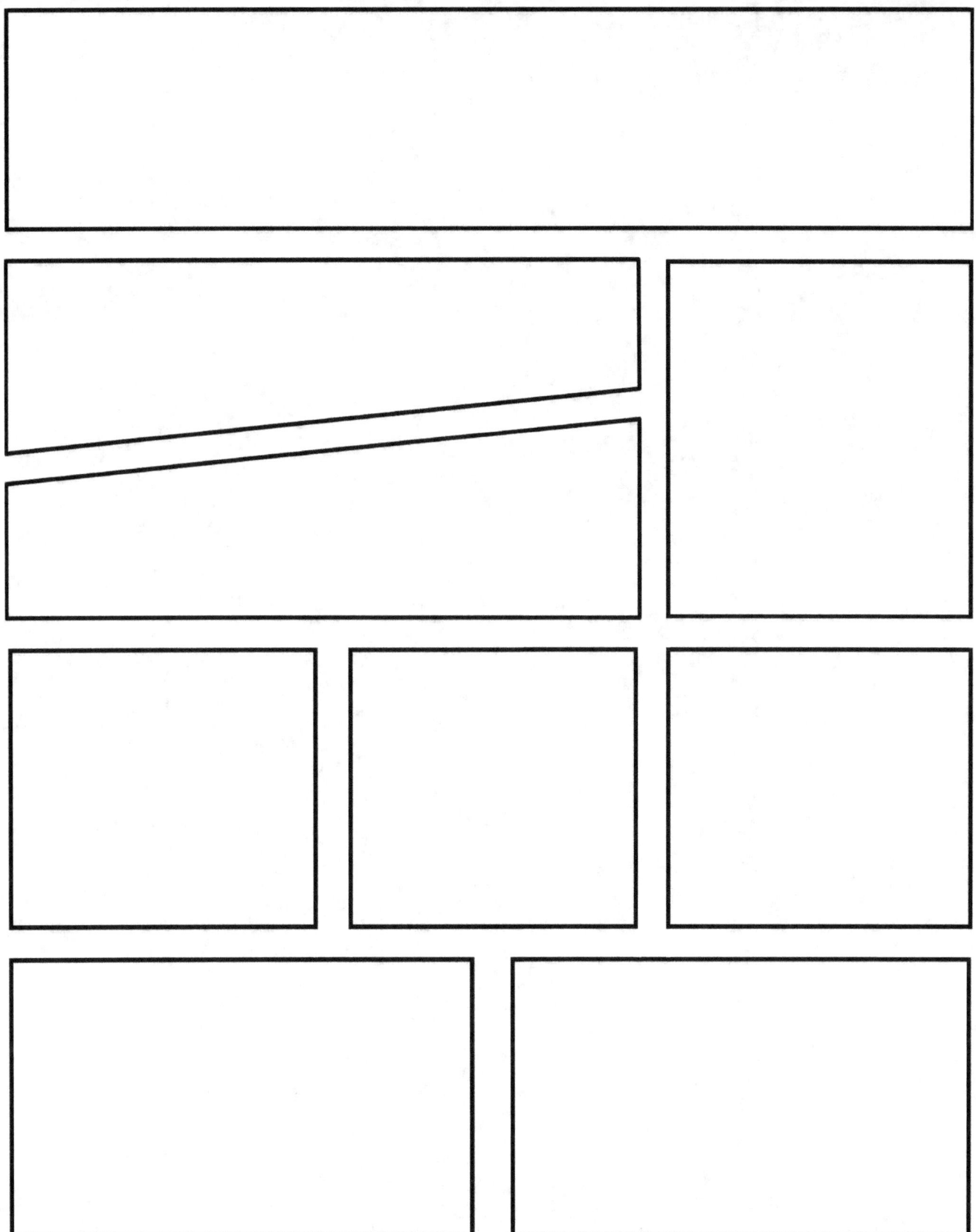

Blank Comic Book

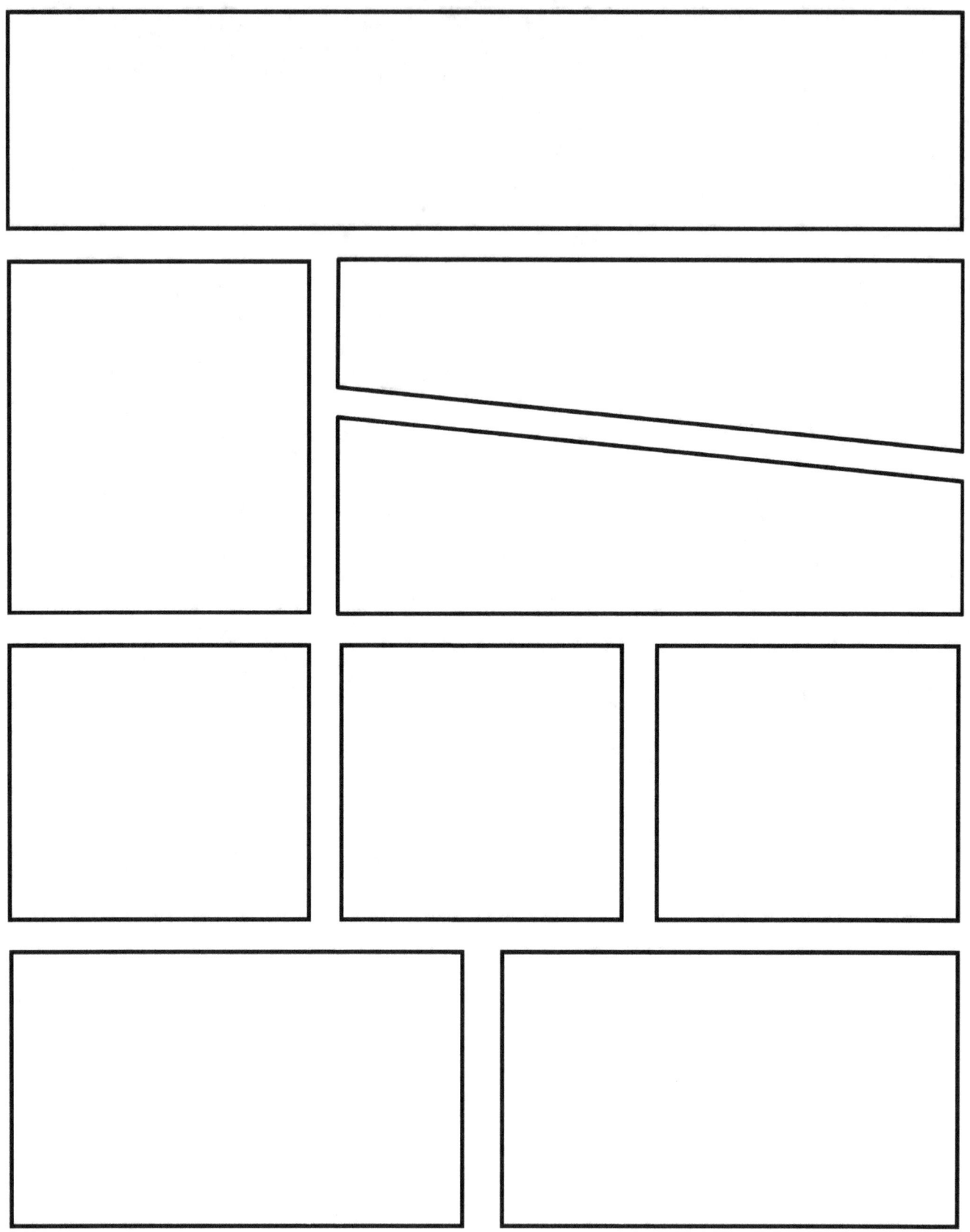

Blank Comic Book

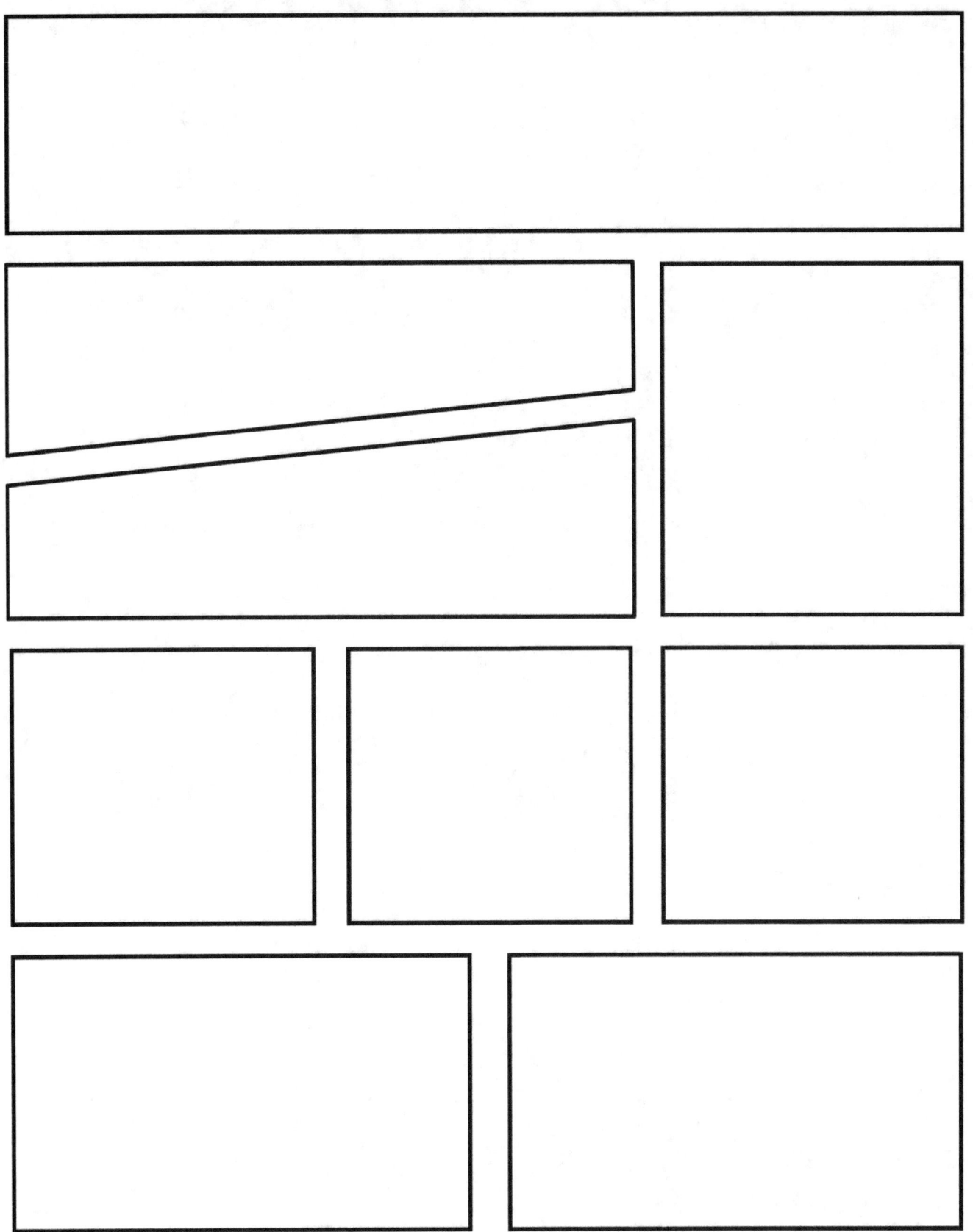

69

Blank Comic Book

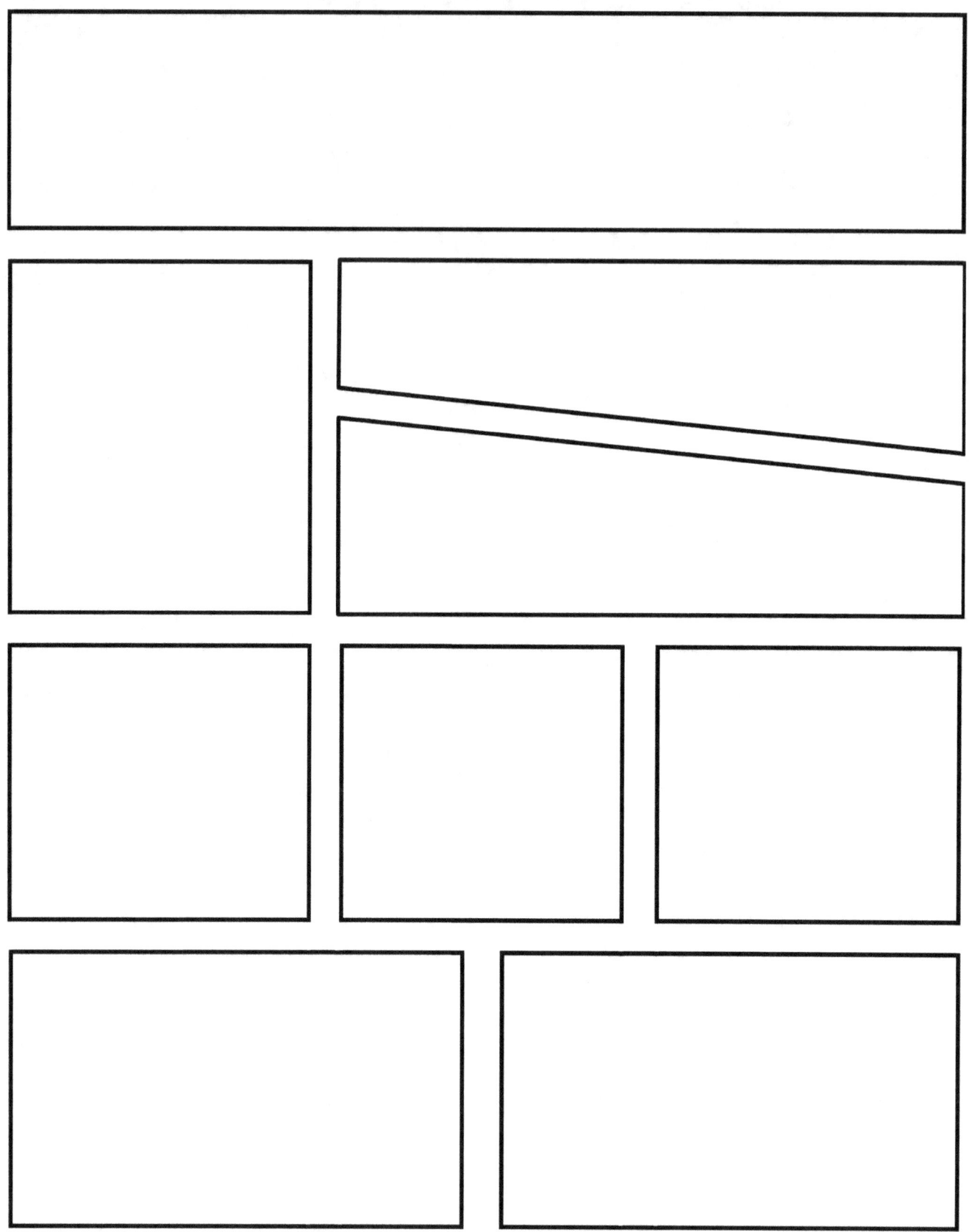

Blank Comic Book

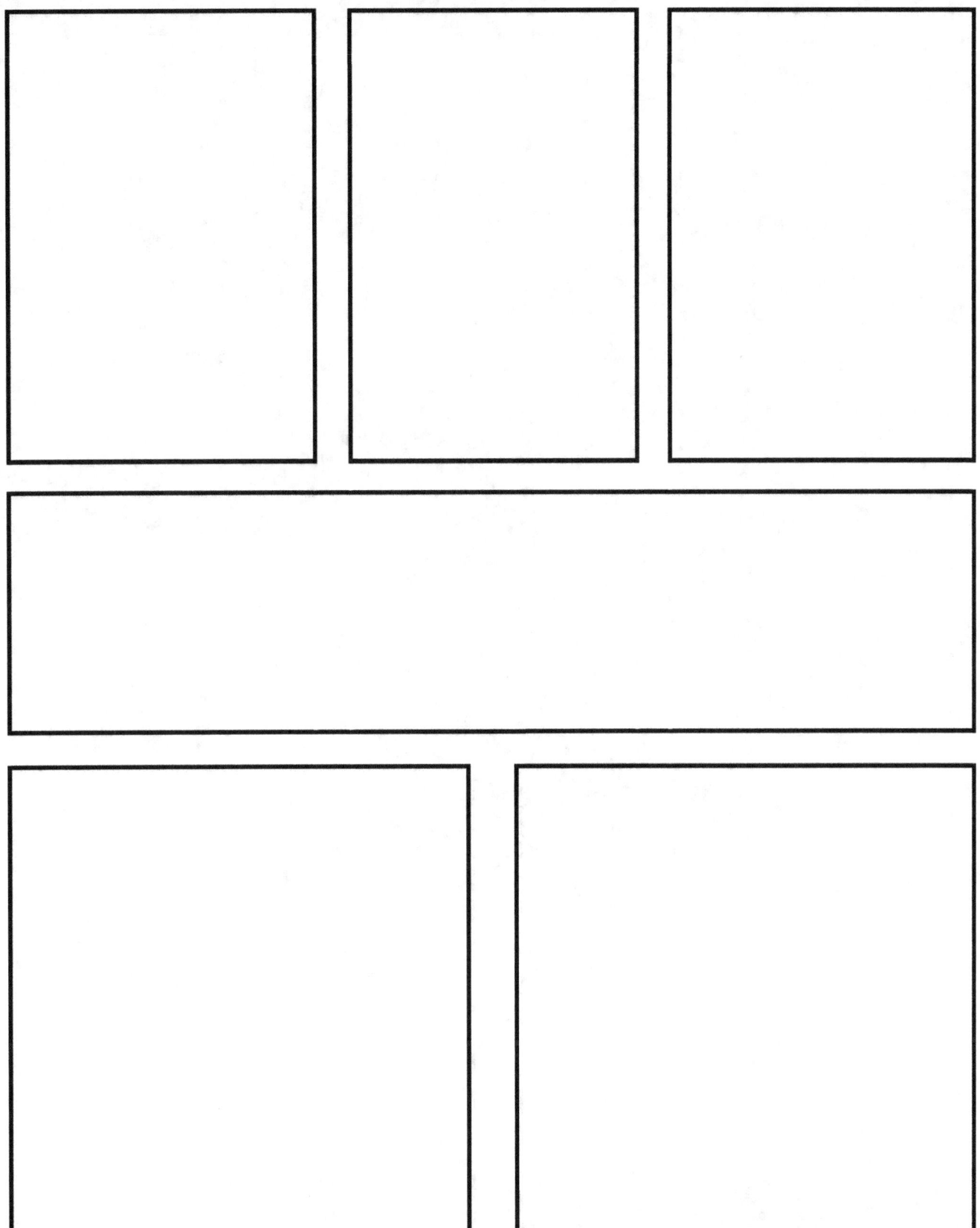

Blank Comic Book

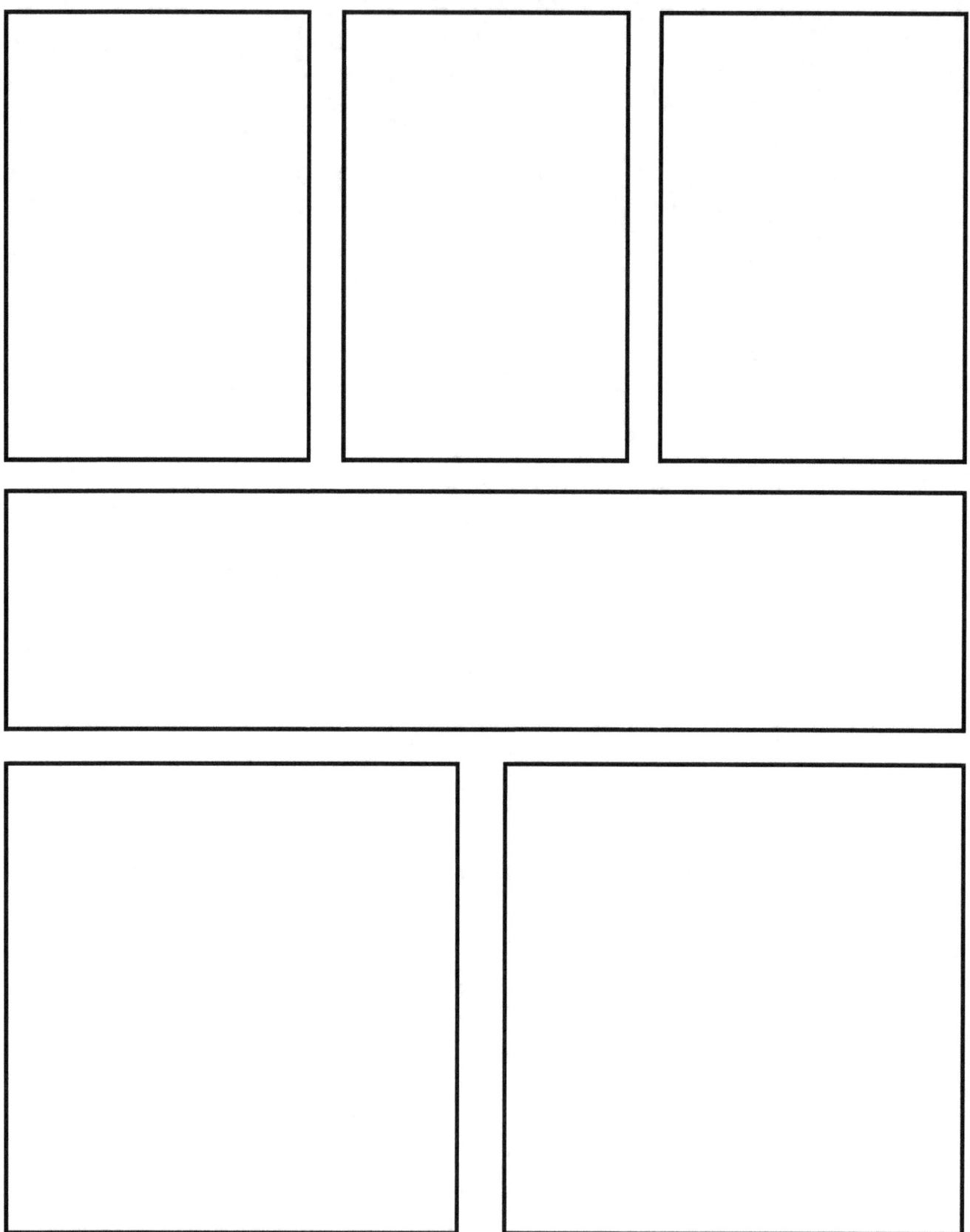

72

Blank Comic Book

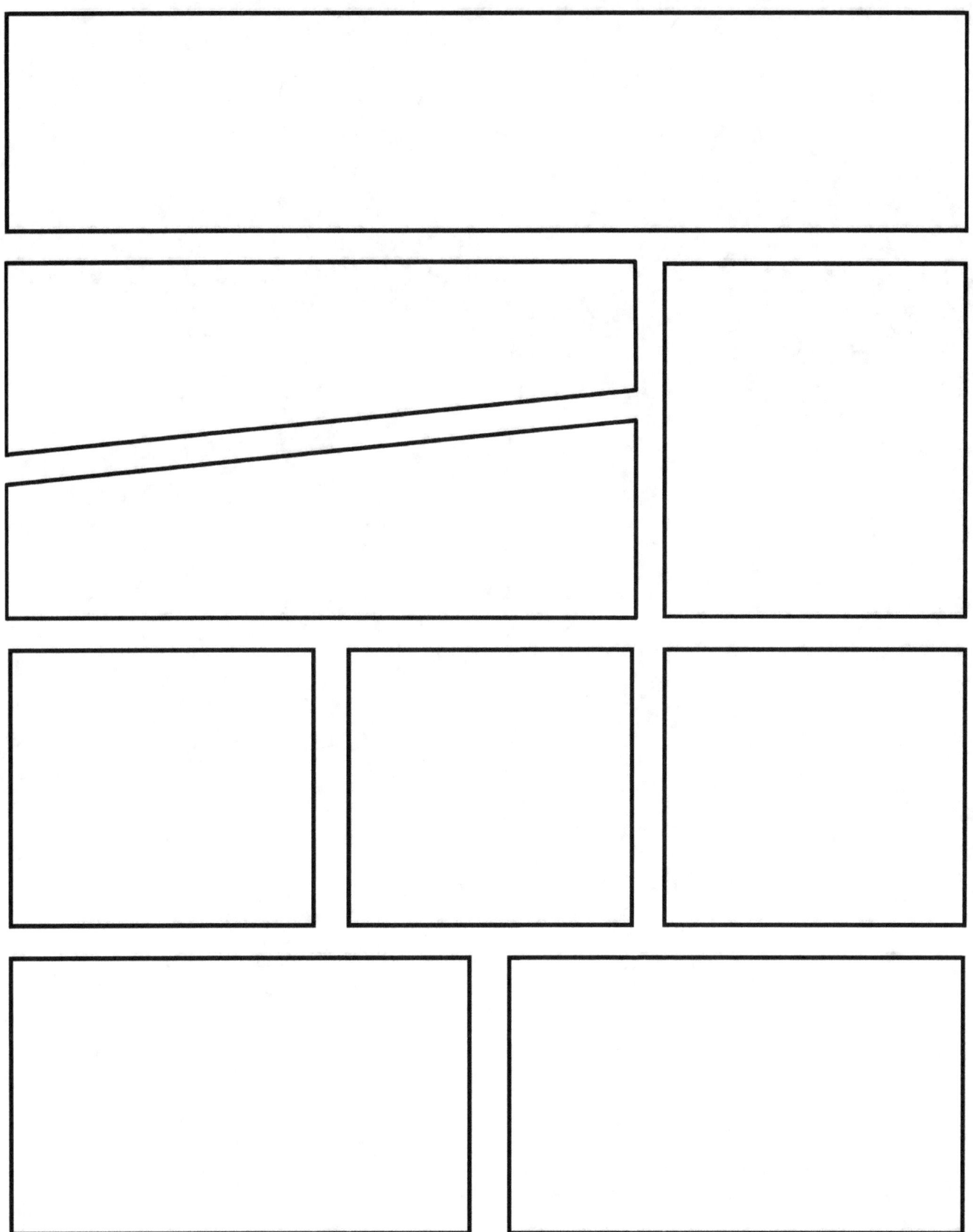

73

Blank Comic Book

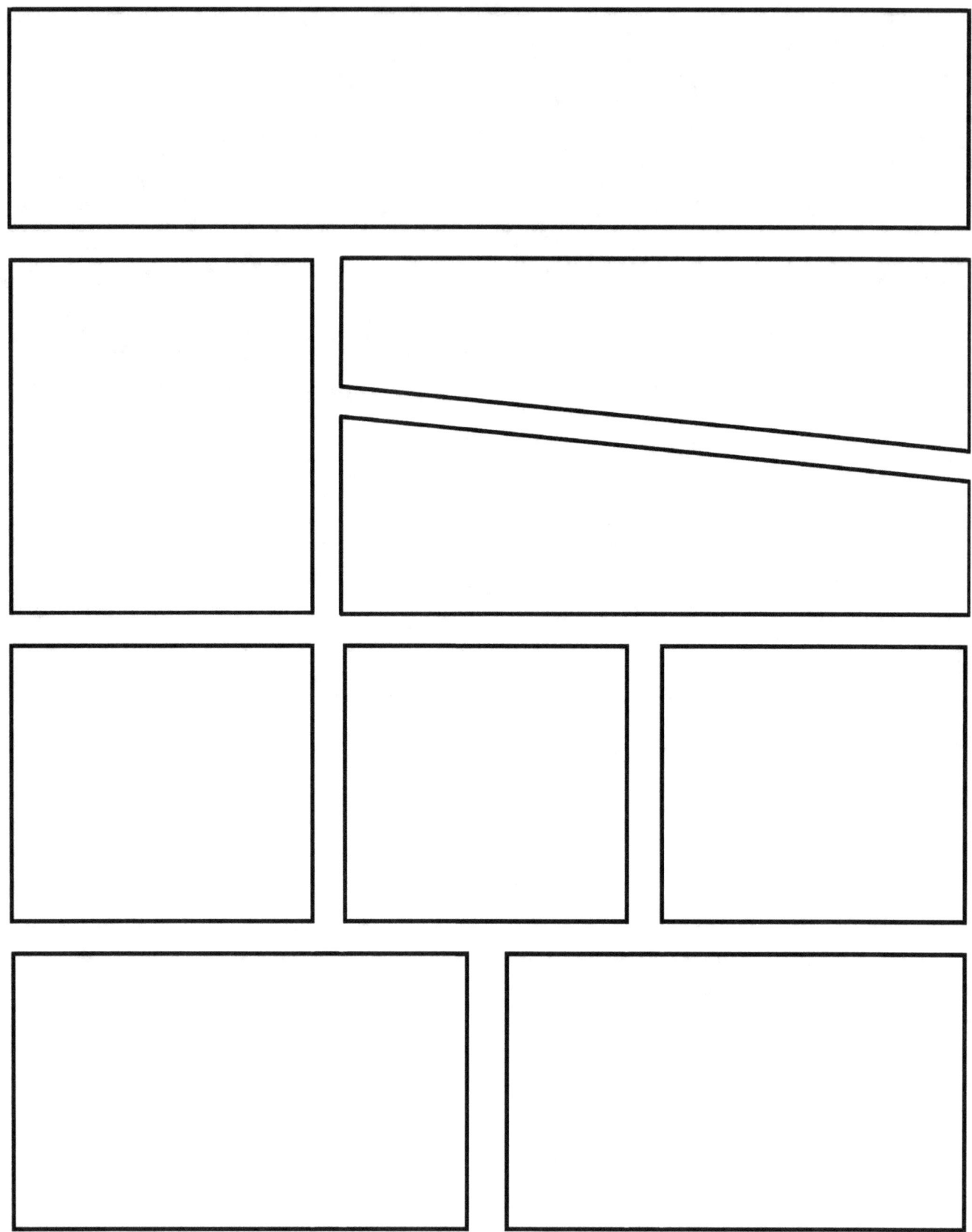

74

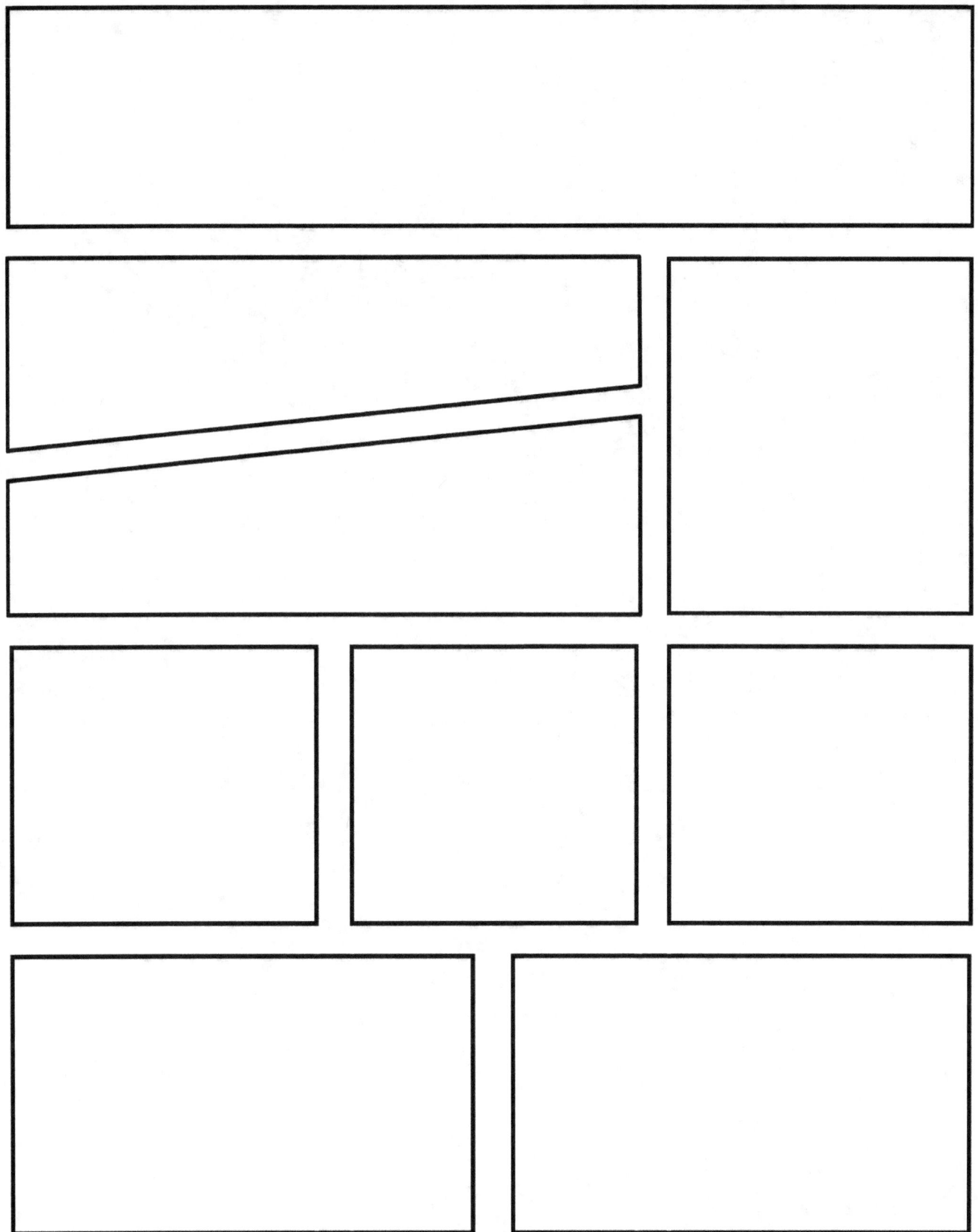

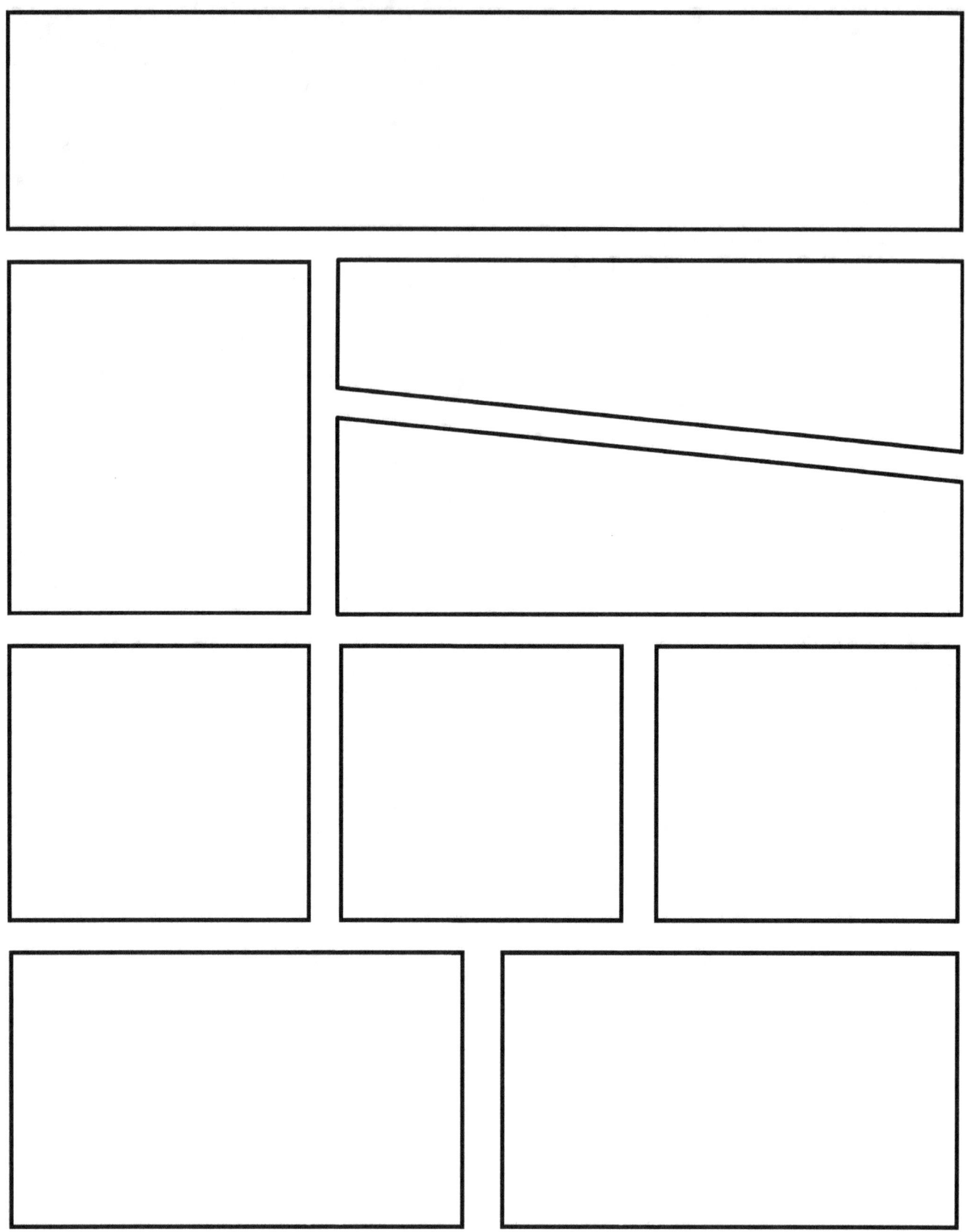

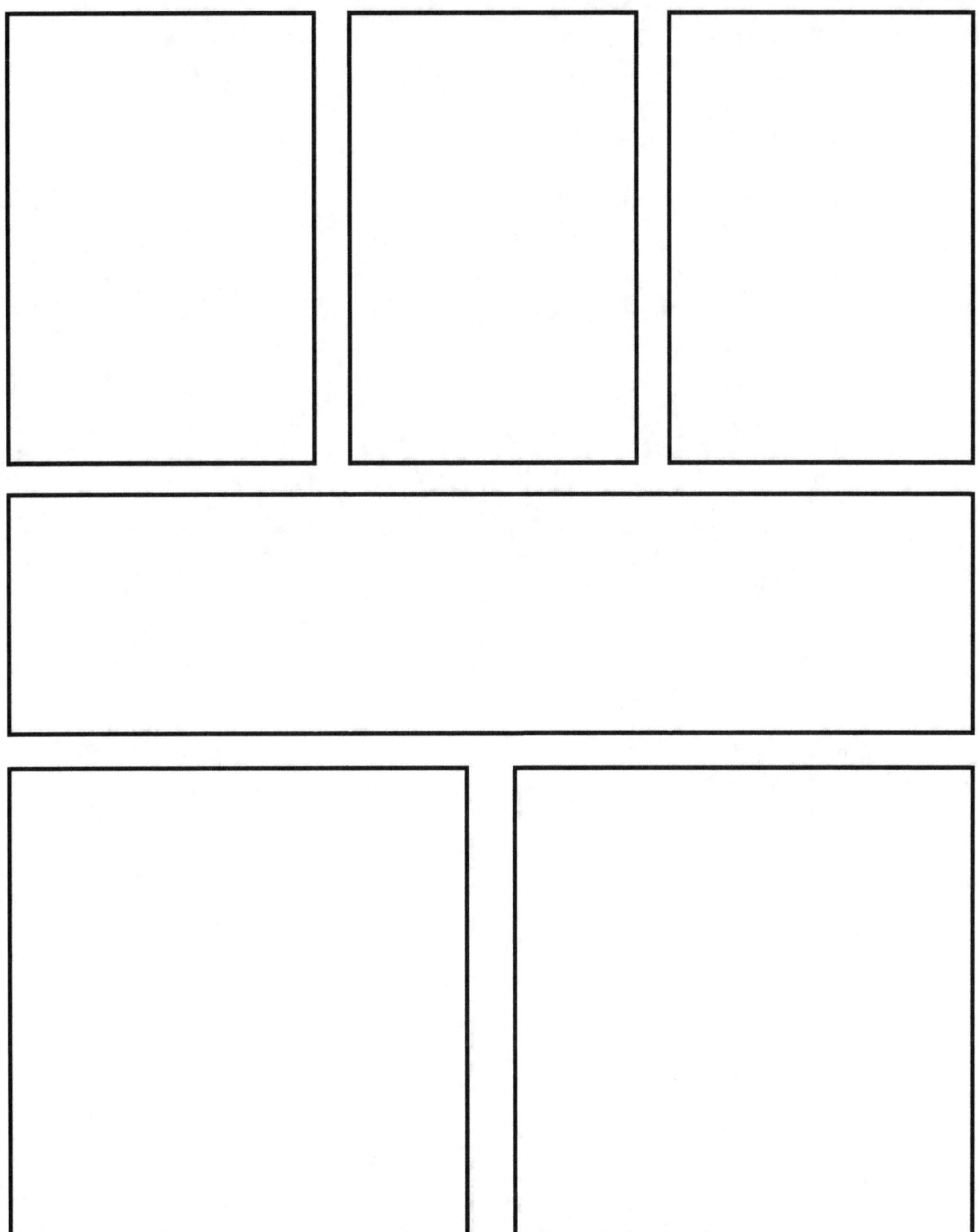

Blank Comic Book

78

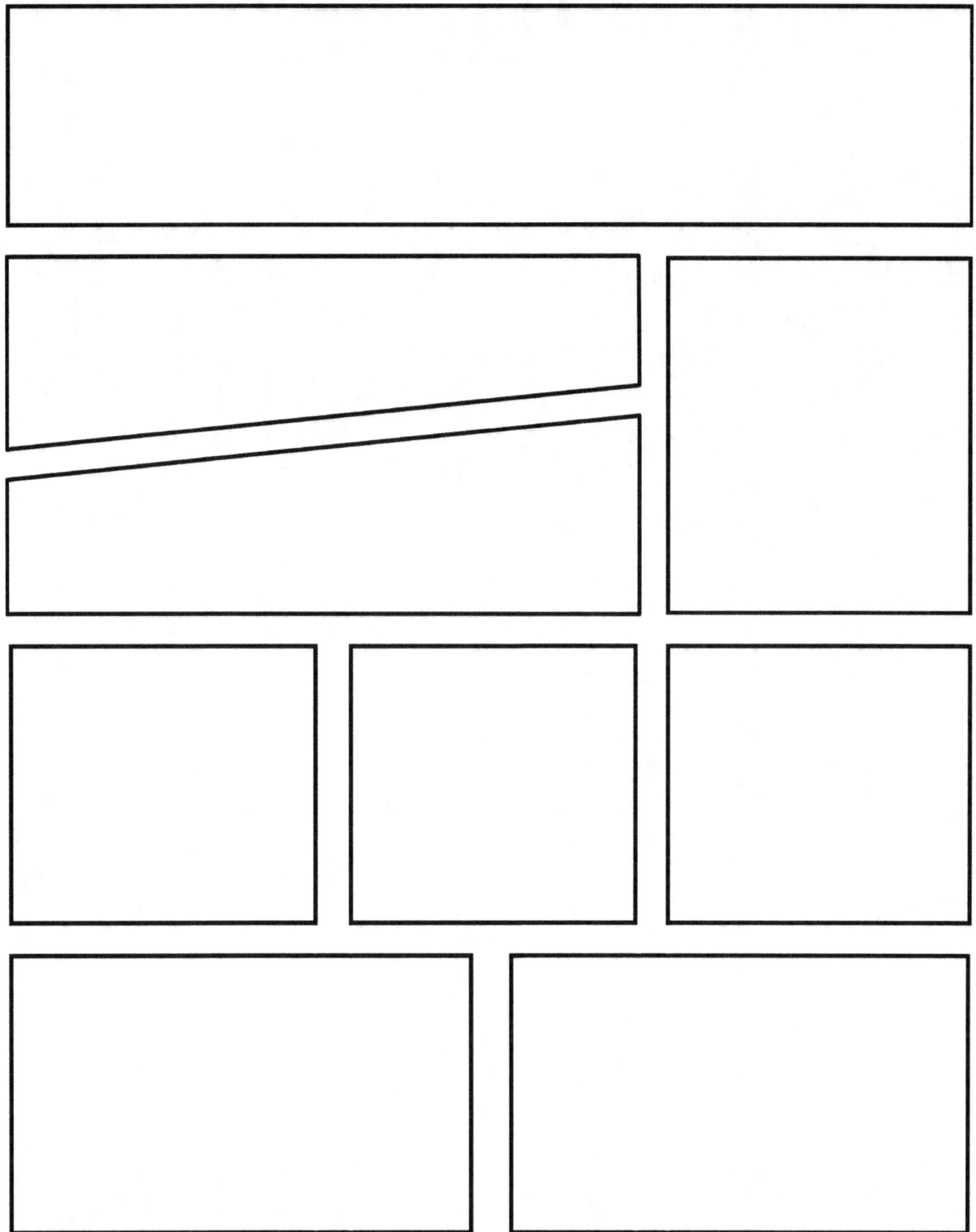

Blank Comic Book

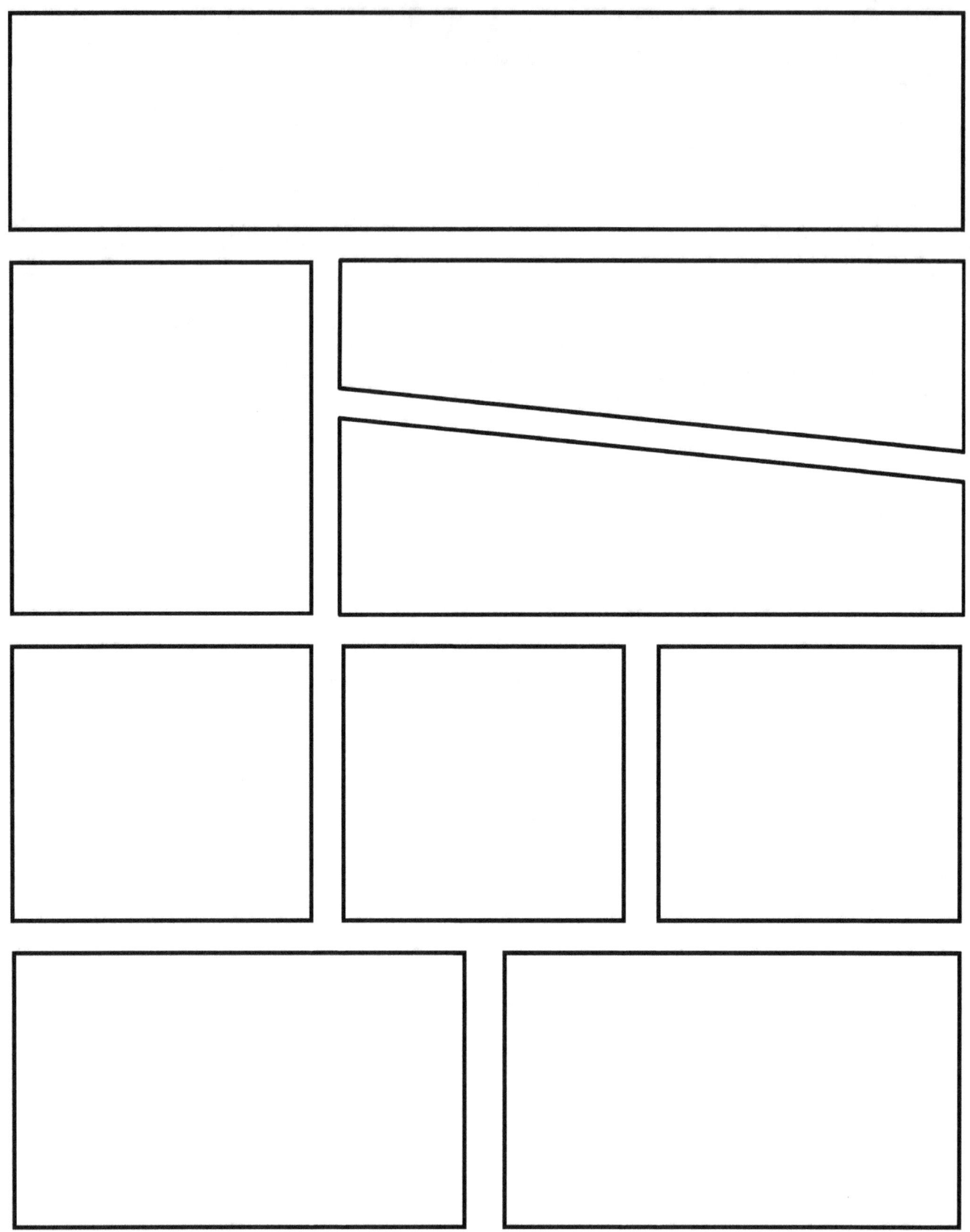

80

Blank Comic Book

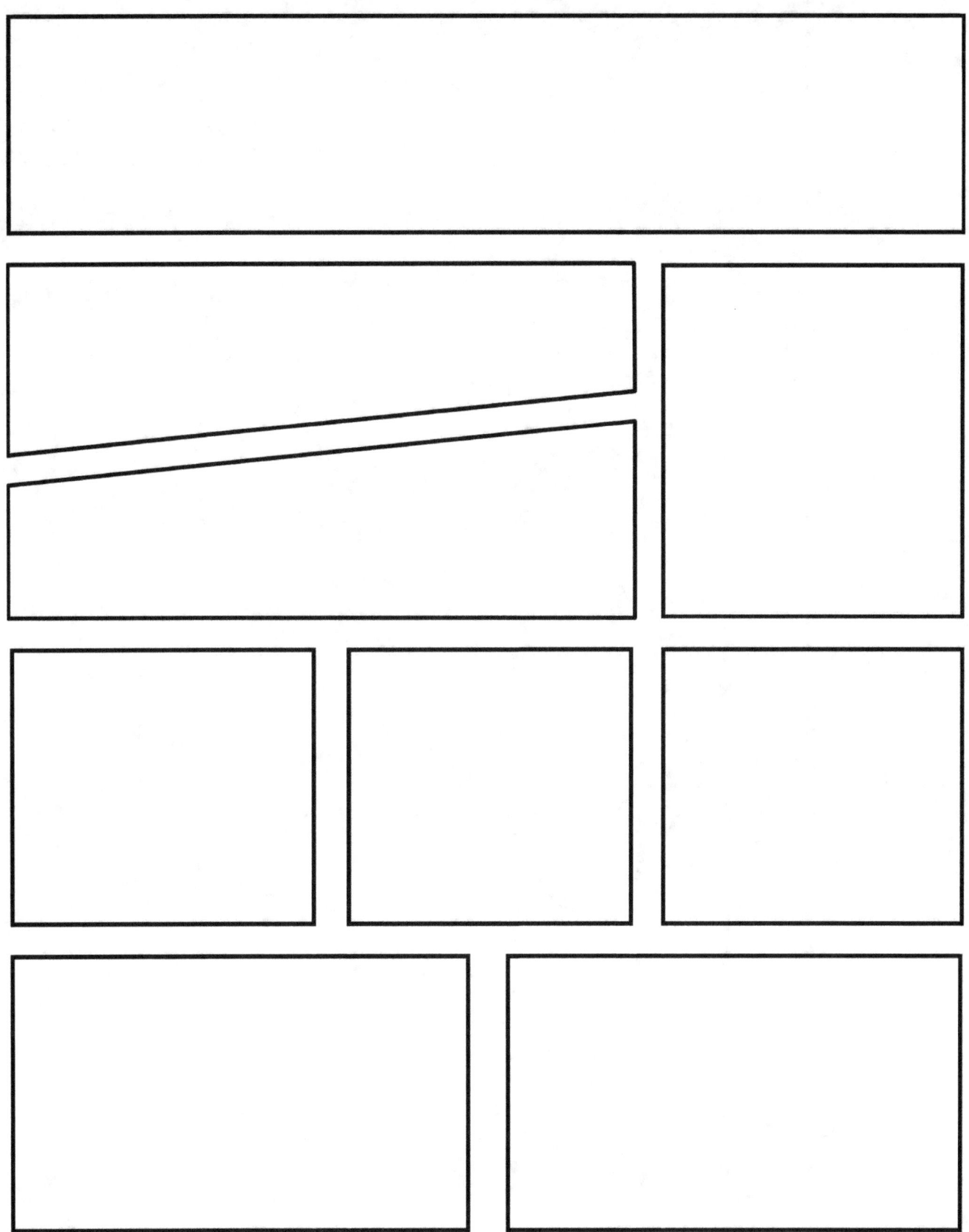

81

Blank Comic Book

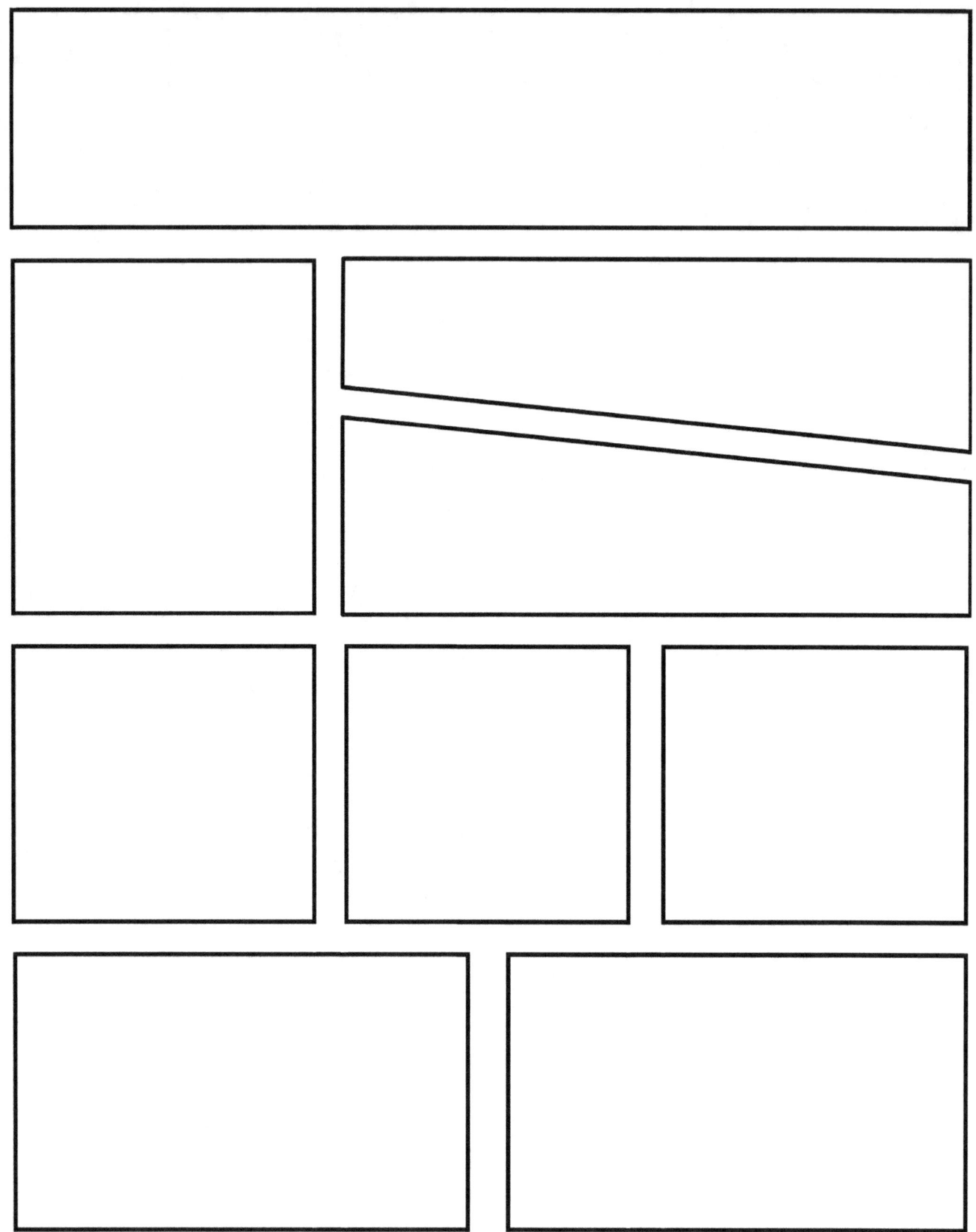

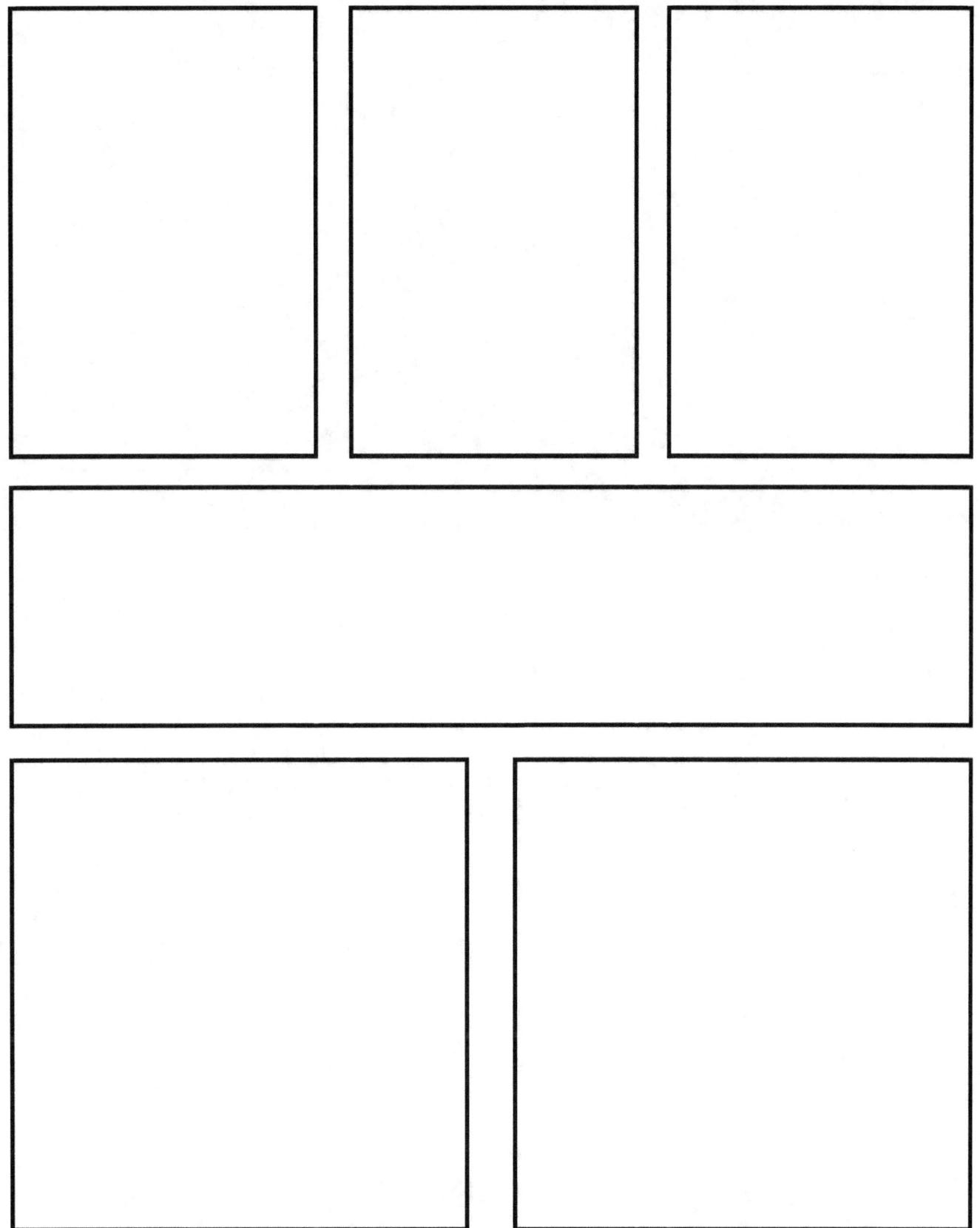

Blank Comic Book

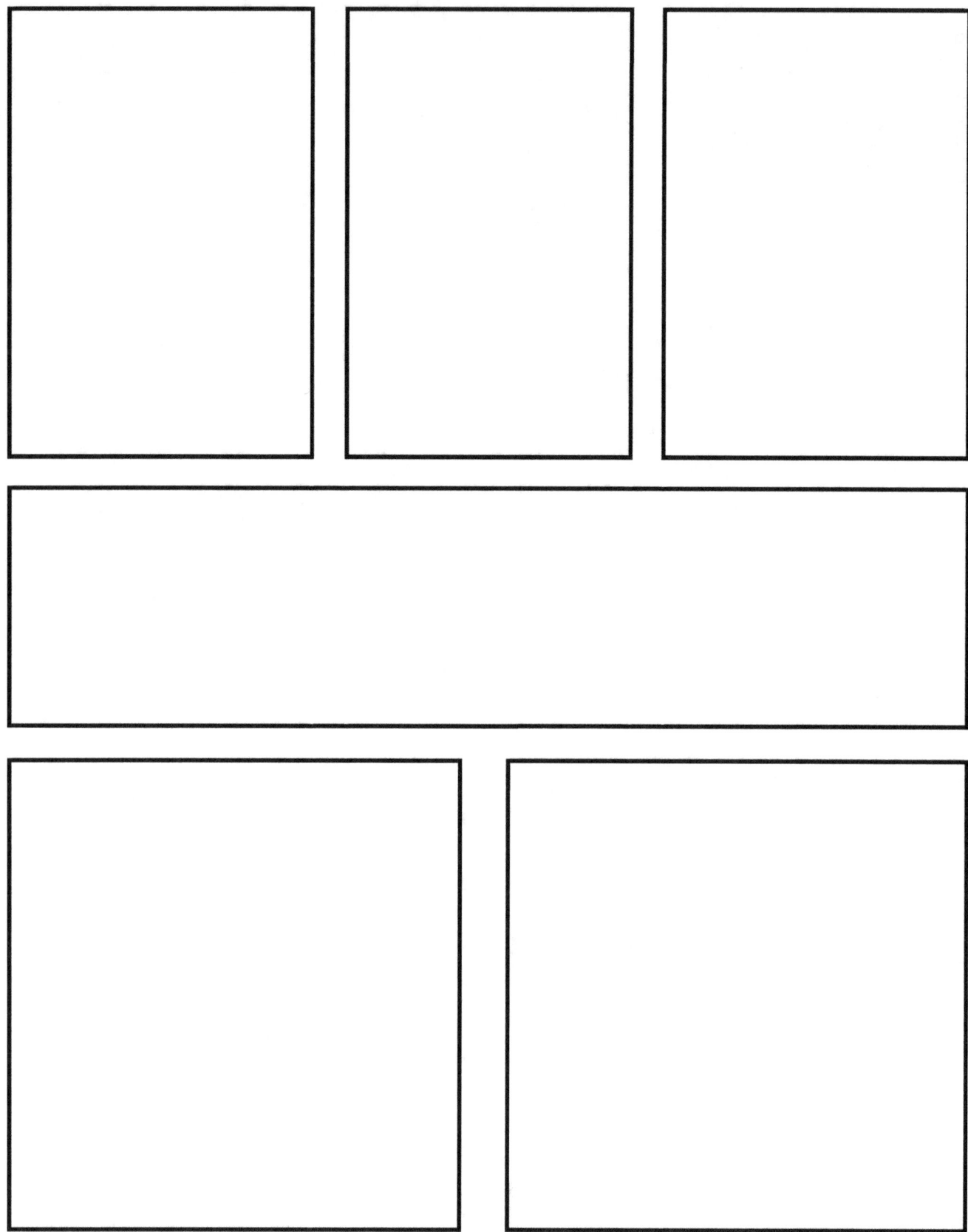

84

Blank Comic Book

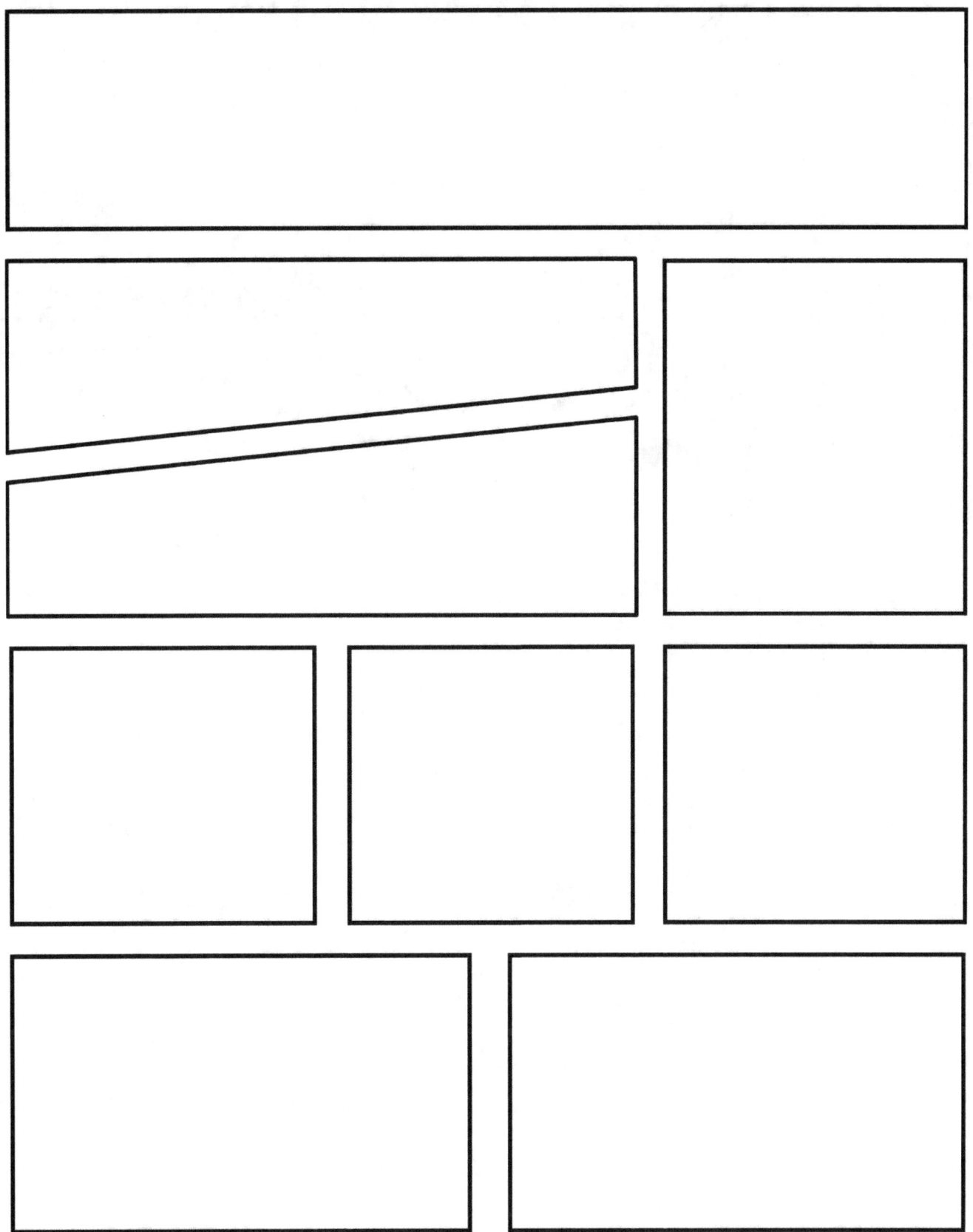

85

Blank Comic Book

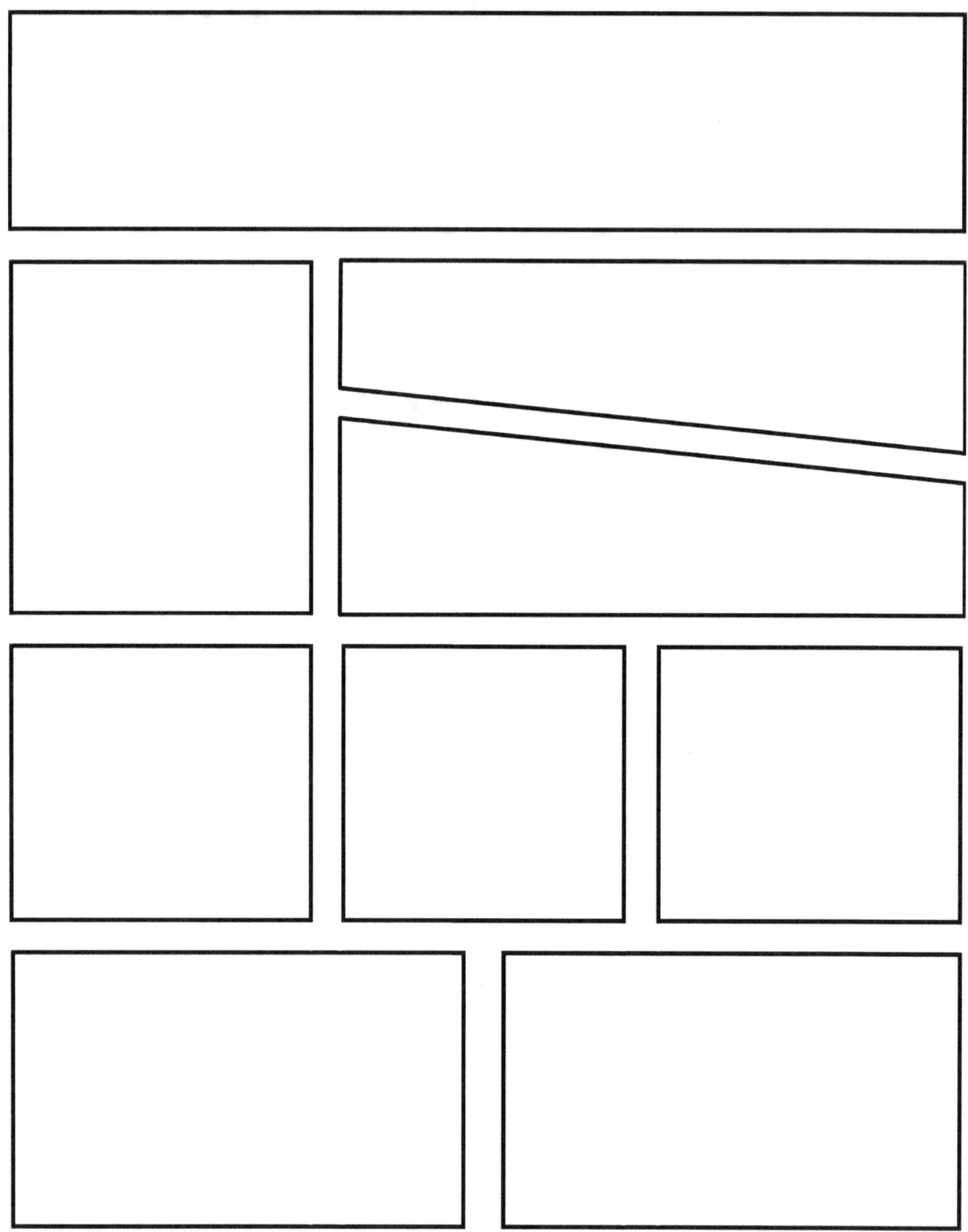

Blank Comic Book

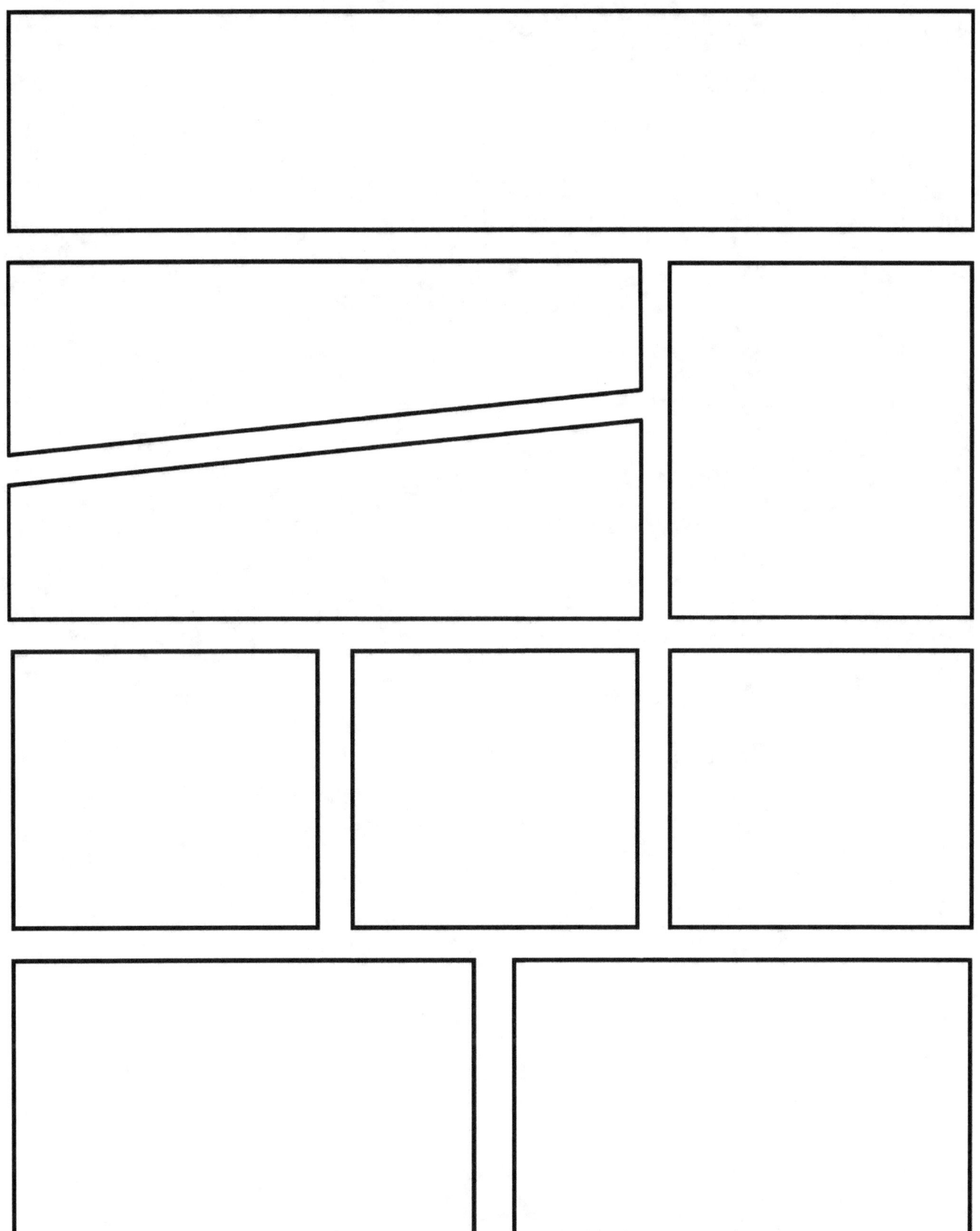

87

Blank Comic Book

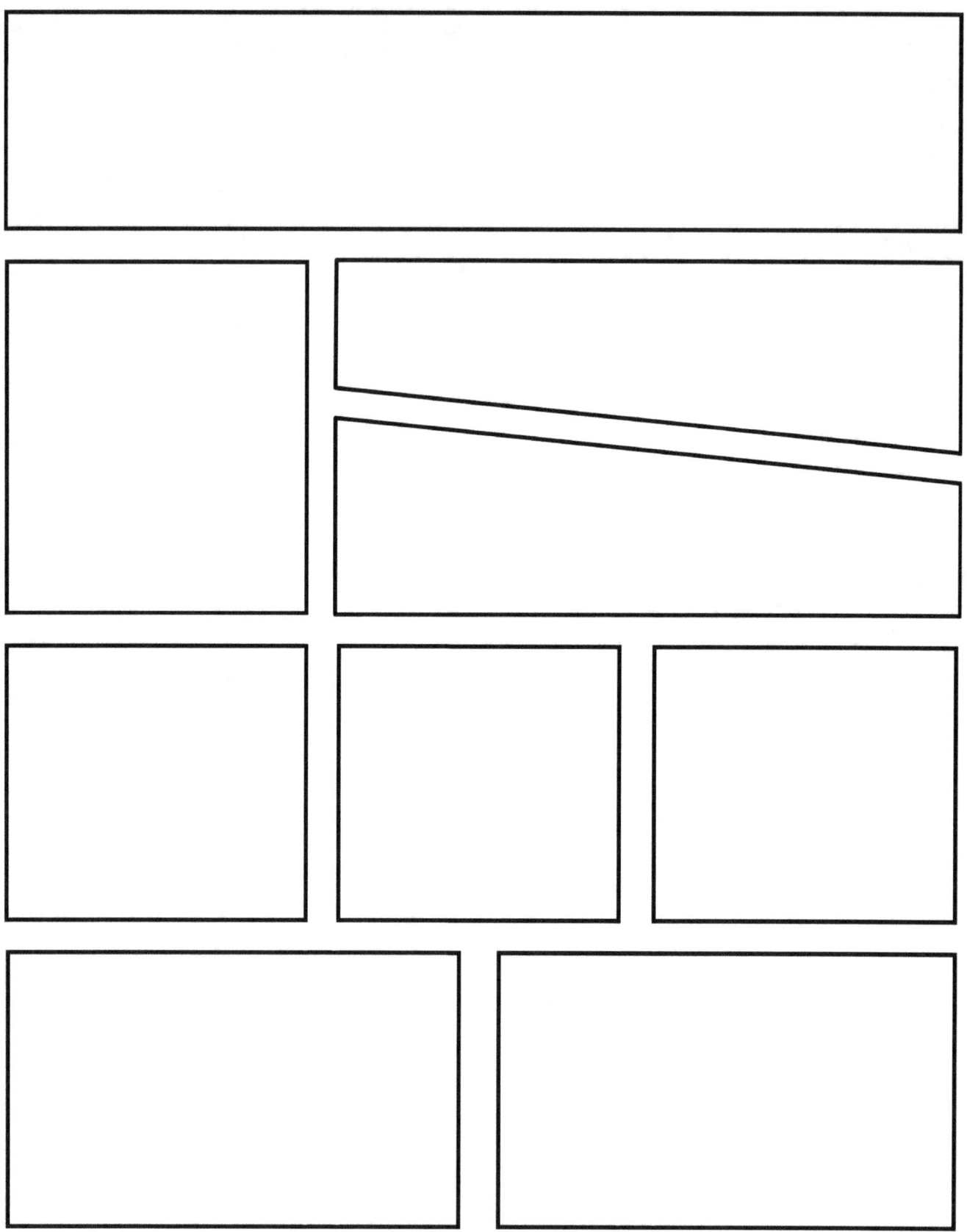

88

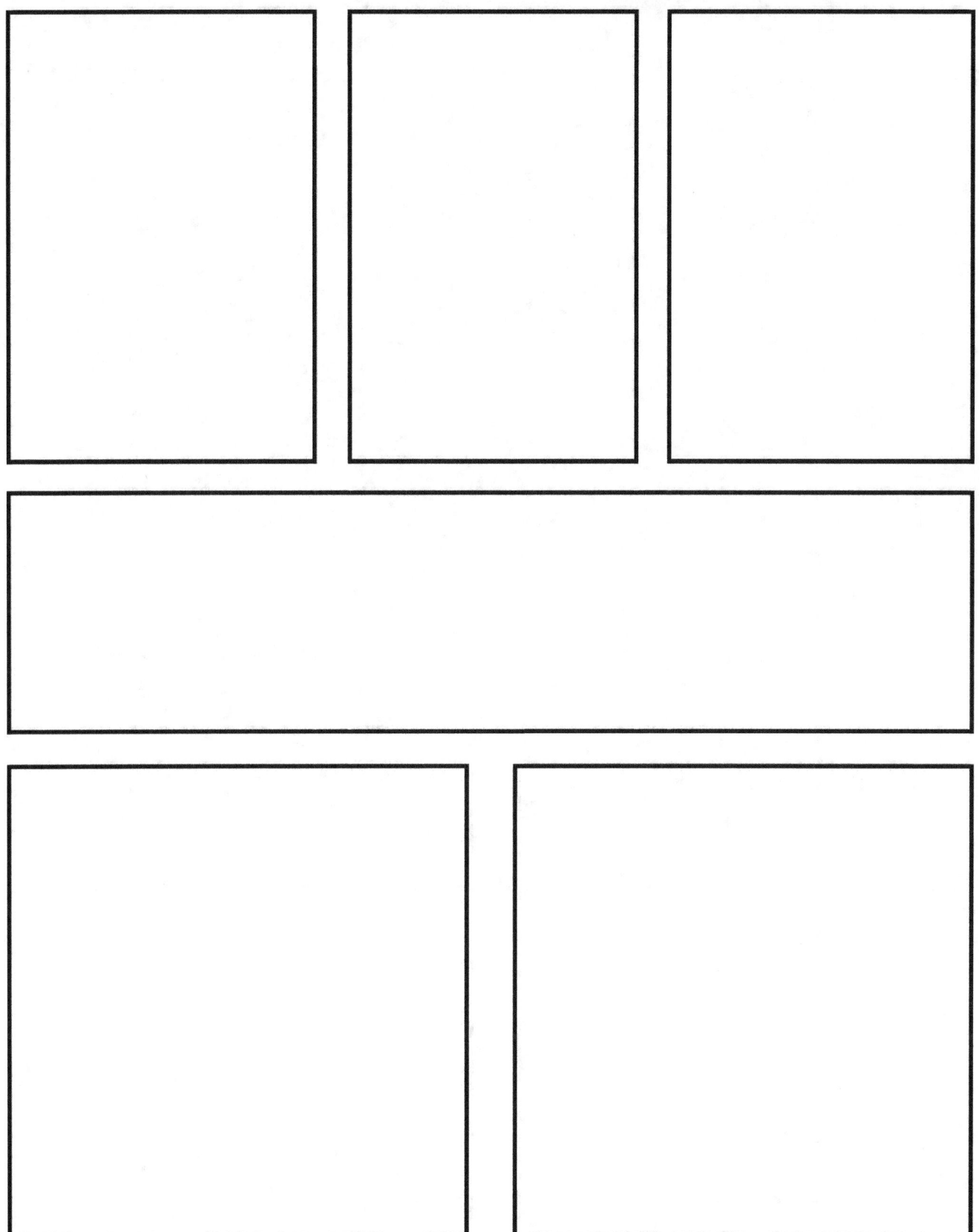

Blank Comic Book

Blank Comic Book

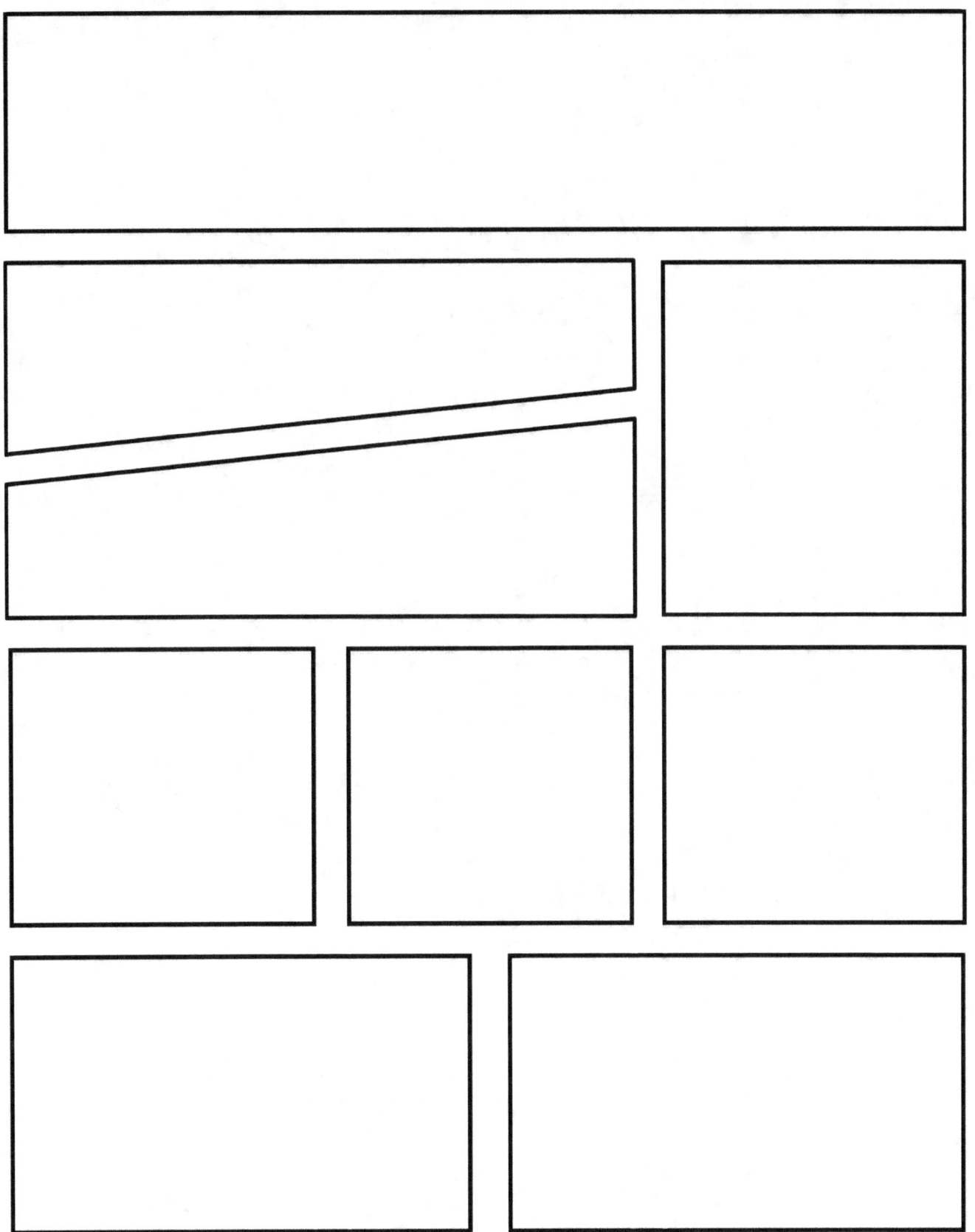

91

Blank Comic Book

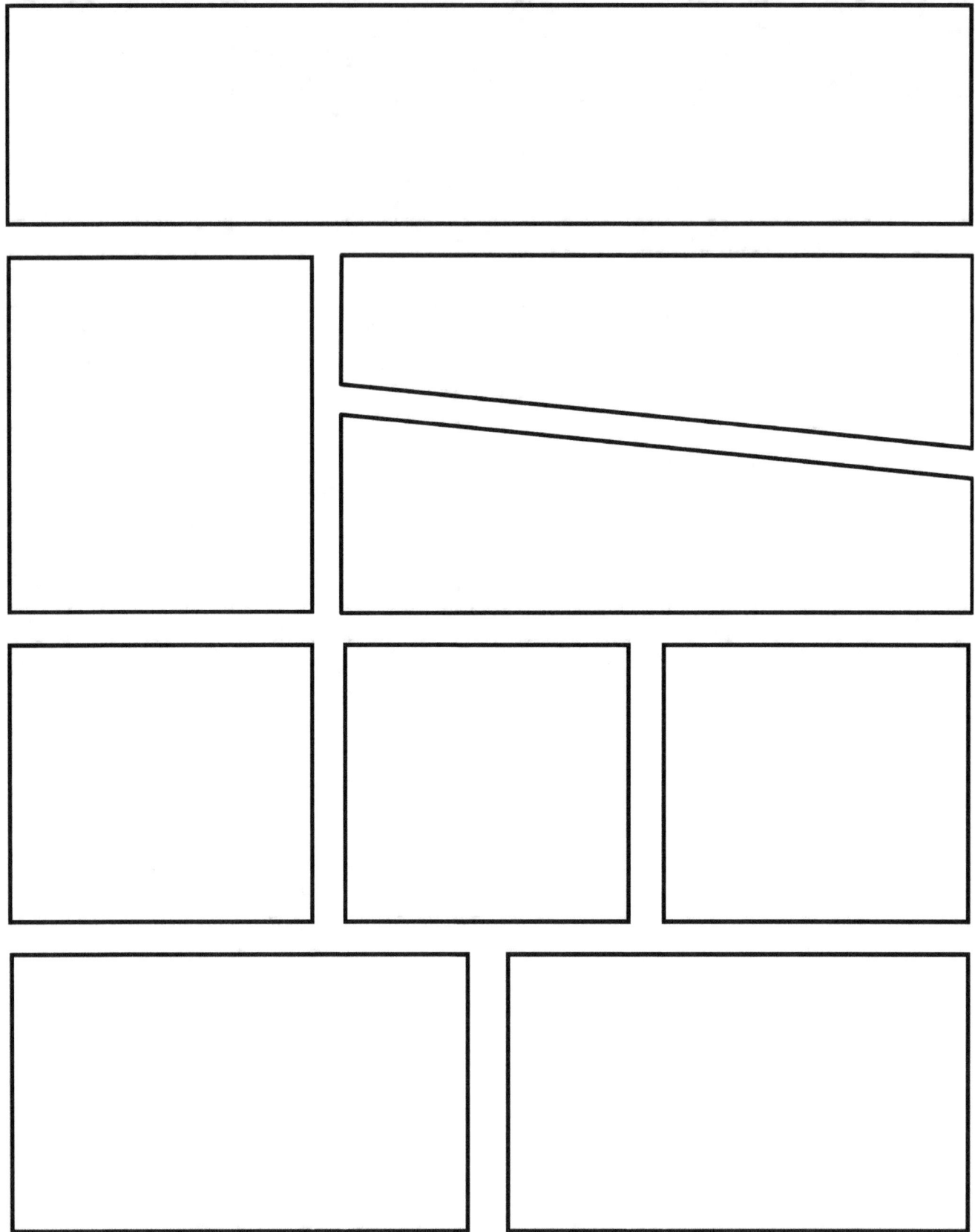

Blank Comic Book

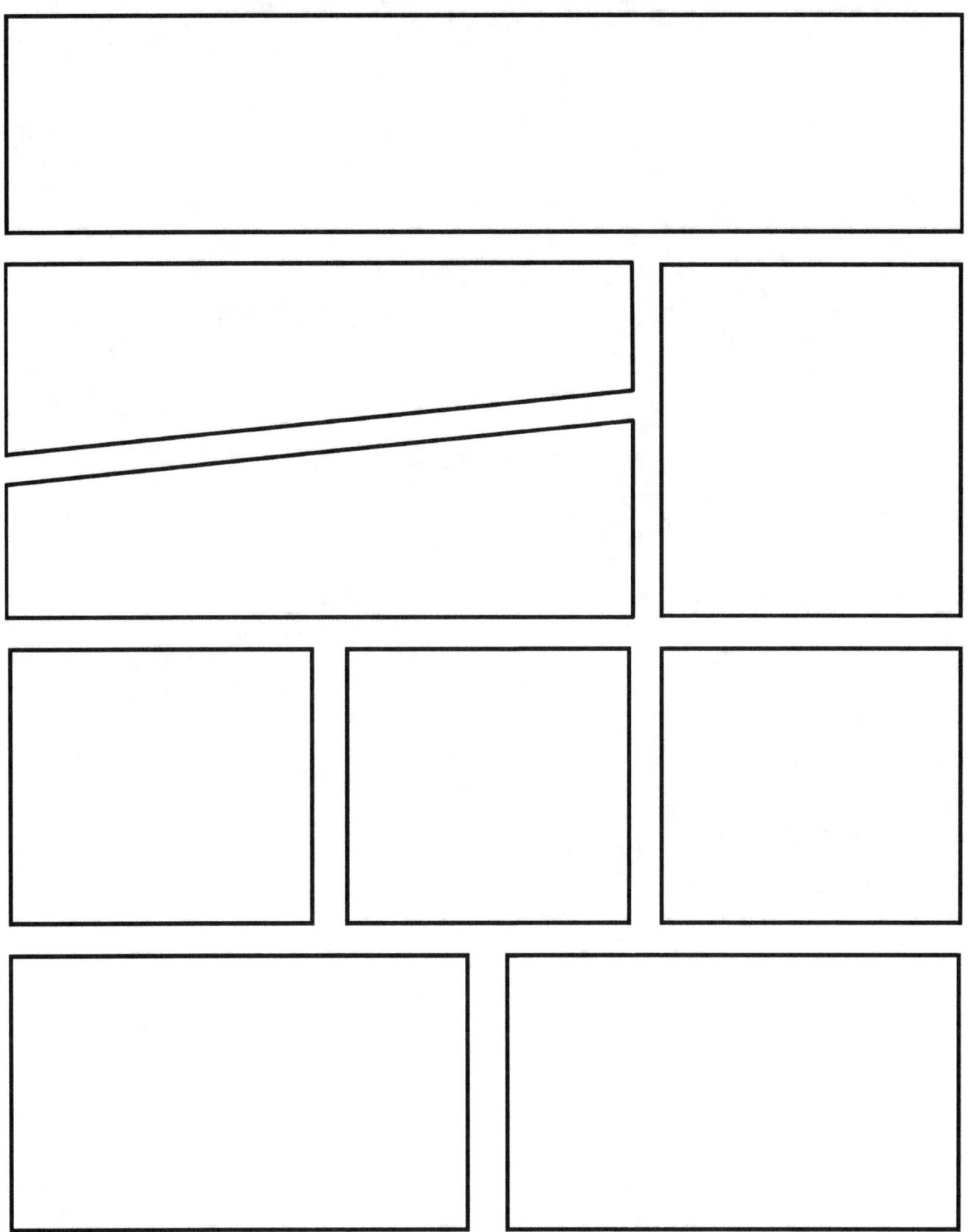

Blank Comic Book

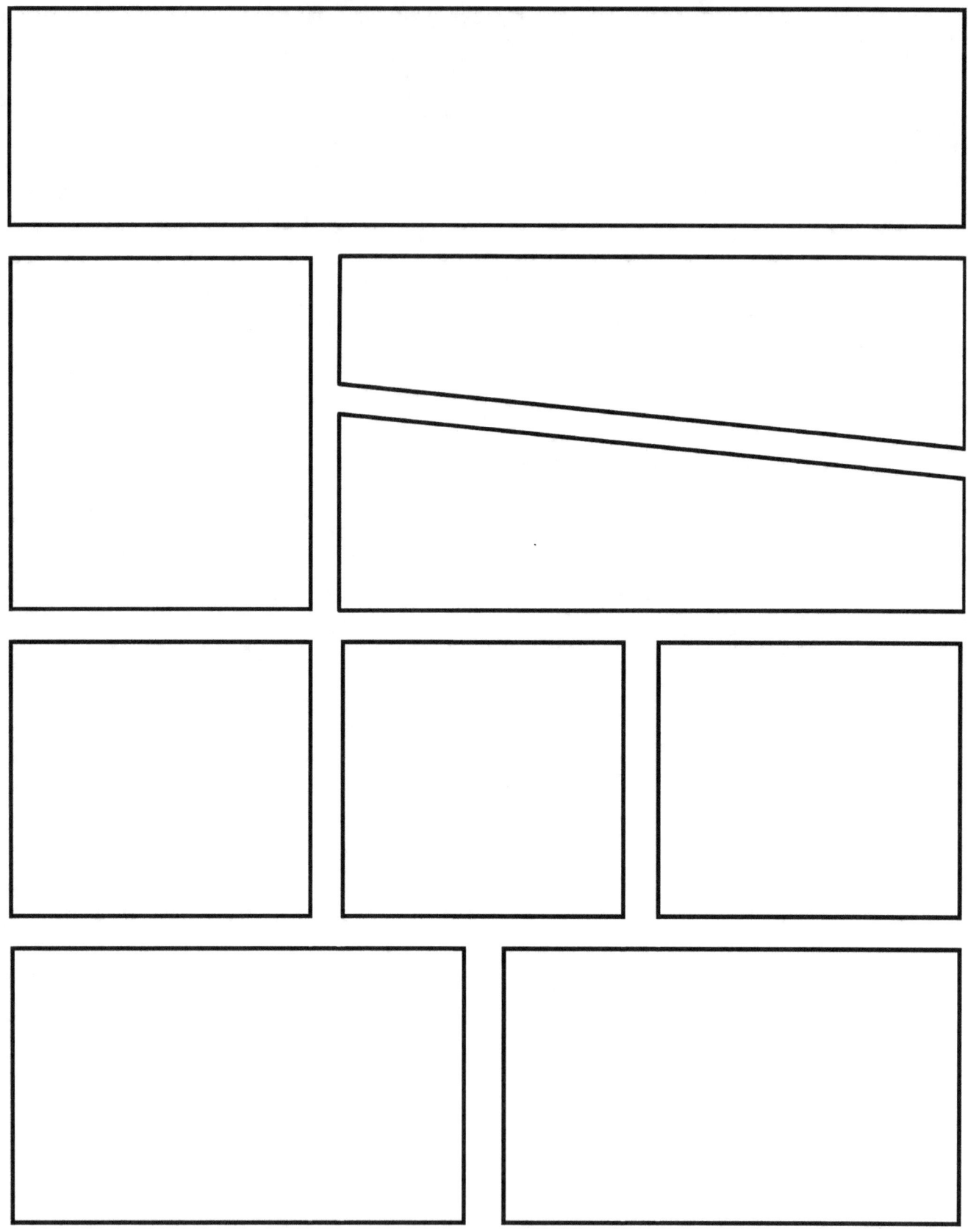

Blank Comic Book

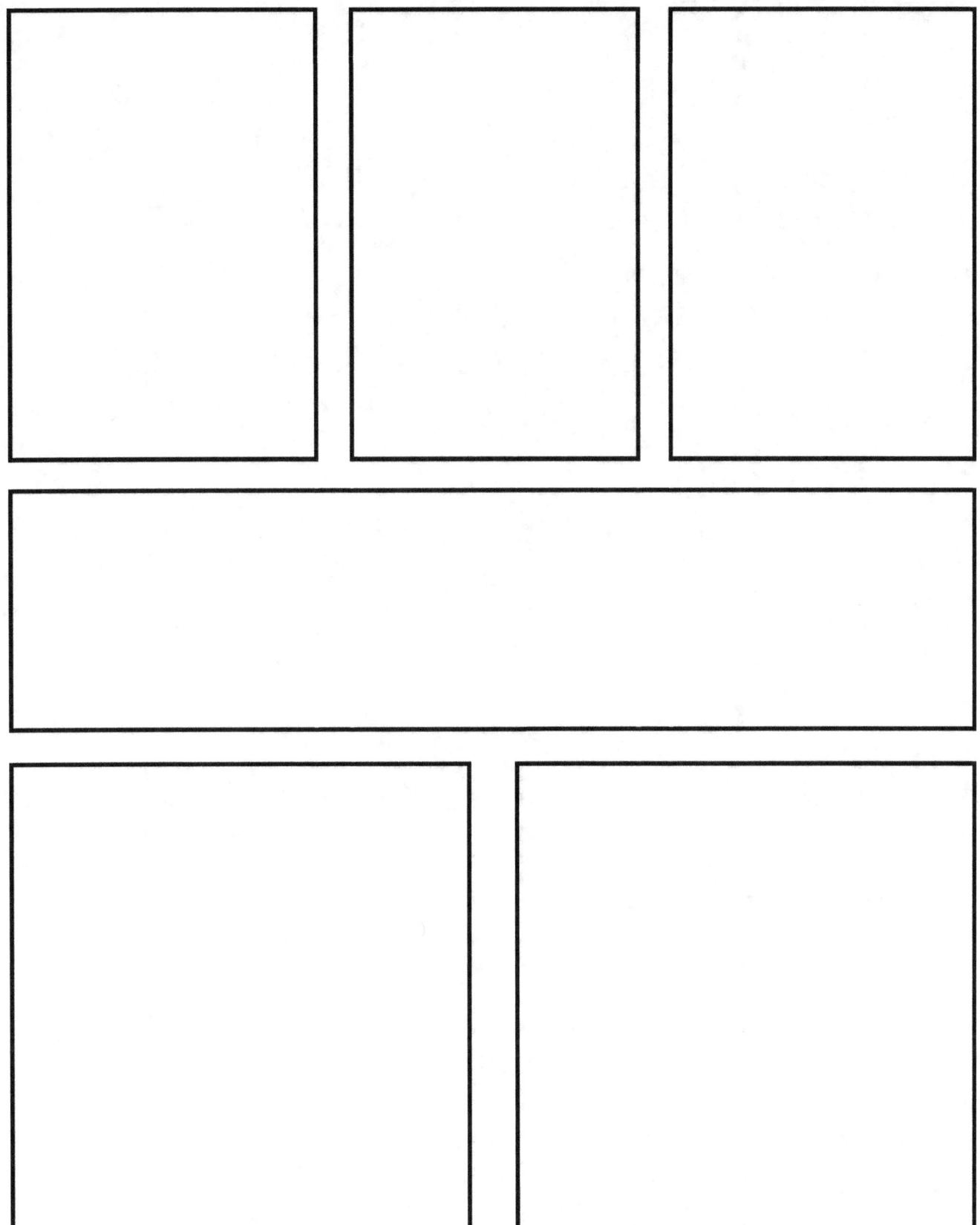

95

Blank Comic Book

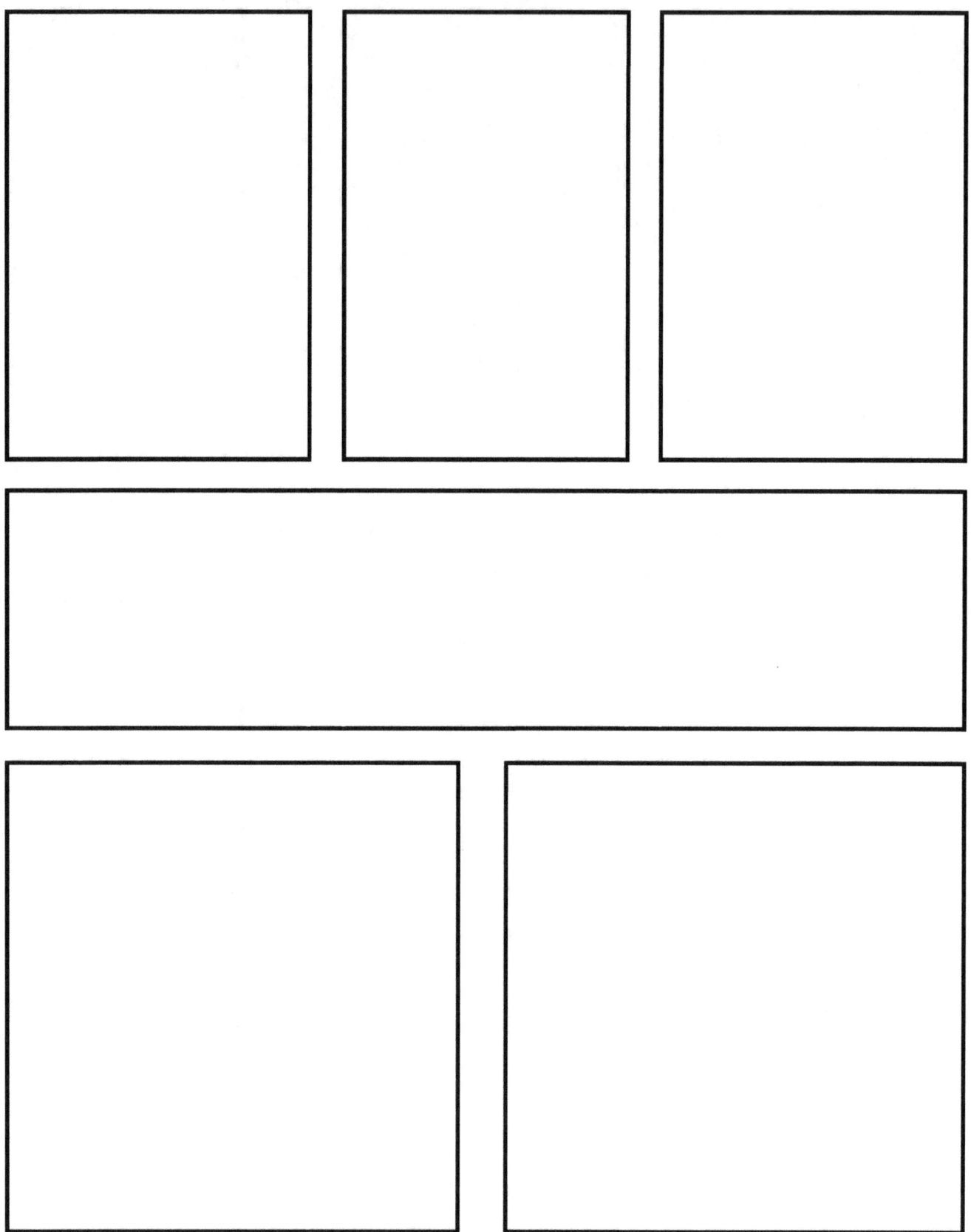

96

Blank Comic Book

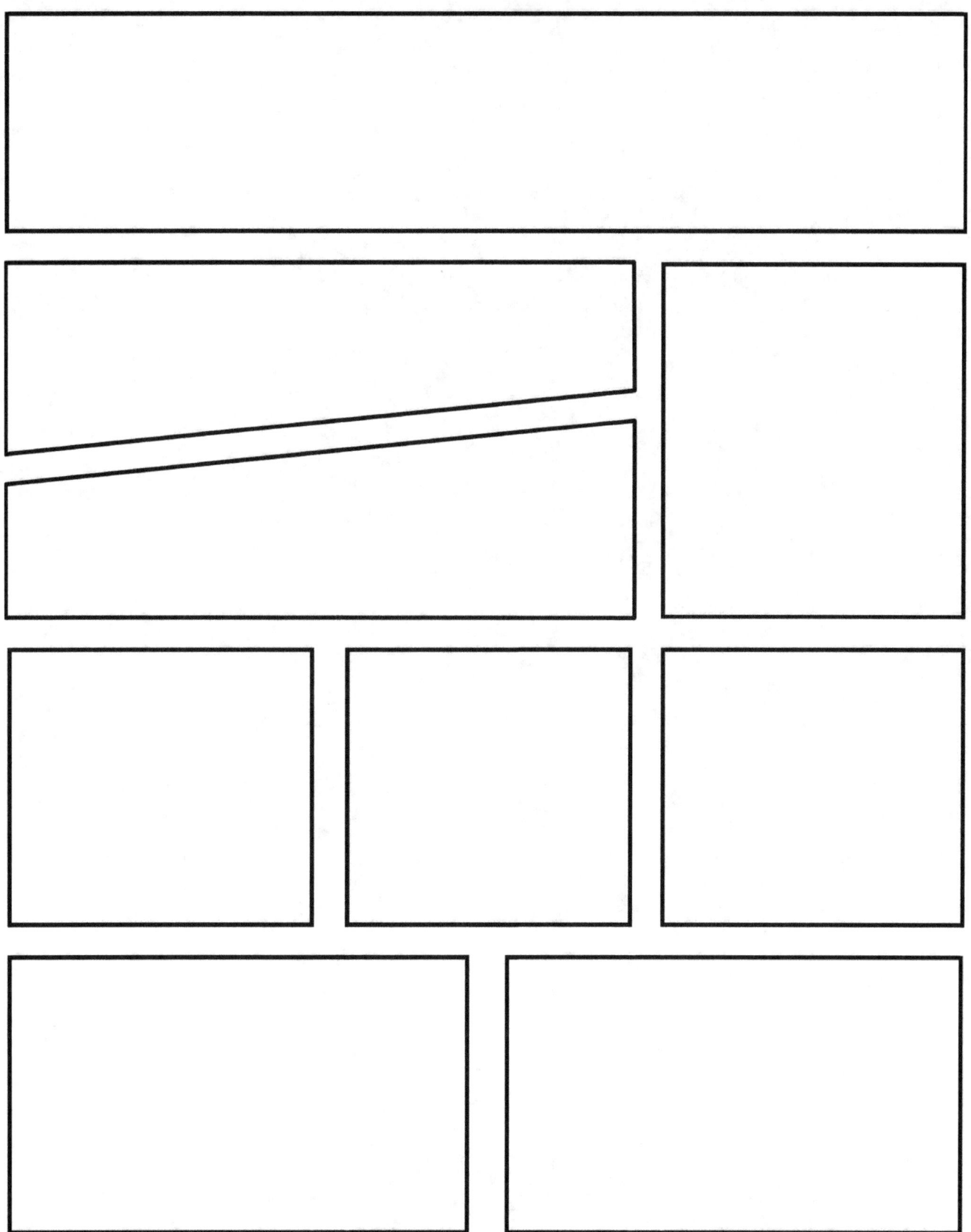

Blank Comic Book

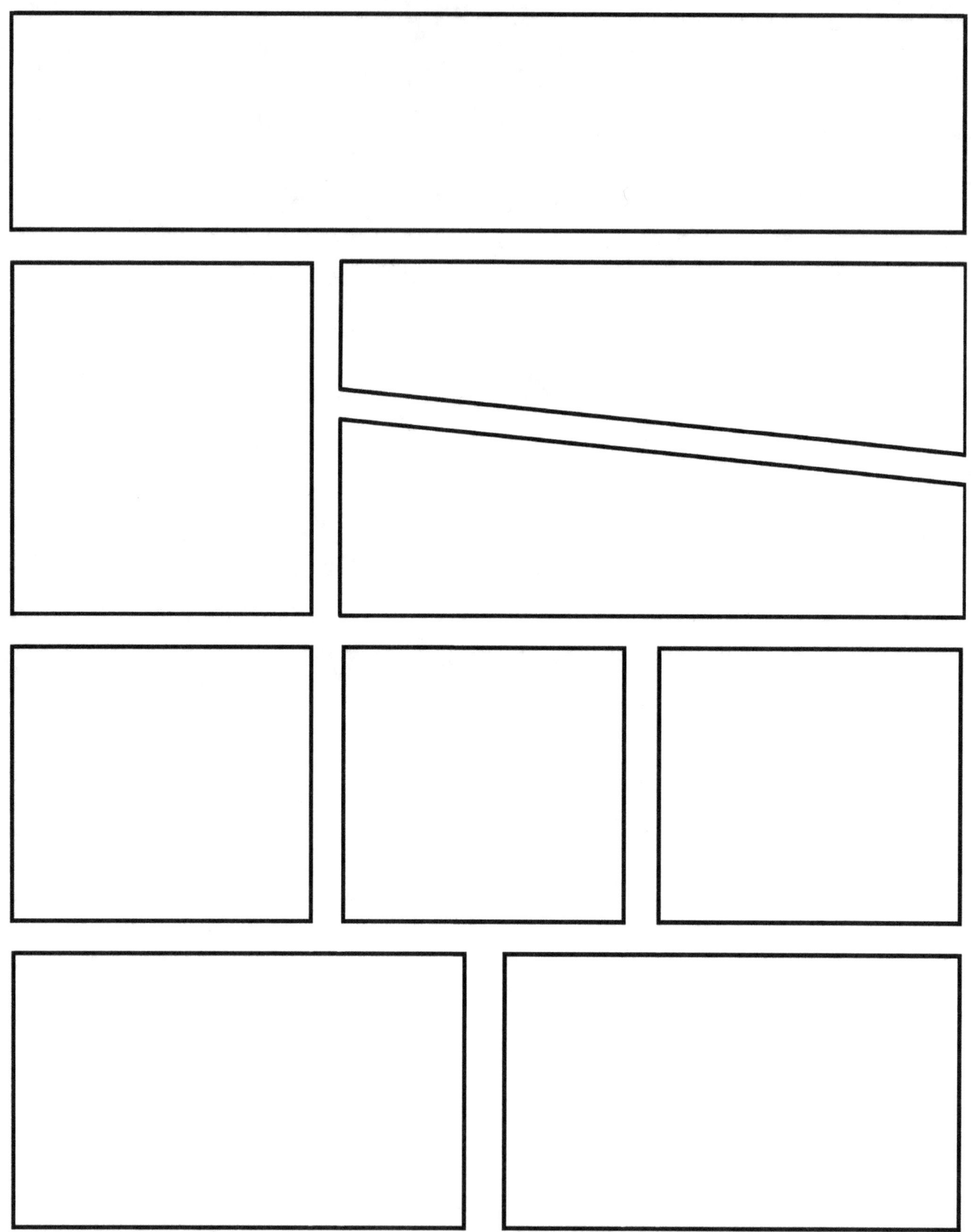

Blank Comic Book

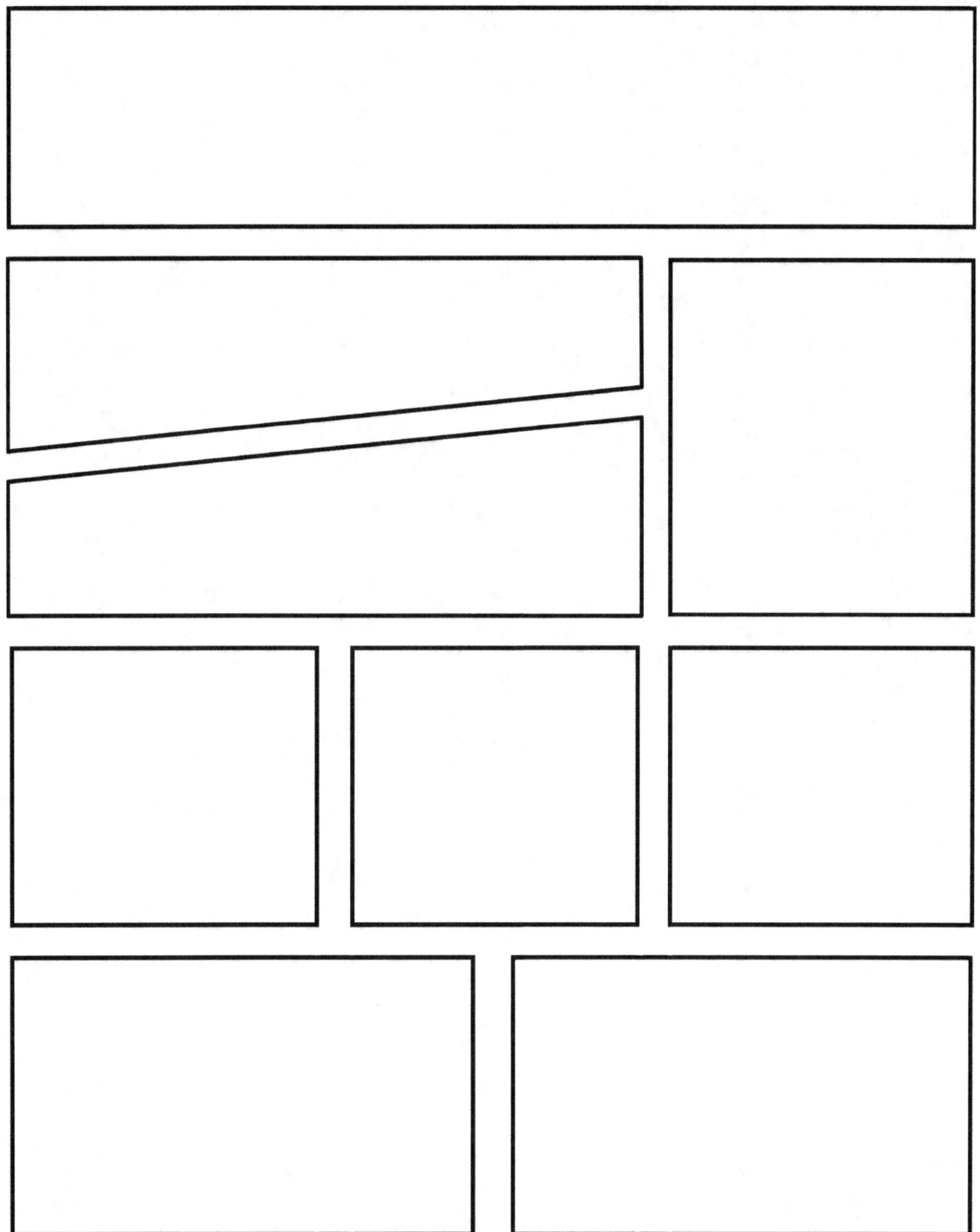

99

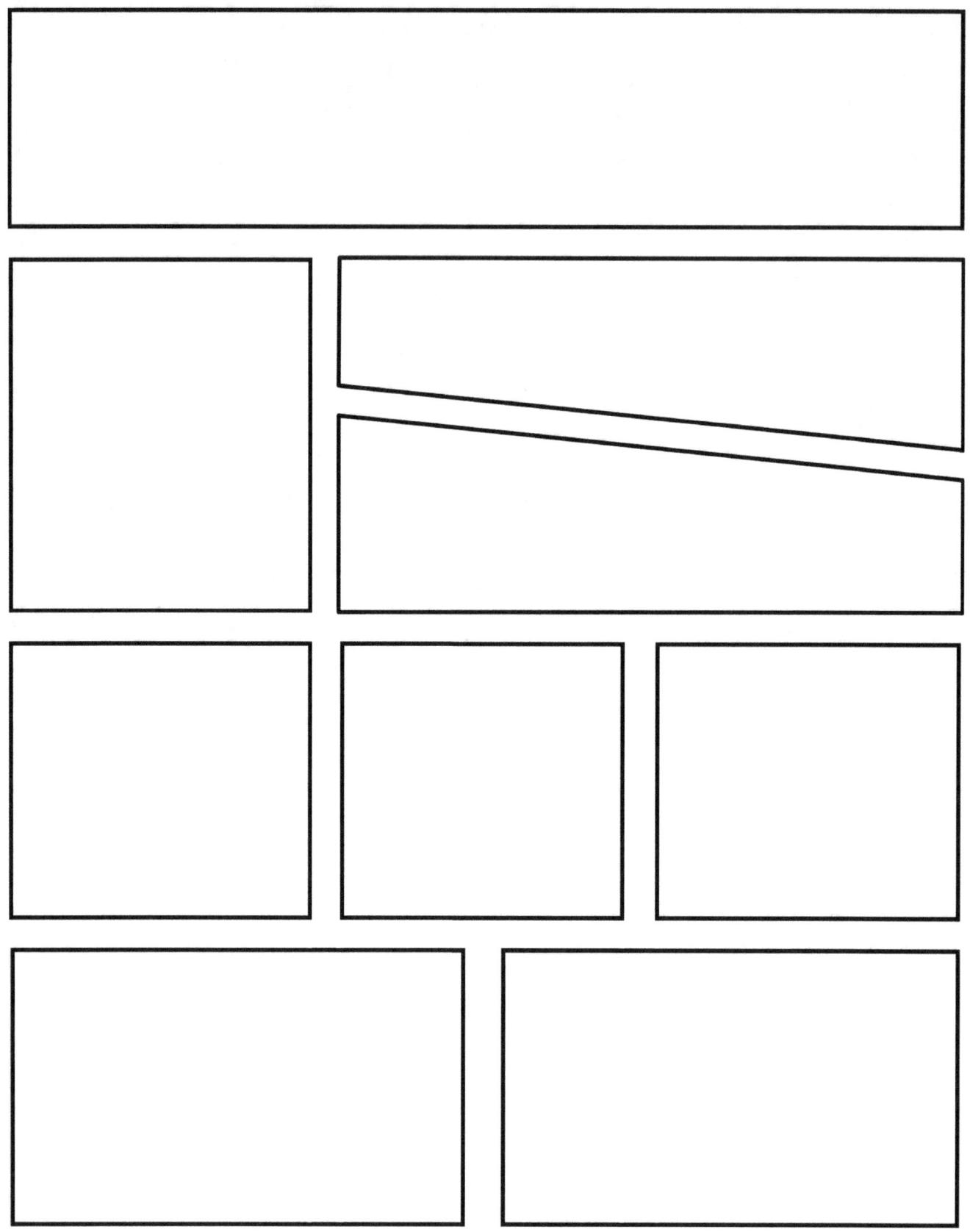

Blank Comic Book

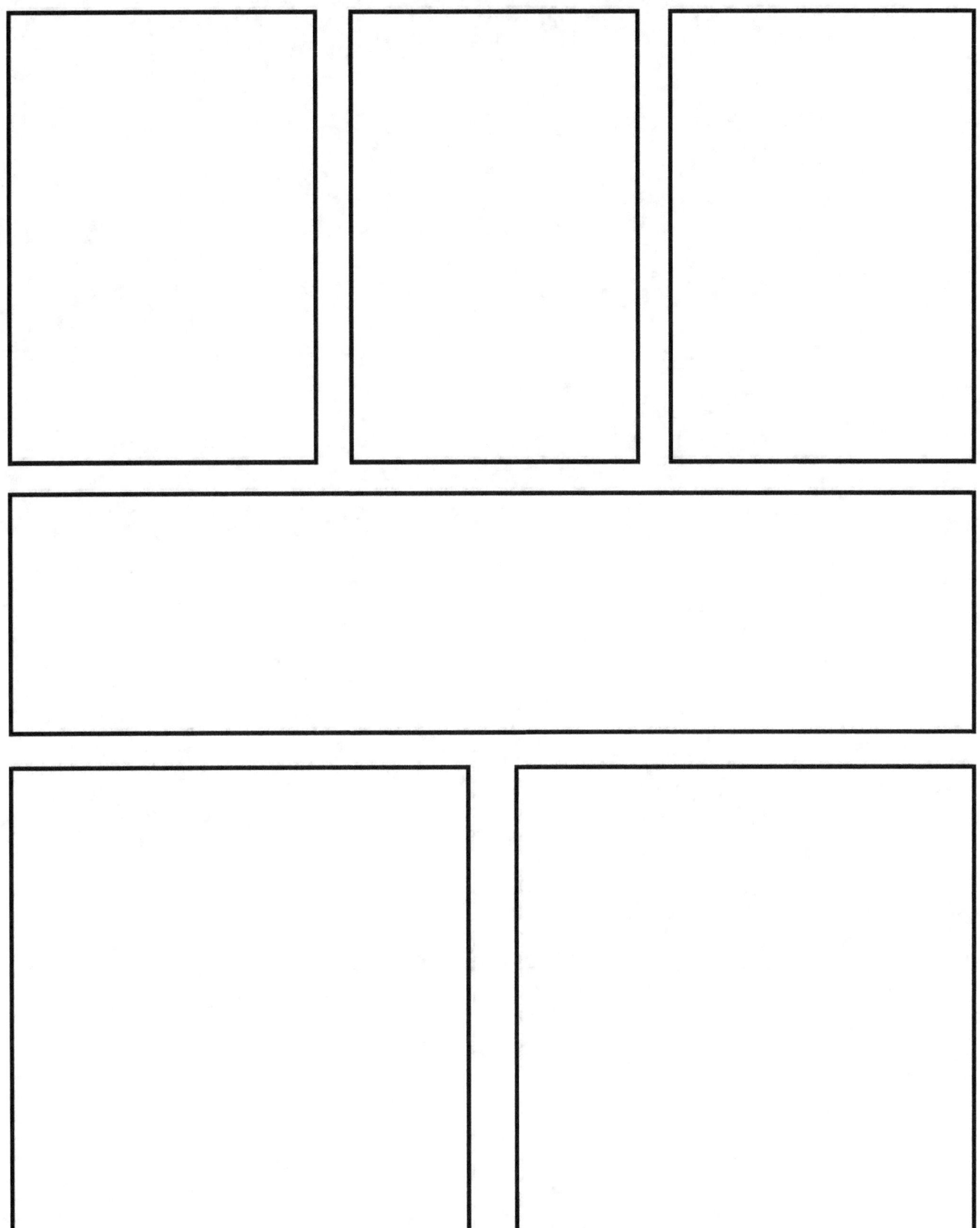

101

Blank Comic Book

Blank Comic Book

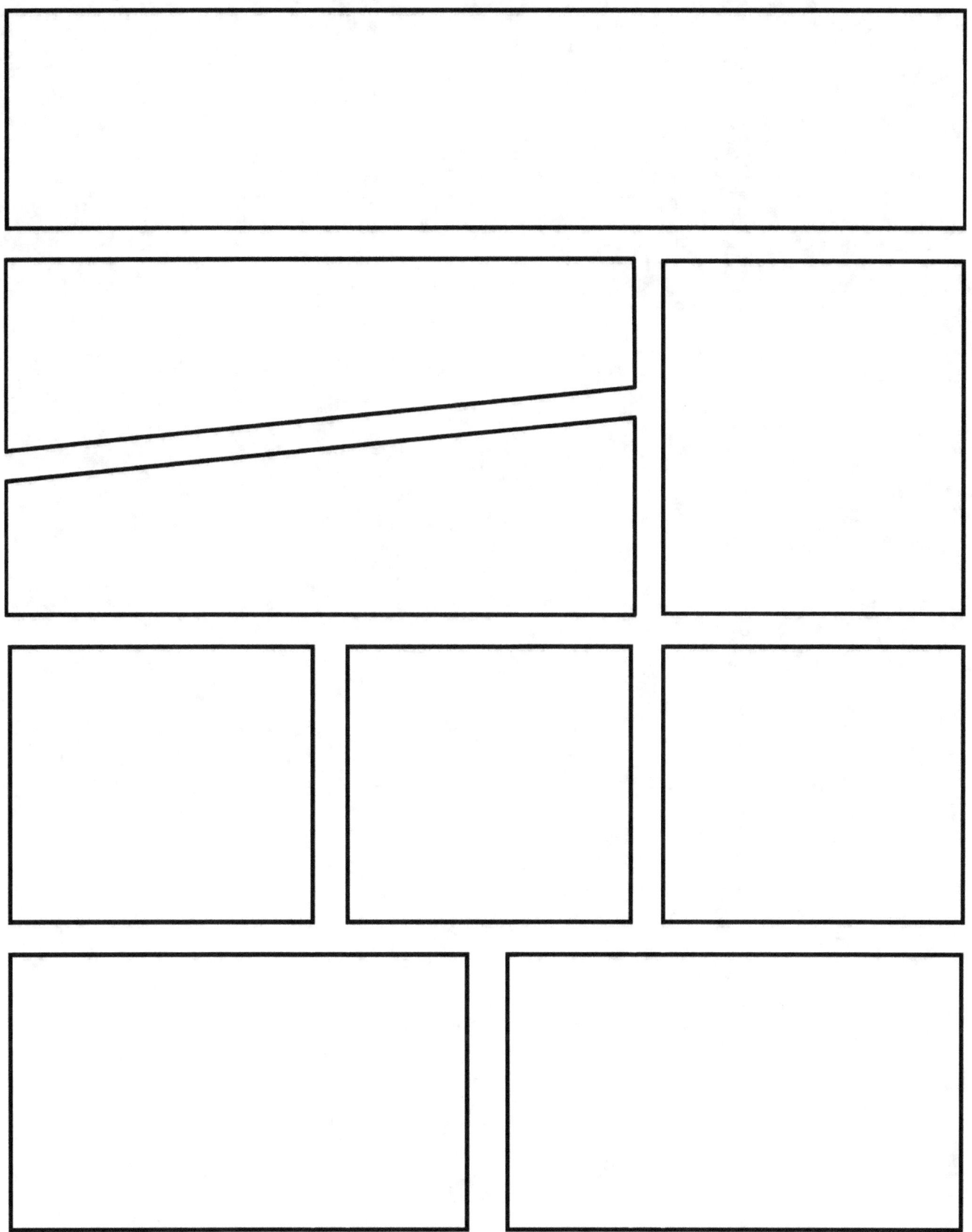

103

Blank Comic Book

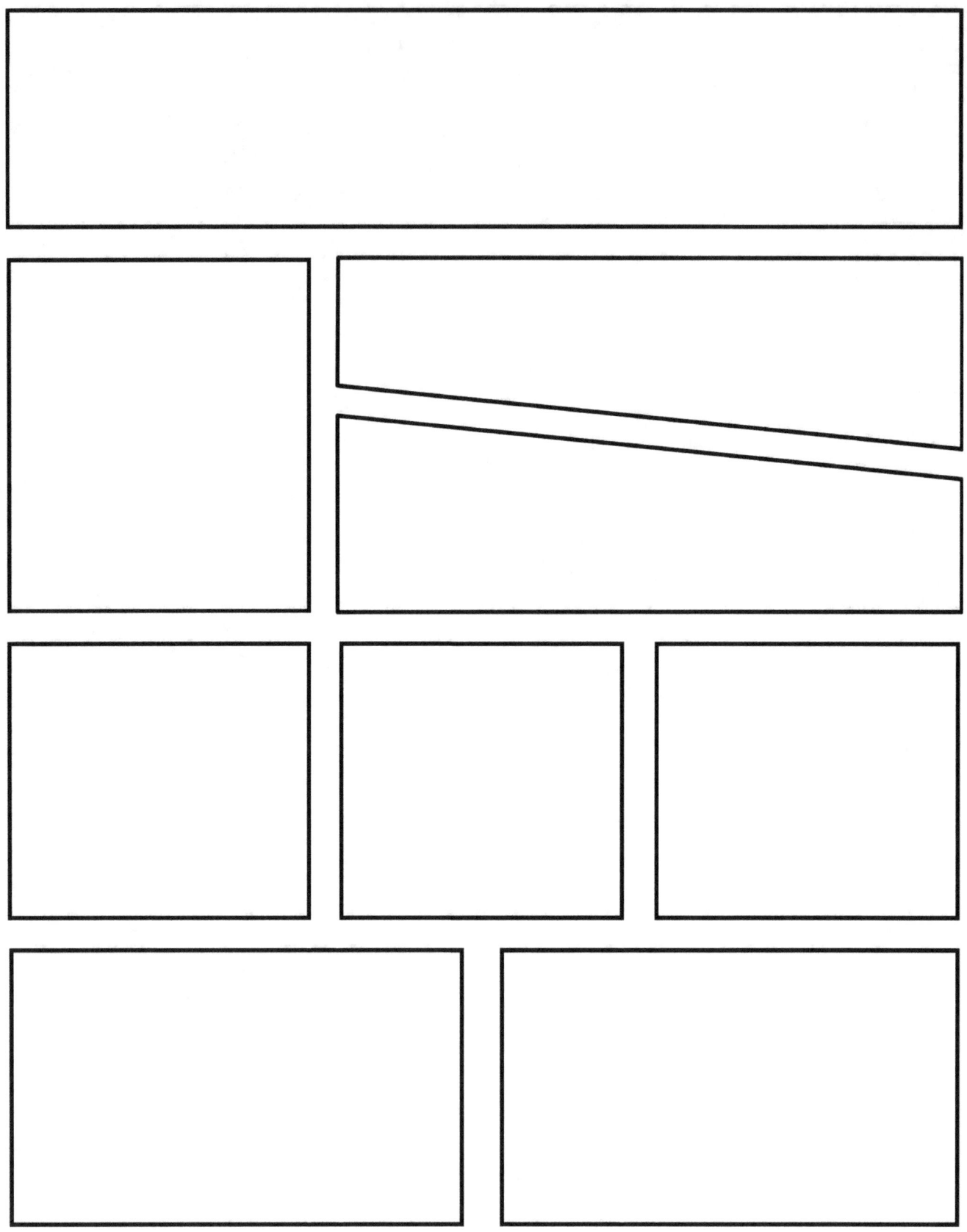

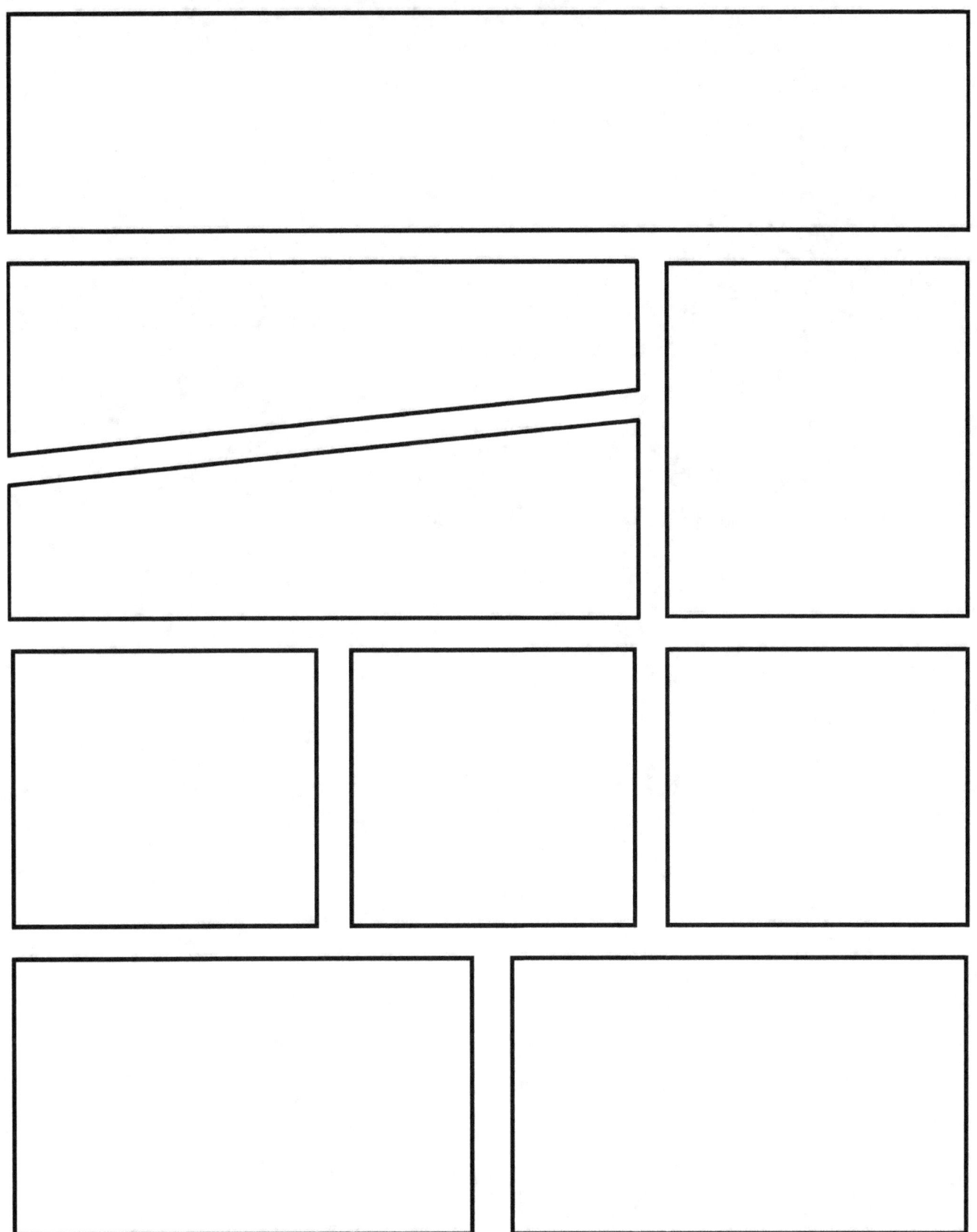

Blank Comic Book

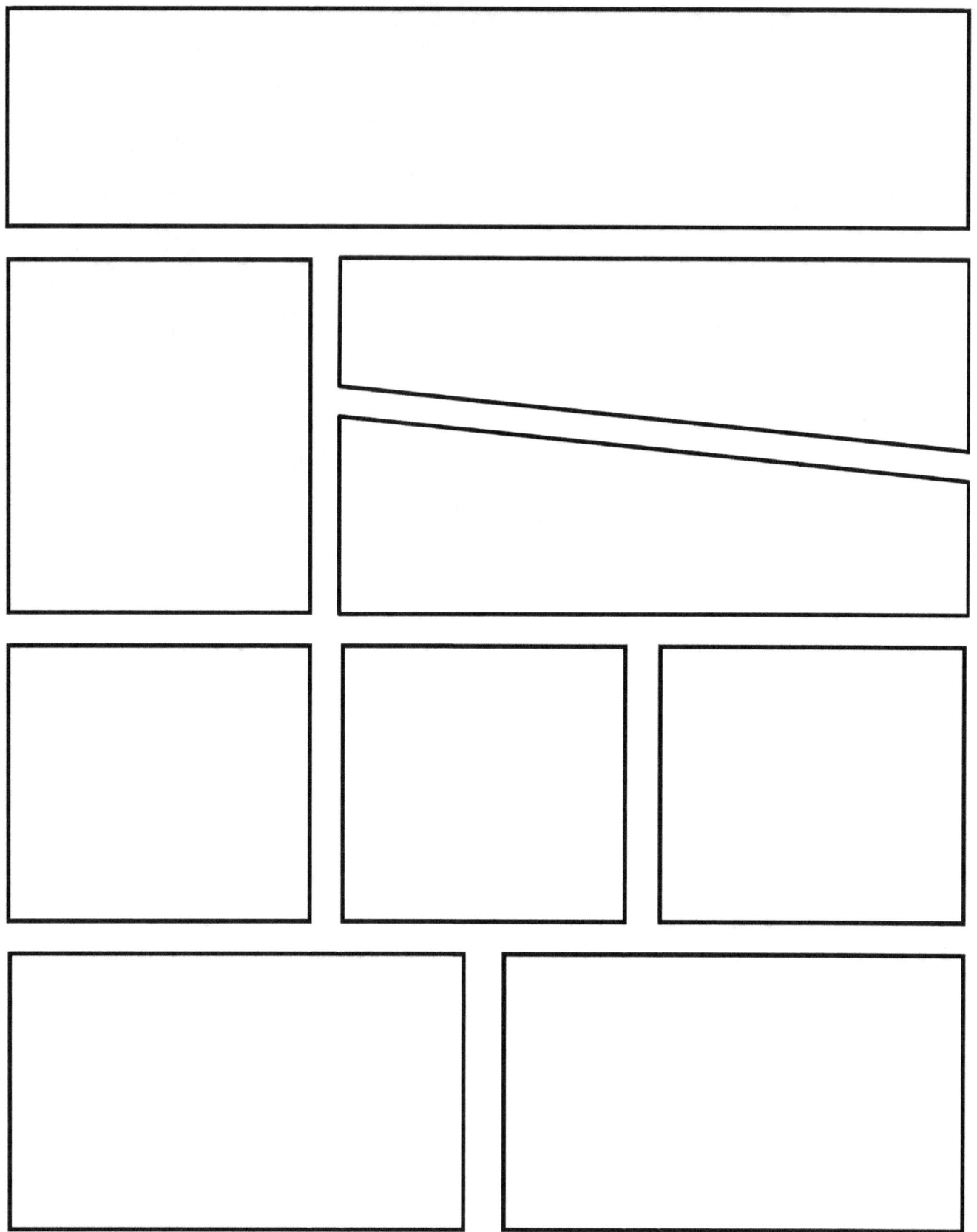

106

Blank Comic Book

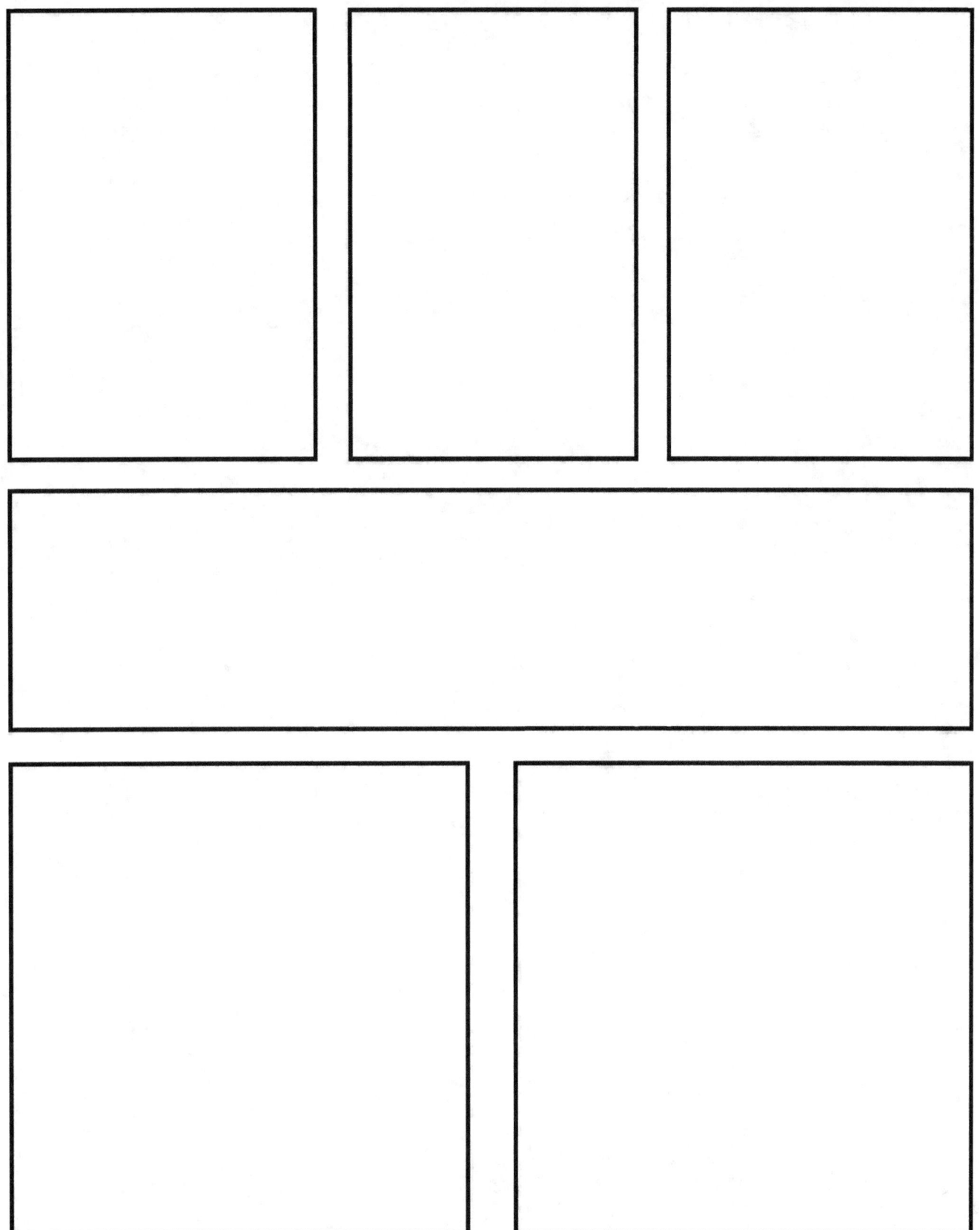

Blank Comic Book

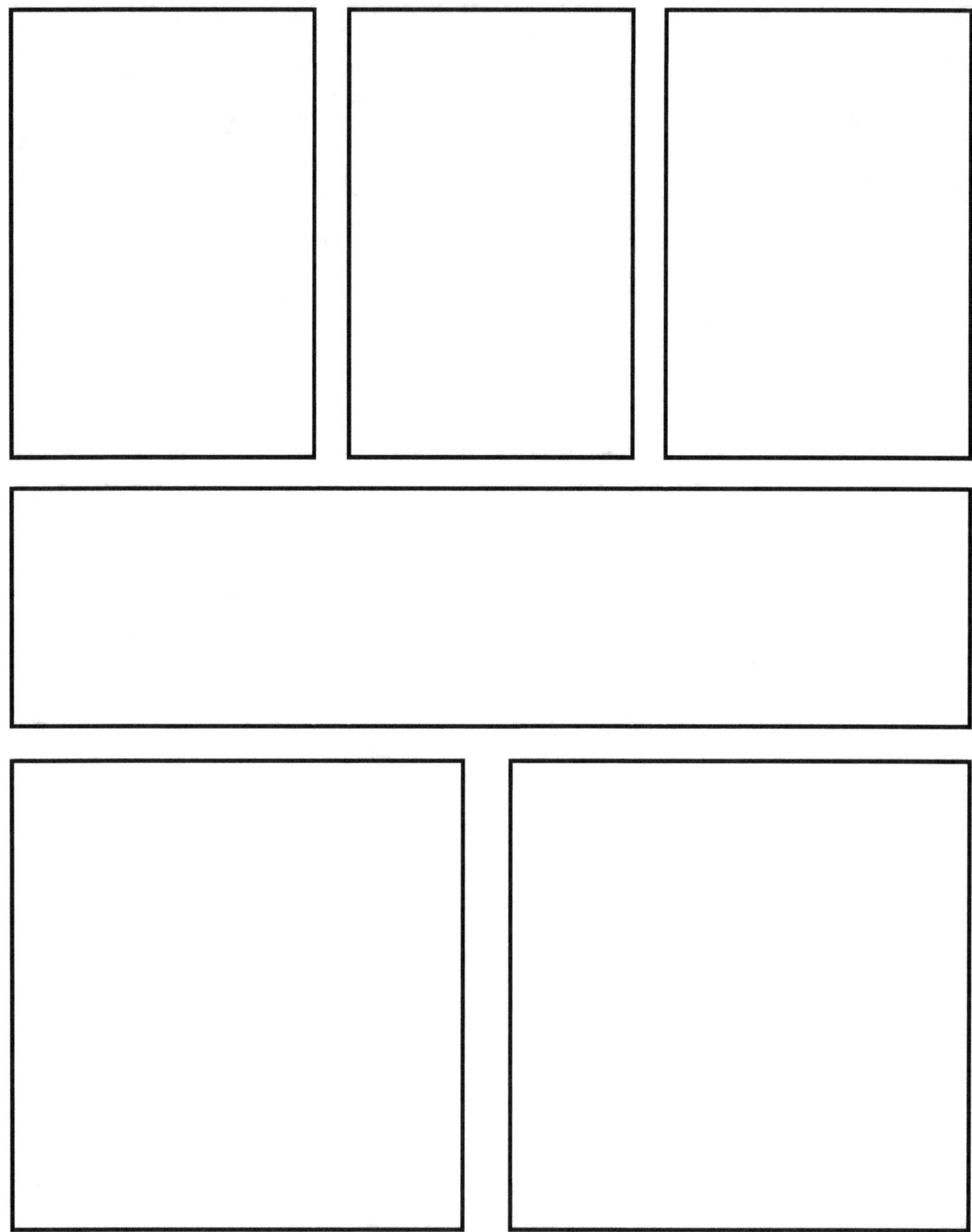

Blank Comic Book

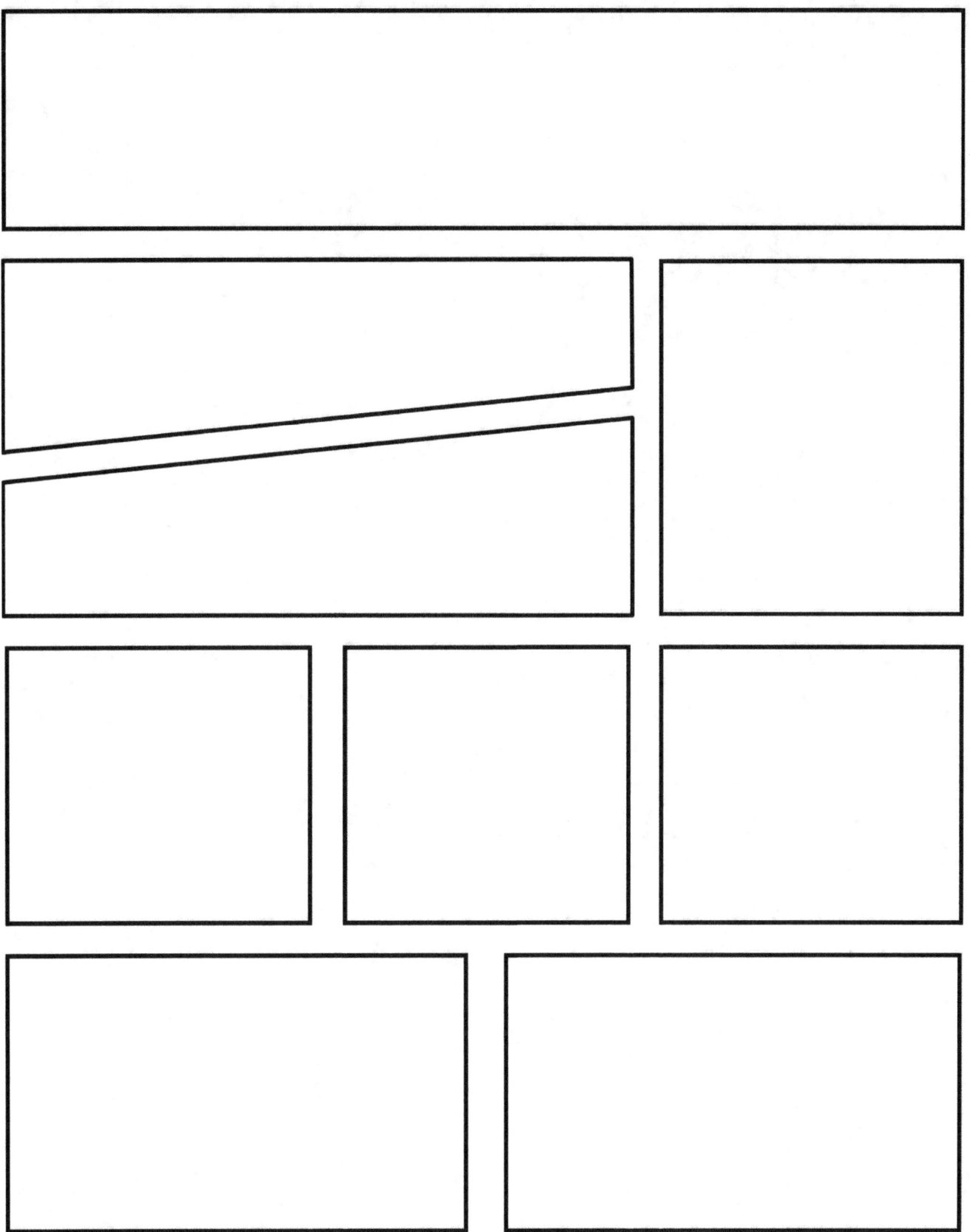

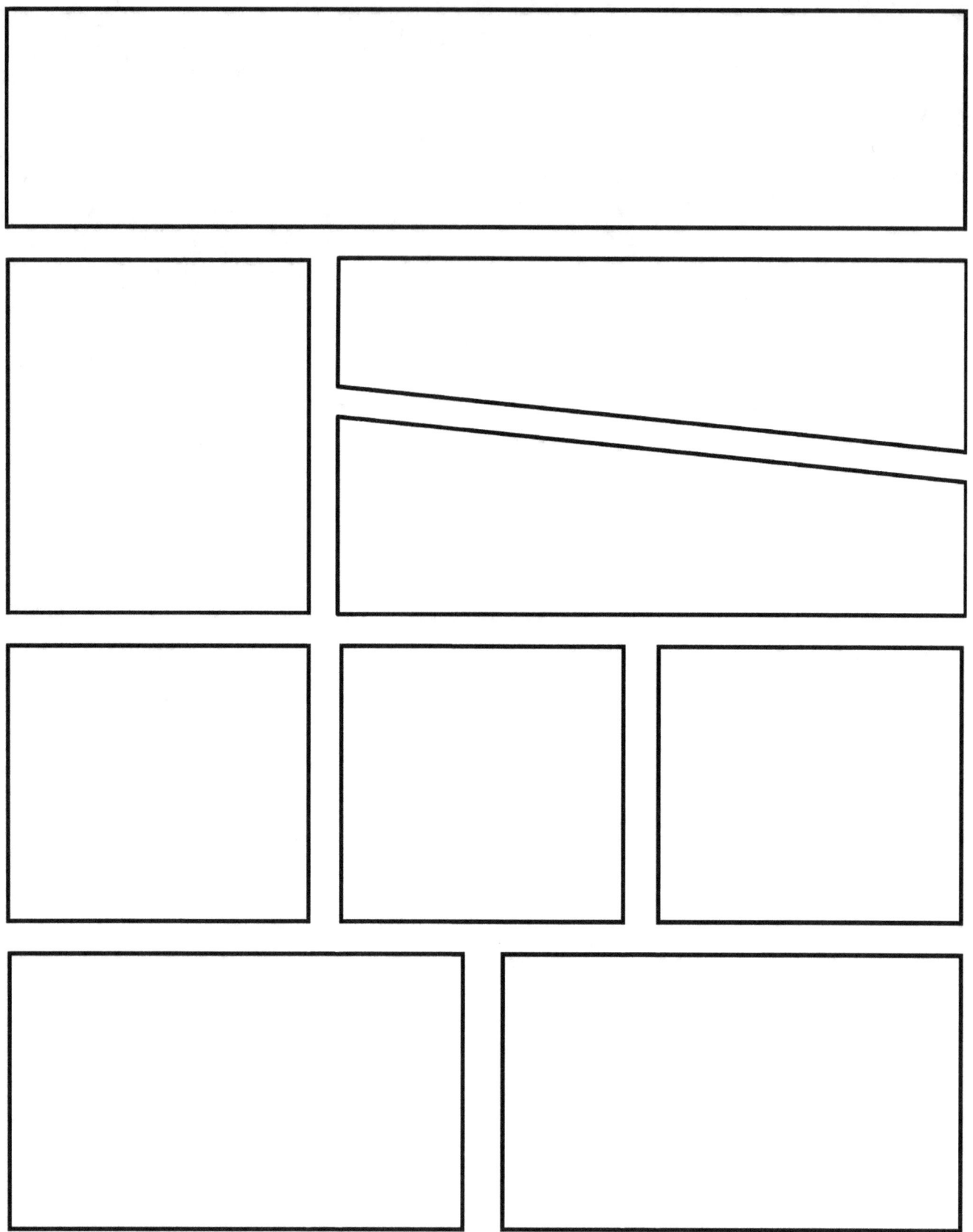

Blank Comic Book

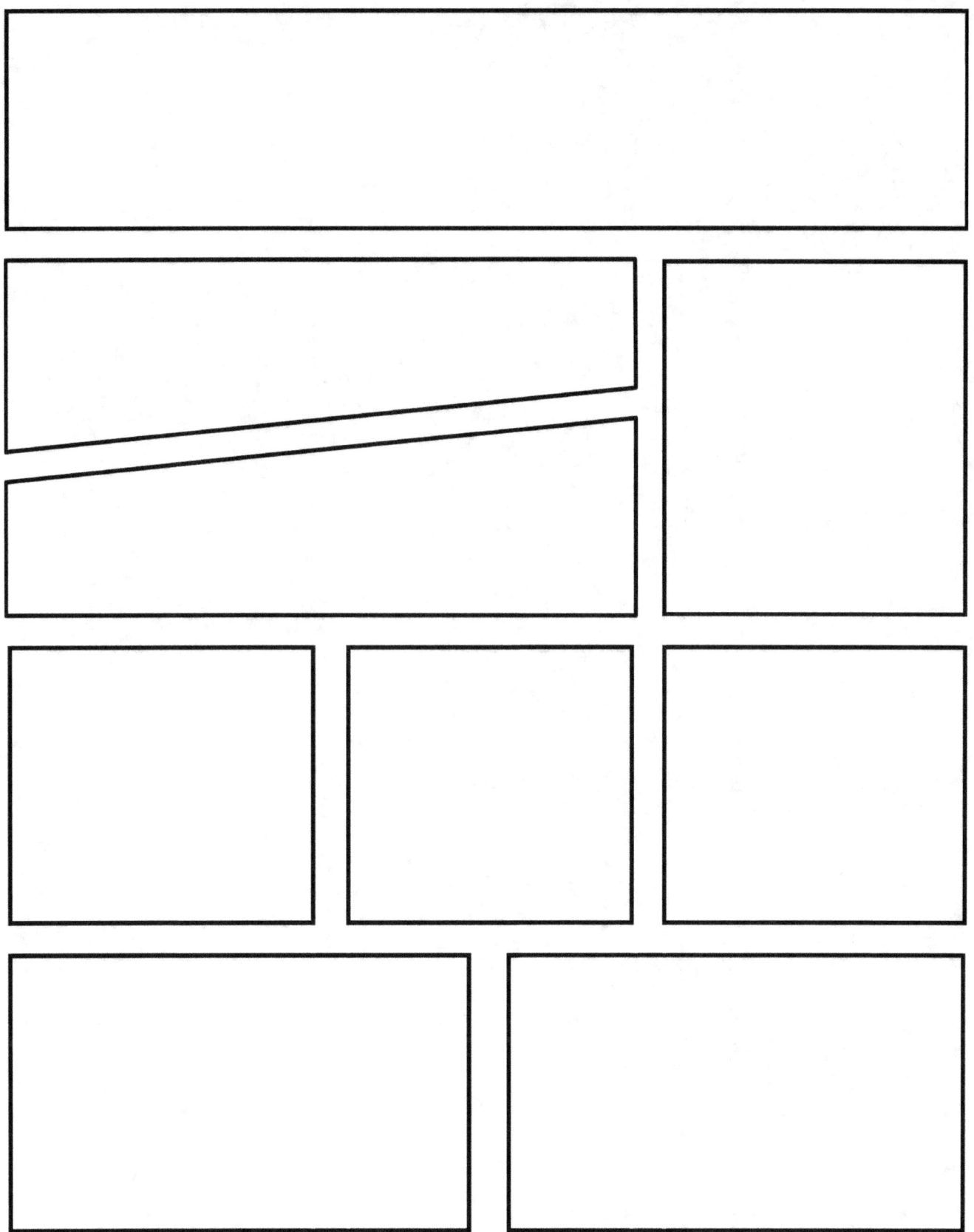

111

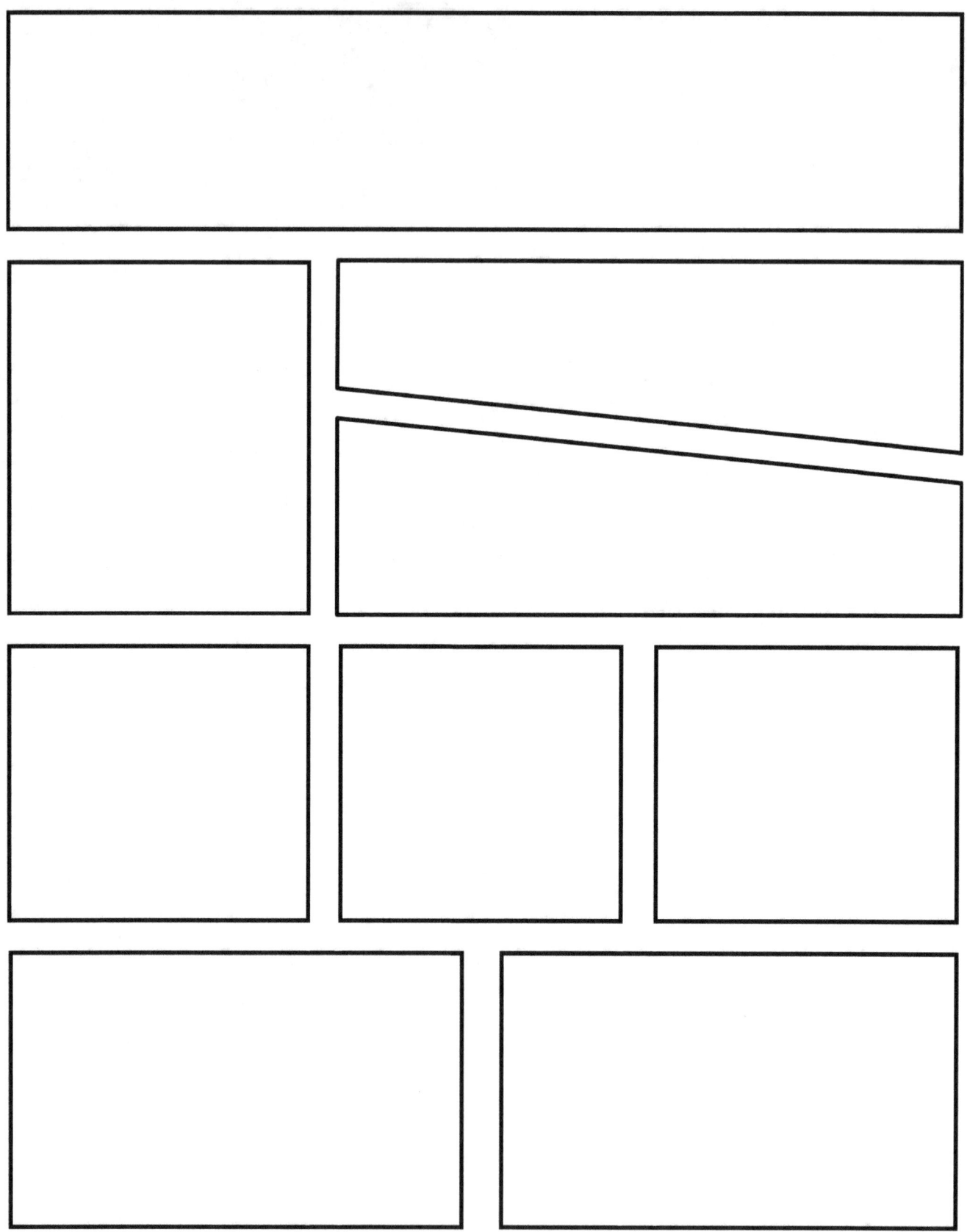

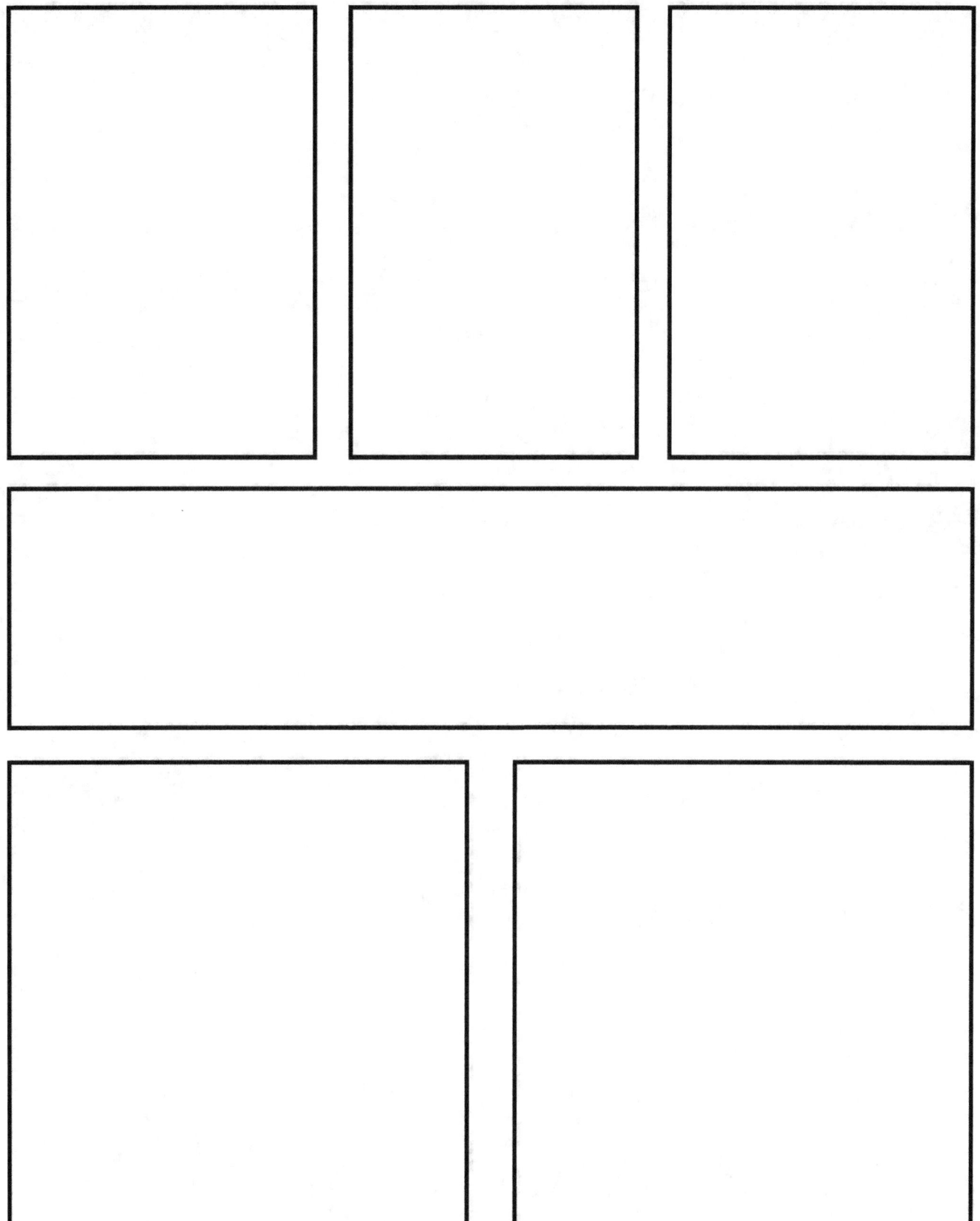

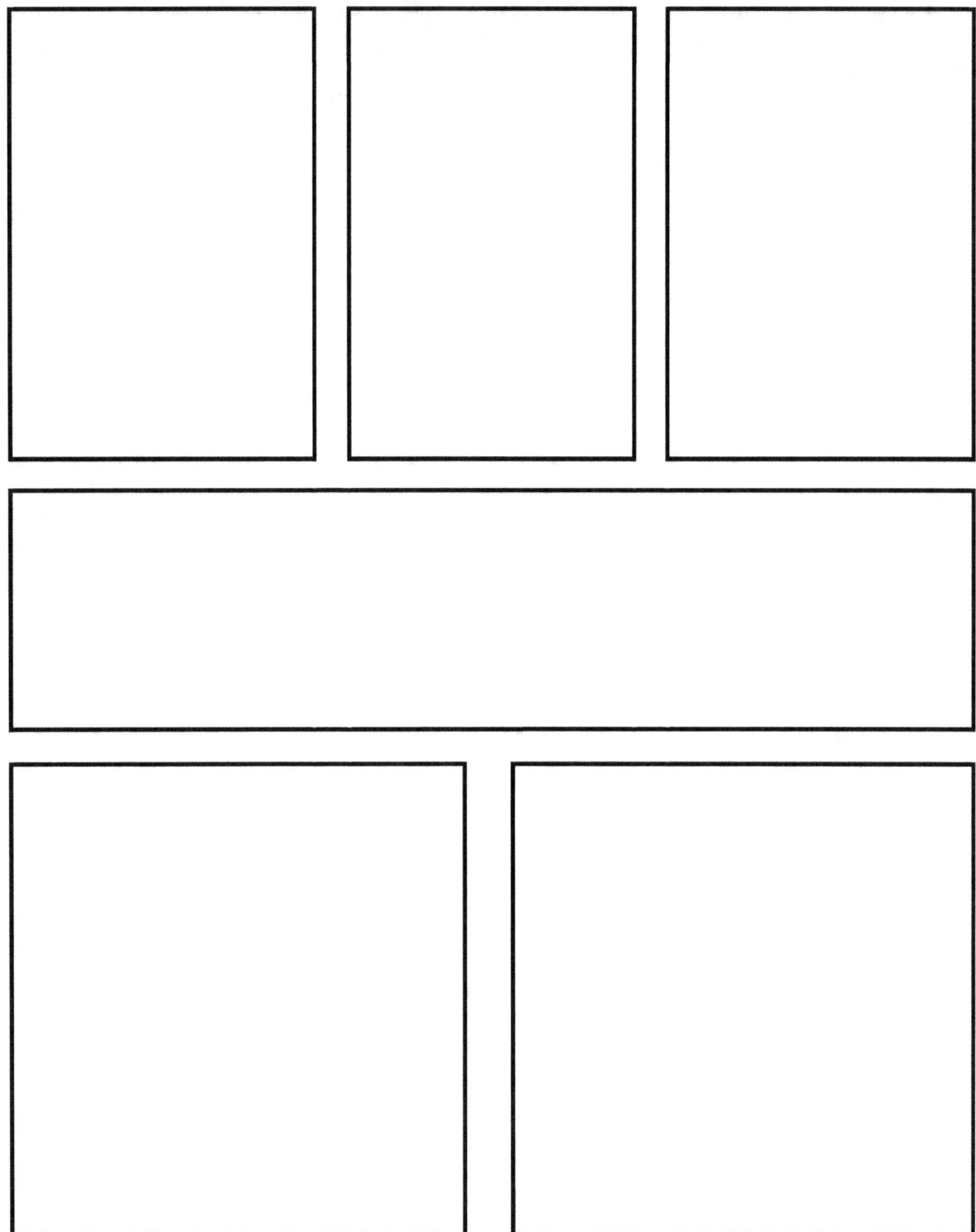

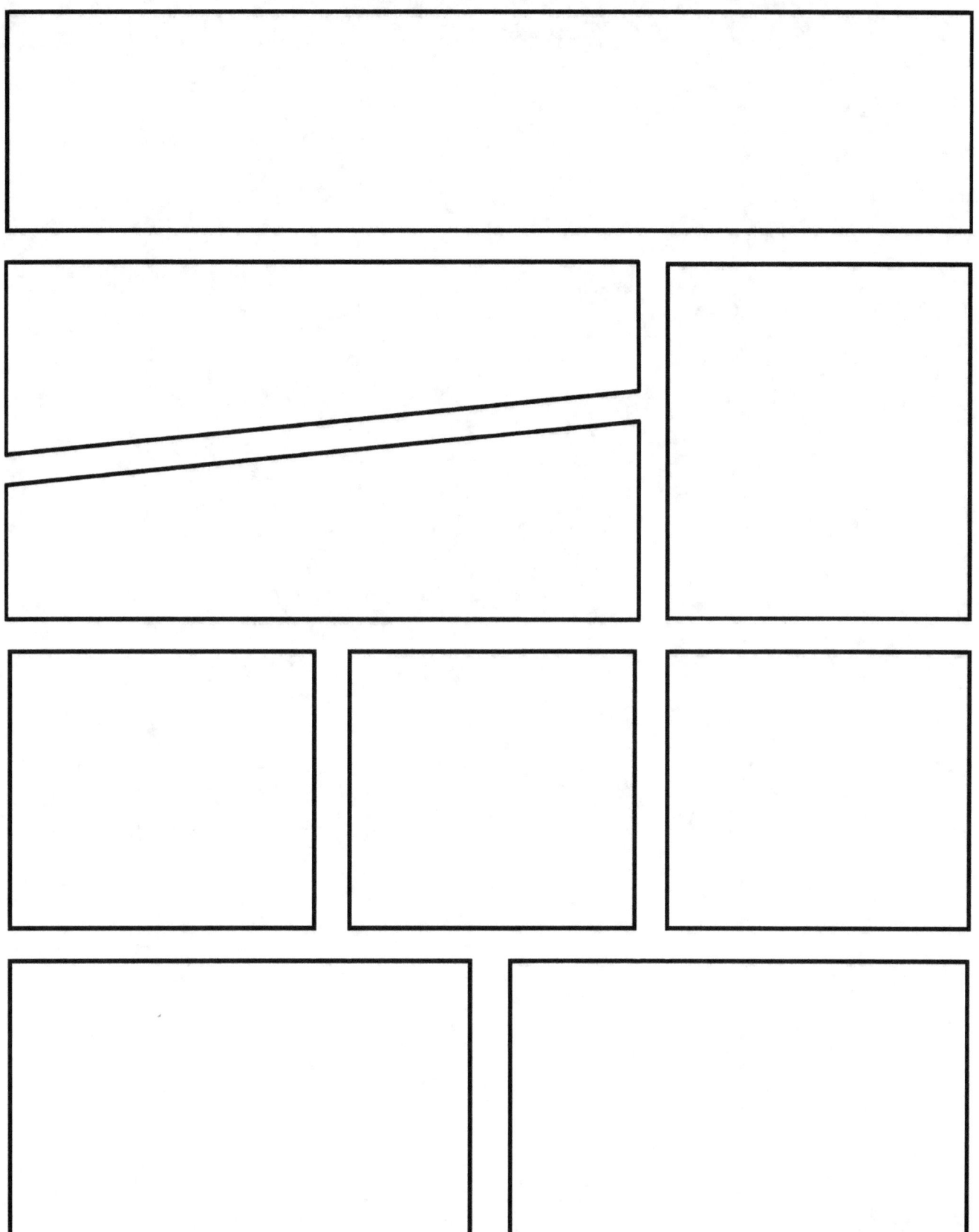

Blank Comic Book

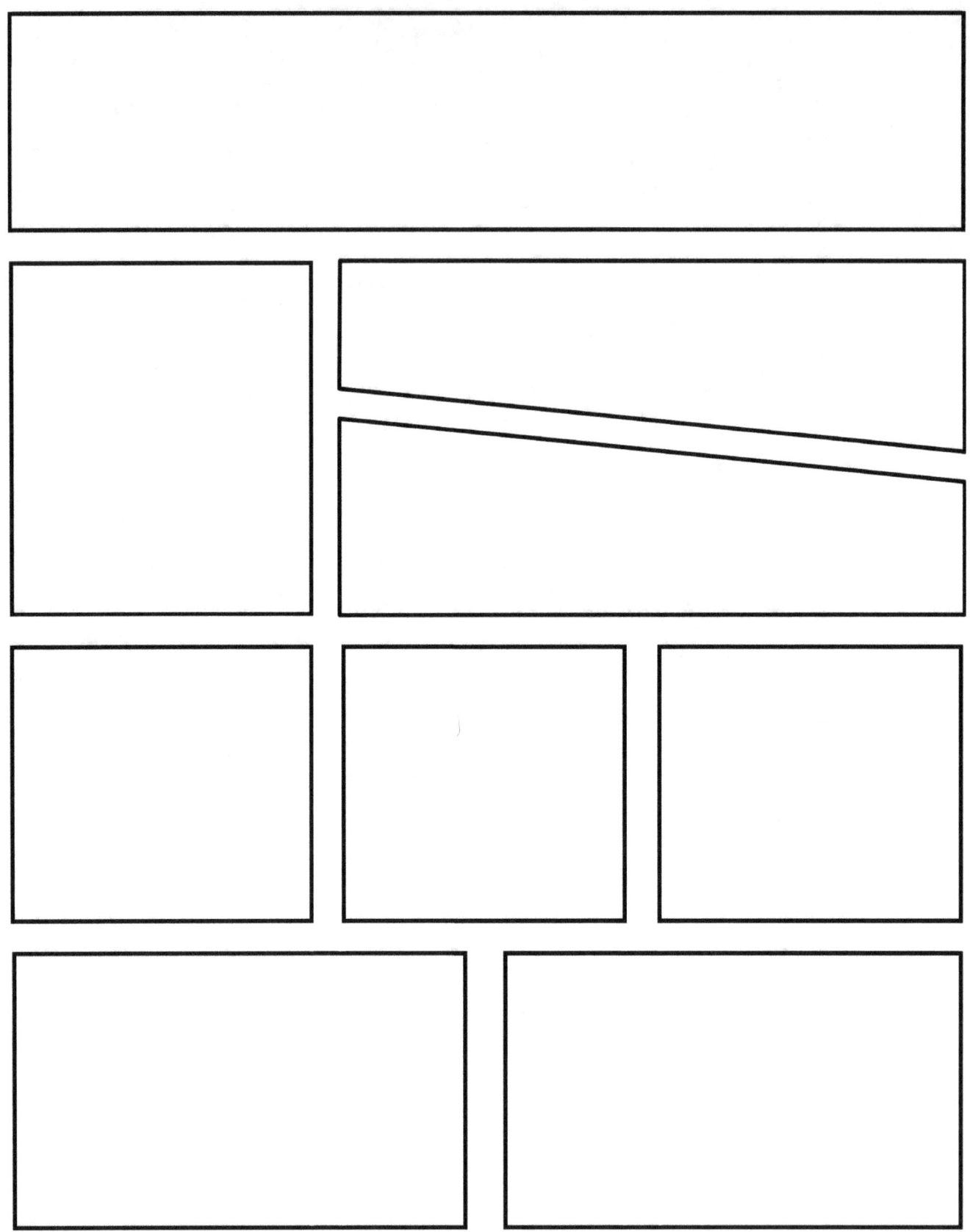

116

Blank Comic Book

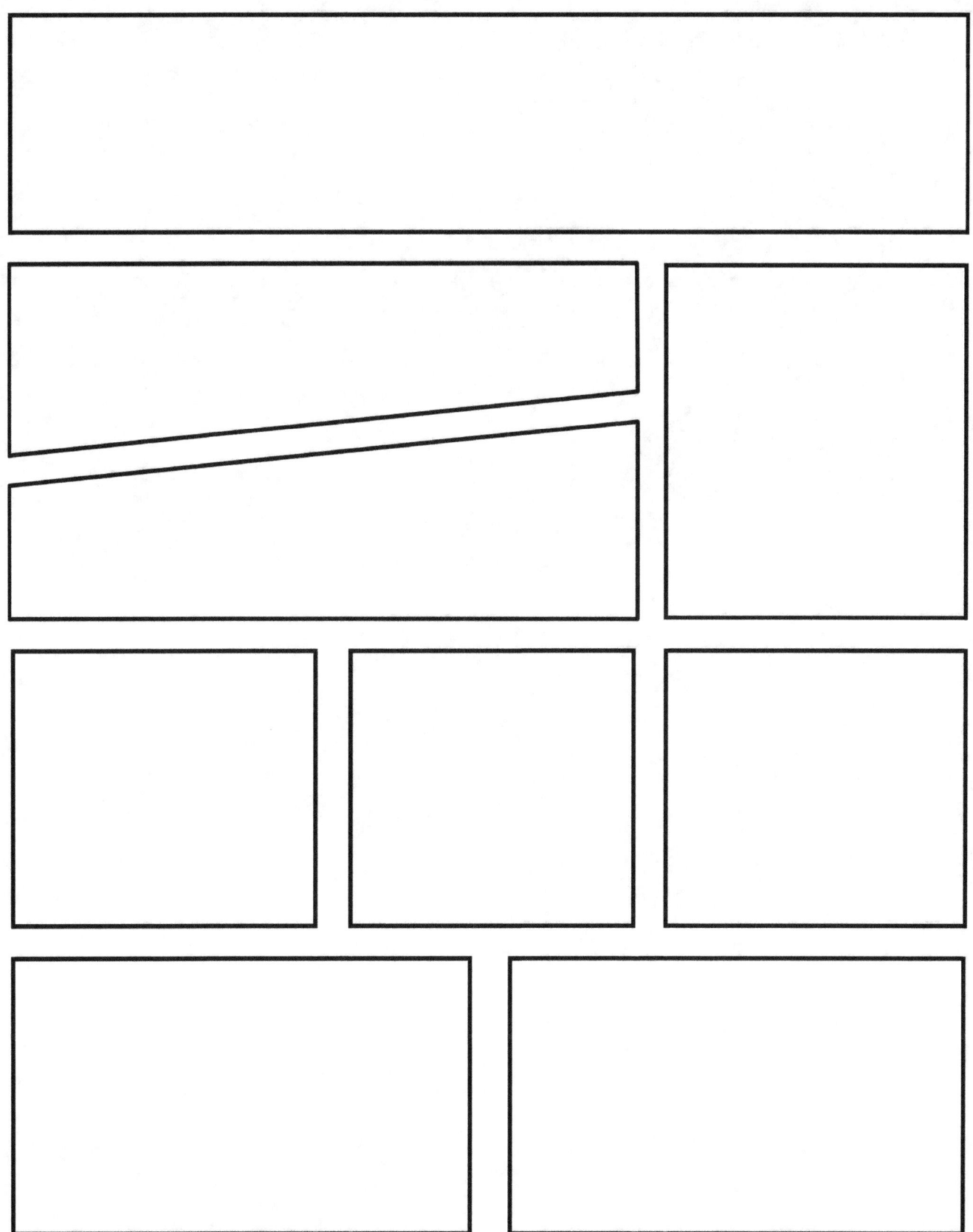

117

Blank Comic Book

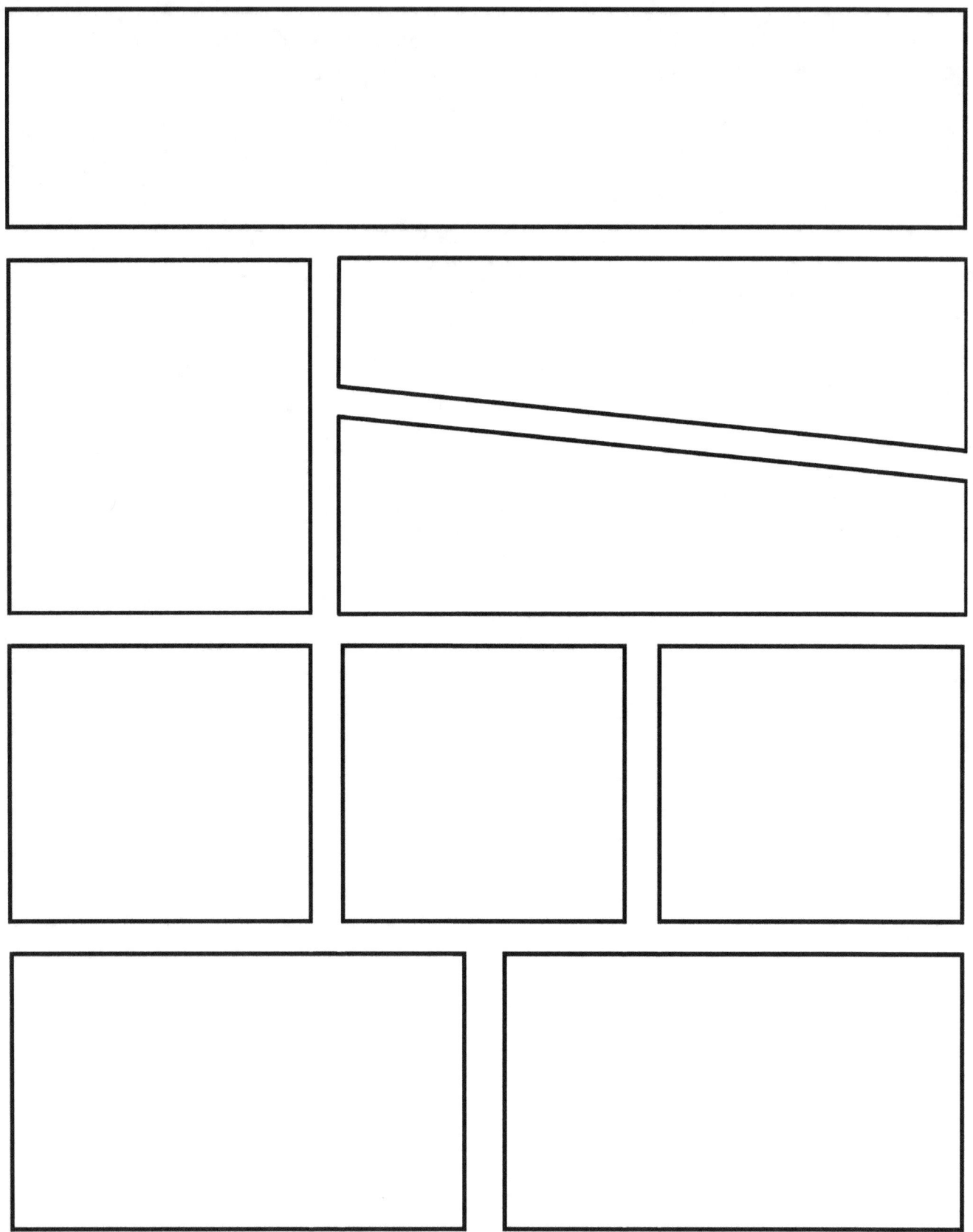

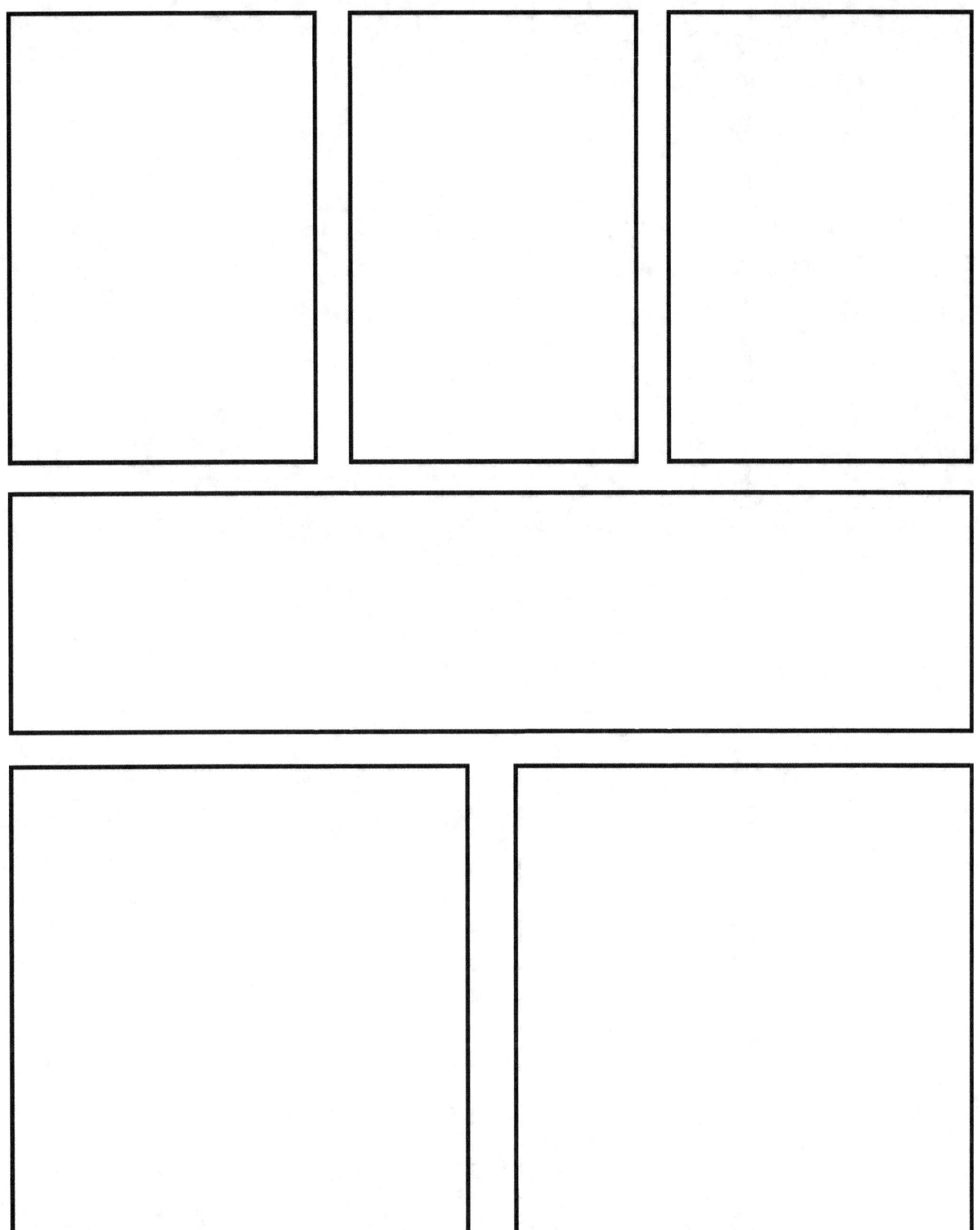

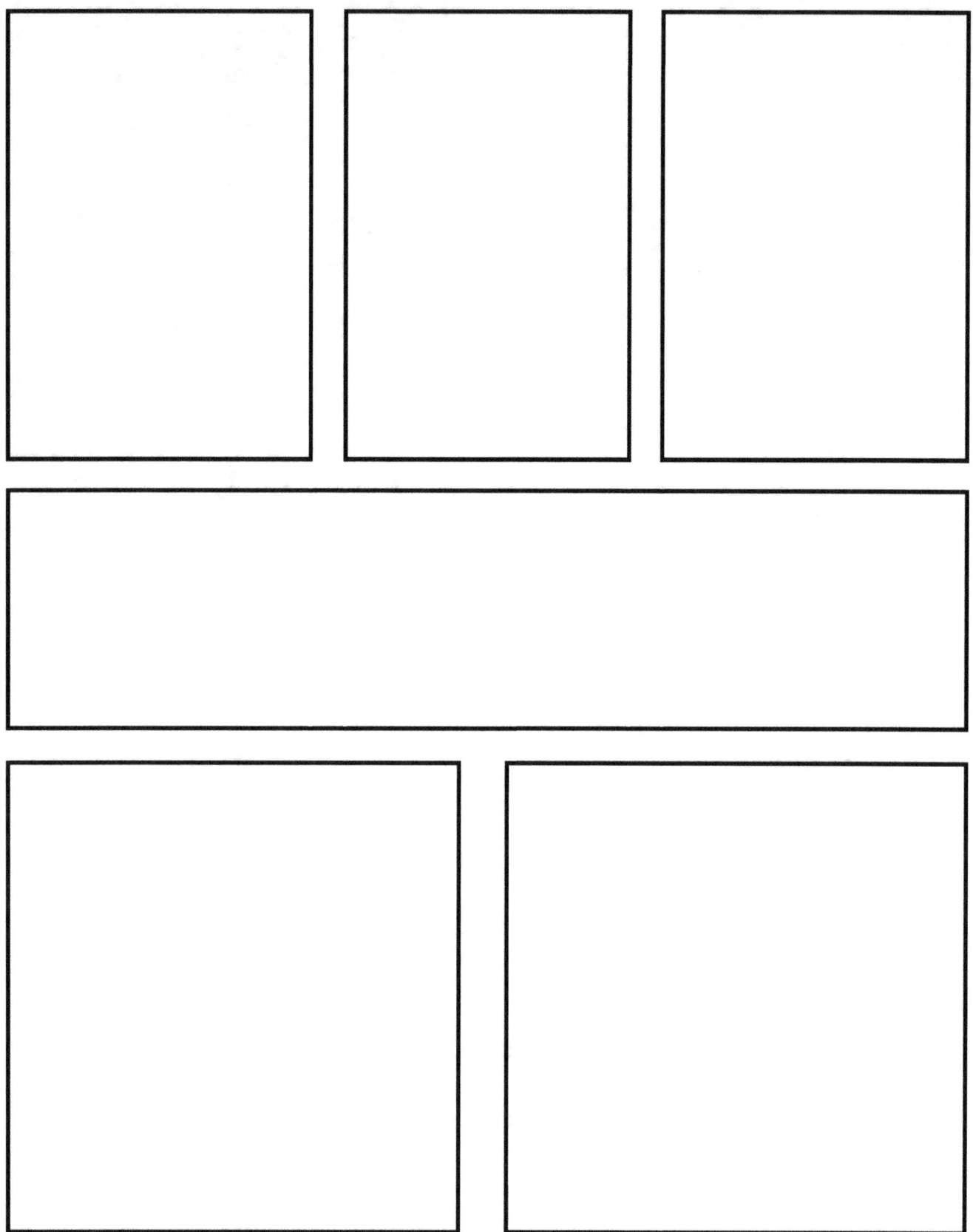

www.ingramcontent.com/pod-product-compliance
Lightning Source LLC
Chambersburg PA
CBHW060420220526
45465CB00008B/2964